PRÁH

TERJE B. ENGLUND

The Czechs
in a Nutshell

A User's Manual for Foreigners

About the author:

TERJE B. ENGLUND is a Norwegian journalist, writer and translator. Educated at the University of Oslo and the Institute of Slavonic Studies at Charles University, he has been based in Prague since 1993, covering Central and Eastern Europe for Scandinavian media. Englund is an affectionate cyclist, mountaineer and diver, and he also enjoys the company of his French bulldog, Gaston.

(czechnutshells@centrum.cz)

Obálka: Tomáš Řízek
Grafická úprava: Karel Kárász
Sazba a litografie: AG Design, spol s r. o., Praha
Redakce: Vladislav Dudák
Lektorace: Karsten Korbøl,
Susan Legro a Katrine Lundgren
Tisk: Finidr s.r.o., Český Těšín

Adresa nakladatelství:
Práh s.r.o., Patočkova 85, 169 00 Praha 6
www.prah.cz

ISBN 978-80-7252-266-8

Contents

Gypsies – See: **Roma**

Hašek, Jaroslav – See: **Švejk, The Good Soldier**

Havel, Václav / 136

Hedonism / 139

Heroes – See: **Charter 77; Cimrman, Jára; Gott, Karel; Havel, Václav; Horáková, Milada; Hus, Jan; Ice Hockey; Mácha, Karel Hynek; Masaryk, Tomáš Garriuge; Palach, Jan; Švejk, The Good Soldier**

Homosexuals / 140

Horáková, Milada / 142

Hospoda / 145

Hungarians / 148

Hus, Jan / 152

Ice Hockey / 157

Intruders – See: **Foreigners; World**

Iron Curtain – See: **Curtains**

Jews / 160

Kafka, Franz / 165

Kajínek, Jiří / 169

Klaus, Václav / 171

Knedlík – See: **Czech Cuisine**

Kundera, Milan / 176

Libuše, Czech Princess – See: **Feminism**

Lustration / 179

Mácha, Karel Hynek / 182

Masaryk, Jan – See: **Denefestration**

Masaryk, Tomáš G. / 185

Matriarchy – See: **Feminism**

Miniskirts – See: **Sandals and Socks**

Mogilevich, Semyon Yudkovich / 188

Preface

I had been living in Prague for half a year when a colleague invited me to visit him and his family. Eager to make the impression that I was perfectly used to visiting Czech homes, I turned up with flowers for my friend's wife and presents for each of his four children. So, when I saw the impressive collection of boots that were neatly lined up outside the doorstep, I immediately started to untie my muddy sneakers.

"Oh no, please don't take your shoes off!" the entire family yelled in unison.

Not knowing that many Czechs on some specific occasions say one thing while they actually mean something totally different (see: **Communication**), I marched my boots across the wall-to-wall-carpet with a blissful grin. Notwithstanding the flowers and the presents I brought, the visit turned out to be a disaster, and my colleague got a clear order from his wife never to invite another Ψ↓Δℵ! **foreigner** to their home.

Some months later, I was sitting in a *hospoda* with a pimpled dentist from Sweden and an astonishingly beautiful and succulent brunette (I know, you might think it sounds chauvinistic to praise a woman's looks so ostentatiously, but if you intend to stay for a while among Czechs without suffering too many nervous breakdowns, just get used to this sexism. And besides that – it's all true!). Since she was studying literature, I decided to try to charm her with my "thorough" knowledge of the writer **Milan Kundera**.

"His novels certainly represent a highlight in modern European literature," I babbled shamelessly. It was the most stupid thing I could have said. Not because I actually hadn't read more than one of Kundera's novels, but because I didn't have the faintest idea that 99.5 percent of Czech intellectuals regard it as a matter of honour to despise the now-French-writing novelist. When I finally learned my lesson, the beauty was already married to the red-faced Swede.

Amazingly enough, there are foreigners who have committed even bigger blunders than I have. Such as the East-Asian businessman who had just taken up the position of managing director at a Czech company. The first day in the new job, he was offered some *knedlíks* – the dumplings that represent the zenith of **Czech cuisine** – at a welcome dinner arranged by his new colleagues. Convinced that it was a small refreshing towel, the poor fellow started rubbing his face with a dumpling. Needless to say, he had a hard time regaining his employees' respect after that performance...

Human consideration prevents me from mentioning even more juicy examples of foreigners making complete fools of themselves simply because they don't understand the Czechs and their culture or don't know the historic background and the main political events that have shaped their prevailing **world**-view.

This manual is a modest attempt to meet such a demand, and also to warn non-Czechs about numerous pitfalls that threaten them. Some of you will probably object that it is too negativistic and critical, but believe me, this is peanuts compared to the flagellation most Czechs every day practice both on themselves, and to others. Their historical fate as a small nation in the middle of Europe, which for more than a millennium has been subjected to enormous political pressure from its surroundings, has rendered most Czechs rather cynical and often also disillusioned. Instead of asking how this or that catastrophe could ever happen, a Czech will ask instead why it hasn't happened far more often.

My immediate motive is to help fellow foreigners, be they **tourists** or longer-term residents, to avoid some of the numerous blunders I have committed. In addition, I hope to share my affinity for a culture and a nation that spans the amusing and the ludicrous, the ingenious and the infantile, the modest and the megalomaniac, the open-minded and the completely xenophobic, with a reach that appears to be broader than in most other European countries.

Terje B. Englund,
Prague, August 2004

Academic Titles

On a cold December day in 1996, the atmosphere in the Czech Parliament's Chamber of Deputies was tense. Rumours were flying that Jan Kalvoda, Minister of Justice and Vice Premier, had committed a shocking and unforgivable sin. Now he was standing on the rostrum in front of 200 curious representatives.

What awful crime would this serious and respected **politician** confess to? Had he exposed himself indecently in a park late at night? Had Kalvoda, as had so many Czech politicians, been caught **driving** drunk? Or, heaven forbid, had the Minister of Justice accepted an envelope stuffed with banknotes (see: **Corruption**) from some lugubrious business people?

It turned out to be much worse. As an educated lawyer, Kalvoda was fully entitled to call himself *Magistr* – a Master of Law. But on several occasions, Kalvoda had been unfortunate enough to call himself *JUDr.* – a Doctor of Law. He had even misused the title when he signed official documents. For Kalvoda, there was only one thing to do: to commit hara-kiri publicly. In front of the flabbergasted parliamentarians, Kalvoda declared that he was immediately resigned from the government, and that his political career was finished forever.

For many **foreigners**, political suicide might seem a somewhat exaggerated punishment for just "upgrading" a *Magistr* to a *Doktor*. Not so for the Czechs. In this country, academic titles are indeed a serious matter. And, what's more, they are almost a prerequisite for those who wish to make a career in politics or business, which, of course, indicates that Kalvoda is not the only title-abuser in this country.

The Czechs' title craze has been explained by several theories. The Swedish writer and diplomat Ingmar Karlsson, for instance, believes it is a legacy from the Habsburg monarchy, when the Czechs, as a matter of national pride, did their utmost not to lag behind the similarly title-fixated **Austrians**. Another explanation is the importance that Czechoslovakia's **First Republic** and its founder, president **Tomáš G. Masaryk**, attached to education as a means of strengthening the young state. And, finally, the communist regime's foolish attempt to create a "classless society" resulted in an incredible inflation of titles, since people used them deliberately to signal that they, although moneyless and materially deprived, at least not were a part of the ruling proletariat.

However comic this title-mania may seem, a foreigner should take it deadly seriously. Not in the sense that an academic title actually guarantees that its bearer is an educated person. Some of the most vociferous racists in this country sport pompous academic titles (Jiří Karas, a parliamentarian who describes **homosexuals** as people who need urgent treatment, is both an *Ing.* and a *JUDr.*) and at least one member of the government plus several other big-shots have acquired titles for academic thesis' which they very likely didn't write themselves.

The problem is that you may commit a social blunder of significant magnitude if you do not address a Czech with his or her proper title. Actually, more title-crazed individuals (which practically means a vast majority of the population) may even interpret your omission as a deliberate insult.

But don't despair – such blunders can be avoided by applying one simple precaution: don't hesitate to address any person who doesn't exercise an apparently manual profession as *Pane inženýre* or *Paní doktorko*. Of course, you might have a problem when meeting a person with two or even three titles *(pane docente-kandidáte věd)*, and there is an obvious risk that you could unintentionally "upgrade" a *Magistr* or *Inženýr*. But as the Kalvoda affair and countless similar cases have proven, the Czechs are as happy as any other people to strut in borrowed plumes.

Albright, Madeleine

Outside the Czech Republic, it's not commonly known that the first woman to become the United States' equivalent of Minister of Foreign Affaires (Secretary of State from 1997 to 2001) is actually Czech by birth and that the **Czech language** is her mother tongue. Marie Jana Körbelová was born in Prague's Smíchov district in May 1937 as the daughter of Czechoslovak diplomat Josef Körbel, who fled to England with his family after the **Munich Agreement** in 1938.

In 1948, the Körbels once more fled Czechoslovakia when another totalitarian ideology came to power (see: **Communism**). They settled in Colorado, and like thousands of other educated and democratically-minded Czechs who left everything they owned to live in freedom, Marie Jana – who changed her first name to Madeleine – and her family tried their best to make a living and become good citizens of their new homelands.

In many ways, this is a typical story about a brainy and ambitious Czech **emigrant**, who fights tremendous hardships and reaches **world** fame. Yet Albright's story is unique. Not only because of her astonishing professional career, but because her background as a political refugee from **Central Europe** strongly influenced her in the job as the world's most important foreign policy executive.

In her memoirs, Albright explains how her personal experience from the appeasement policy that led to the disastrous Munich Agreement and subsequently the Second World War and Holocaust (because they were Czech **Jews**, three of Albright's grandparents were murdered in **German** concentration camps) made her a firm – and in the beginning a sole – advocate of a military action against Slobodan Milošević's regime in Yugoslavia in 1999. She also hints that it was her personal influence, combined with president **Václav Havel's** international prestige, that eventually ensured a somewhat-indifferent Czech Republic (see: **Scepticism**) membership in NATO.

Curiously enough, Madeleine Albright has not met the Czech emigrant's traditional fate in her mother country – negligence, oblivion or even envy.

Instead, she was mentioned as a possible successor to president Václav Havel (which she politely declined). What's more, to millions of Czech women (see: **Feminism**) she has proven that it's possible to have almost any professional career, if you are only ambitious and bull-headed enough. And thirdly, she personifies the fate of thousands of Czechoslovak Jews born in the liberal **First Republic**, who were so thoroughly assimilated that they didn't even know about their Jewish origins.

Alcoholics

One might think that Czech alcoholics are not particularly different from alcoholics in any other part of Europe. Which would basically be true, if it not were for their two national peculiarities: their imposing number, and their easy life.

The percentage of the population suffering from alcoholism (see: **Beer**) dwarfs that of most other countries on the continent, but thanks to the extremely generous spread of watering holes (see: **Hospoda**) combined with a correspondingly generous tolerance towards drunkards, many Czech alcoholics manage to survive socially and, perhaps more surprisingly, also professionally. Unfortunately, their frequent appearance behind the steering wheel is less successful (see: **Driving a Car**).

The term alcoholic is, admittedly, pretty woolly. The Welsh writer (and heavy drinker) Dylan Thomas once sarcastically pointed out that the pejorative "alcoholic" is used about a person you don't like, but who drinks as much as you do. It's not known which definition is used by Prague's Apolinář Hospital, the country's leading research institution in the field of alcohol addiction, but doctors there estimate that some

300,000 Czechs deserve the label full-fledged alcoholics, while another 2 million persons are regarded as heavy drinkers, although not (yet) alcoholics. In other words, almost 25 percent of the Czech population has a drinking problem.

When the total consumption of alcoholic beverages is broken down in litres of pure ethanol per capita, each and every citizen in this country pours down more than nine litres annually, which places the Czechs among Europe's most soggy nations – after the French, Portuguese and **Hungarians**. But those are the official statistics. If you also include all the hooch, which is distilled and subsequently drunken in private homes – the inhabitants of **Moravia** are especially vigorous – the Czechs probably come out as medal winners of the European Drunkards' League.

As already mentioned, there are some rather obvious reasons for this wild boozing. Just like other manifestations of **hedonism**, the commonly respected moral code treats drunkenness with extreme tolerance (see: **Urination**). As the famous photographer Jan Saudek puts it – *I don't have any drinking problem. I just drink, get drunk, and fall asleep. That's no problem.*

This attitude was widely cultivated during the years of **communism**, when cheap and easily accessible alcohol was one of the goodies with which the regime rewarded the population for their "loyalty". Symptomatically, the Czech Republic is still one of those rare European countries where bars and restaurants charge more for non-alcoholic beverages than for beer.

As expected, the **Velvet Revolution** in 1989 didn't make the Czechs less thirsty. On the contrary, they started to booze even more (particularly women, who currently represent almost one third of all treated alcoholics). A similar development was also witnessed in Portugal after the fall of the military dictatorship in 1974: the newly-acquired freedom created an exhilarated atmosphere, which enhanced neither temperance nor limitations.

In the Czechs' instance, this post-totalitarian euphoria has manifested itself in a virtually omnipresent sale of alcoholic beverages and a deep-rooted conviction that unlimited access to booze is one of democracy's most basic pillars.

When a member of the Parliament's Chamber of Deputies in late 2003 got so drunk that he didn't manage to press the correct voting button, the media questioned whether the people's elected representatives really needed five on-site bars and restaurants serving alcohol for a price next to nothing. They were immediately put in their place by the Chamber's President, who maintained that "he would be ashamed" to receive foreign visitors and not be able to serve them a stiff drink.

To be fair, the Czechs' long and rich boozing traditions have also brought about some positive results; for instance, in developing a medical treatment for alcoholism. Prague was, in 1952, allegedly the first city in Europe to open a detention station to take care of dead-drunks who were picked up at public places. A few years later, a strong-willed and unorthodox medical doctor, Jaroslav Skála, opened a clinic for alcoholics at the Apolinář Hospital in Prague.

Contrary to the Western attitude, where boozers are treated with meek understanding and friendly therapy, the now-legendary Doctor Skála introduced a three-month cure with a draconian regime resembling the Foreign Legion. Patients were forced to start every day with a jog, and they had to earn themselves points by exemplary behaviour to gain even the smallest privileges.

To establish disgust towards alcohol, Doctor Skála even gave his patients pills that caused strong vomiting. The smelly bucket in which the poor fellows had puked in was used the next day when the patients washed the floor to earn privilege points.

Notwithstanding its masochistic elements, the Skála Therapy has proved surprisingly successful. Bar the forced vomiting, it is still applied by most of the institutions that offer alcoholics medical treatment in this country. Consequently, **foreigners** who develop a drinking problem during their stay in the Czech Republic have two options: either do as most locals, i.e. choose the untroubled attitude and keep on boozing as long as your liver lets you. Or join the smaller but often quite prominent group of graduates of Doctor Skála's anti-alcoholic survival course.

Austrians

When the Lower House of the Austrian Parliament in December 2003 voted to accept the enlargement of the EU, it was in reality a formal matter. After all of the international hullabaloo caused by the right-wing populist Jörg Haider and his Freedom Party the Austrians certainly wouldn't tease Brussels by blocking the former communist countries from becoming "a part of Europe".

Yet they took great care in giving the Czech Republic significantly fewer votes than any of the other eight candidate countries. The Czechs, for their part, shrugged their shoulders as if nothing had really happened, but off the record officials admitted they were scared to death that the Austrians would be more than delighted to cause serious troubles with their EU accession.

All in all, this is a fairly accurate picture of the relations between the two neighbours: the Czechs and the Austrians (in sharp contrast to the **Hungarians** and the Austrians) simply love if not to hate, so at least to provoke each other. Bi-national brawls take place with impressive regularity, and as soon as the consequences of one clash start to be forgotten, a new one breaks out. However, both partners realize that they can't move apart, and that they have lots of common interests. Thus, despite the not very amicable feelings, they try to behave pragmatically and at bright moments even pretend that they are good friends.

If the Czechs' somewhat ambiguous relations to the **Slovaks**, Hungarians and **Poles** seem strange to you, then the reason for their

distaste for Austrians seems almost as straightforward as that for the **Germans**.

Except for the peculiar name that the Czechs use for their southern neighbours – *Rakousko* is not of Slavonic origin, but propably derives from the name Raabsburg, a fortress by the Rabe river – millions of Czechs immediately associate Austria with niceties such as "national suppression", "hypocritical snobs", "arrogance" and "eco fascists". If you, just to be balanced, ask them to also mention something positive, they'll probably come up with "chocolate cake" or "the Alps".

As one might expect in a region where history is omnipresent, the reason for Austria's shabby image lies in the past – both in its older and more modern chapters.

When Ferdinand of Habsburg ascended to the Czech throne in 1526, the Czech kingdom, politically dominated by Protestants (see: **Hus, Jan**) formally became a part of the strongly Catholic Austrian Empire (see:

Religion). The tensions between the king in Vienna and his quarrelsome subjects in Prague seethed and boiled for almost a century, until they reached their climax with the **Battle of White Mountain** in 1620, where the Czechs were beaten into their boots, and their kingdom was practically reduced to a province of Austria.

The official historiography that emerged with the creation of Czechoslovakia in 1918 depicted – and often still depicts – the three centuries when the Czechs were ruled from Vienna as "the era of darkness". This was certainly a handy slogan for creating a Czech **national identity**, and the inglorious defeat at White Mountain unquestionably brought about some harsh consequences for the Czechs, but compared to real life during those 300 years, it was most probably a dramatic exaggeration.

Bar a period following the 1848 uprising against the Habsburgs, which had stronger public support in Hungary and other parts of the Empire, Vienna enhanced the cultural and economic development of **Bohemia** and **Moravia**. How could Bohemia otherwise become the Empire's industrial hub? Logically, what Vienna didn't support was the demand for Czech sovereignty that emerged during the national revival in the middle of nineteenth century (see: **Czech Language**).

In the slightly nationalistic climate that followed the separation of Czechoslovakia in 1993 it's not a politically correct question, but one can ask whether the broad masses of Czechs were all that dissatisfied as the Emperor's subjects.

What really infuriated them, was **Franz Josef's** decision not to come to Prague to be crowned a Czech king, and also the fact that Hungary, in 1867, was made Austria's equal within the Empire, while the Czechs were not. But basically, the Czechs' ambiguous attitude to the Austro-Hungarian Empire is reminiscent of those two old ladies who went to the manager of the hotel where they were staying to complain about the food. "It's completely inedible," one of them snorted. "And the portions are far too small," the other added.

However, the last years of *kakánie* (a popular Czech renaming of the Empire, based on the frequently used abbreviation *kk – kaiserlich und königlich*, which resembles that verb *kakat* – to take a dump) were far from funny.

When Austria-Hungary in 1914 declared war on Serbia, the Czech population was drawn into a carnage in which they didn't have any political interest (see: **Švejk, The Good Soldier**), and which ultimately cost more than 200.000 young Czechs their lives. Still, almost every city, town and village in Bohemia and Moravia has a monument honouring the huge sacrifice that the Czech nation had to pay "because of those Ψ↓Δא! Austrians".

Only twenty years after Czechoslovakia's **First Republic** was established, hell broke loose once again. Most Austrians were thrilled when their countryman Adolf Hitler in March 1938 incorporated Austria into Nazi Germany, and they were not too sad when Bohemia and Moravia were occupied by Nazi troops a year later (see: **Munich Agreement**). It's not exactly heroic, but perhaps understandable that the Czechs longed for revenge after the war. As soon as **Russian** troops had liberated Southern Moravia, thousands of ethnic Germans – including children, women and old people – were gathered in Brno, and then forced to march more than 50 kilometres without stopping all the way to Austria.

After the **Velvet Revolution**, some very vocal Austrians, most notably Jörg Haider and his supporters, have advocated that the Czechs should do penance for the "death march" and similar atrocities, and also that the subsequent confiscation of the expelled Germans' property needs to be discussed. This is regarded as a caustic provocation by a vast majority of the Czech population, who feel that the Austrians should praise themselves lucky to be considered victims of Nazi aggression, and not as Hitler's enthusiastic supporters, which might be more appropriate.

This goes double for the Czechoslovak Germans expelled to Austria in 1945. They should, as the Czech Republic's former premier Miloš Zeman (see: **Carlsbad English Bitters**) once subtly declared, be "grateful for not being executed as traitors". As a result of these historic resentments, even the smallest and most insignificant Czech-Austrian spat has a tendency to end up as wild discussions about the Second World War.

In recent years, nothing has demonstrated the complexity of the Czechs' troubled relations with their southern neighbours better (or worse, if you like) than the debate about the Czech nuclear power plant Temelín.

The construction of the plant started under the communists in the early 1980s, and both the dimensions of the giant project and the crazy idea of locating it in the most picturesque and untouched part of South Bohemia, truly revealed classic communist sensitivity. But when the Bolsheviks were finally kicked out of power in the Velvet Revolution, so many billions of *korunas* were already invested that the new political leadership in Prague decided, after much hesitation, to complete the "monster project" and to put it into operation.

How did the Austrians react? If you consider that Temelín was originally designed with communist technology, that the **world** still had the Chernobyl catastrophe fresh in its memory and that the Austrians themselves, because of their "anti-nuclear psychosis" had recently decided to scrap their modern and Western-built plant in Zwentendorf, the answer is obvious: with a combination of incredulity and undisguised fury.

Unfortunately, instead of displaying some clever diplomatic footwork, the Czech political elite let historic animosity and emotions take complete control.

If the Austrians are so deadly afraid of nuclear energy, why don't they protest against plants in Germany and Switzerland? And why do the Austrians disregard their own scientists who declare that Temelín, after some initial problems, now meets international standards? Well, that's because those stuck-up Austrians still believe they are imperial *capos*, entitled to boss around the Czechs at their pleasure! But those days are gone! In reality, Austria has fewer inhabitants than the Czech Republic, their industrial output is falling, and they don't even have a nuclear power plant!

Now, add a unique national referendum that Austria in 2000 arranged only to press the Czech Republic to scrap Temelín, a Czech prime minister (once again the golden-tongued Miloš Zeman) who publicly stated that anti-nuclear Austrians were a "bunch of idiots" (see: **Cursing**) plus zealous Austrian demonstrators who, several years after Temelín was put into operation, still regularly blocked crossings along the two countries' 466-kilometre-long border.

Spice the bad, nuclear atmosphere up with lots of grievances from the first years after the Velvet Revolution when Austrian shopkeepers installed signs such as *Czechs, Please don't steal in our Store,* and you understand why many Czechs regard the Austrians as big-mouthed and arrogant parvenus, while Otto von Habsburg, son of Austria-Hungary's last Emperor Karl, didn't hesitate to tell Czech media that "I love all the peoples in the former Dual Empire, well, except the Czechs, of course".

The funny thing, though, is that a **foreigner** regarding the two quarrelsome neighbours from outside might confuse them, because the similarities are striking.

Three centuries in a common state with almost identical educational system, cultural institutions and the same bulging **bureaucracy** have left indelible traces. The architecture of the cities in Lower Austria, the country's most populous state, is almost indiscernible from cities in Southern Moravia and Bohemia. Both Czechs and Austrians pack their joviality and badly concealed **hedonism** into polite formalities, obstinate use of **academic titles** and a common worshipping of ingrained conventions (see: **Dancing Schools**).

Ethnically, the ties are so close that it's almost impossible to tell the two peoples apart. Open Vienna's telephone book to any page, and you'll find it is crowded with Czech-sounding **surnames**. Thanks to the huge influx of Czech and Slovak workers to Vienna by the end of the nineteenth century, some 200,000 Austrians carry family names with roots in the Czech language. And some world-famous Austrians with apparently German names – Sigmund Freud, Gustav Mahler and Rainer Maria Rilke among them – were actually all born in Bohemia or Moravia.

Also on the political level, relations are far more interwoven than historical hangover and the unfortunate Temelín affair might suggest.

When Nikita Khrushchev's political thaw finally reached Stalinist Czechoslovakia in the mid-1960s, Austria gave full backing to Alexander Dubček and his comrade-reformers. One might even claim that Helmut Zilk, the boss of Austrian state television at that time and later Vienna's flamboyant mayor, personally contributed to kick-starting the Prague Spring when he launched a tele-bridge where Czech and Austrian teams competed live. In 1968, when the attempt to reform **communism** ended in tragedy, Premier Bruno Kreisky (check the origin of that name!) personally ensured that Austria for the next two decades adapted a very generous – and in the Czech Republic never fully appreciated – policy towards Czech political **emigrants**.

It's a telling expression of all the misunderstandings and failures accompanying the Czech-Austrian relations that when president **Václav Havel**, in the late 1990s, decided to reward Helmut Zilk with a state order for his personal contribution to help Czechs and Slovaks, it all ended in a scandal. The Czech Ministry of Interior ran a routine check on Vienna's popular and respected mayor and found his name registered among the communist secret police StB's foreign informers (see: **Lustration**). Thus, a well-meant step towards reconciliation turned out to be just another slap in the face.

Ultimately, to understand the Czechs' relations to the Austrians, it's tempting to use a theory, developed by the writer Herman Hesse, that also applies to their relations to the Germans:

If you dislike a person, you dislike something in him that is a part of yourself. Consequently, the Czechs dislike the Austrians even more than they dislike the Germans, because they, thanks to the centuries of Habsburg rule, have even more in common with them. But the difference is not too significant. As every Czech knows – Austrians are basically Germans who wear hats!

Balkans

It happens year after year: when the holiday season starts in July, almost one million Czechs (correct, that's 10 percent of the population!) pack their Škodas full of **beer**, camping gear and food, and head off to the South. After a swift, eight-hour drive, most of them (see: **Driving a Car**) reach a camping site, pension or hotel on Croatia's beautiful Adriatic cost.

Of course, the sea (plus relatively low prices) is what primarily draws all those Czech landlubbers to Croatia. But there are lots of other advantages, too. Croatian is a Slavonic language, and a Czech can, with some effort, communicate in his or her mother tongue. Their respective cultural heritage is not that different, as both the Czechs and the Croatians were for hundreds of years a part of Austria-Hungary, and both nations have experienced a communist regime, although Tito's Yugoslavia was definitely a lighter and more colourful version of one than Husák's grey Czechoslovakia.

This, you might conclude, must make the Czechs feel almost at home in Croatia and mentally very close to the Balkan region. Peculiarly enough, you're both absolutely right and completely wrong. Yes, most Czechs apparently feel almost at home in Croatia. And no, barring the former Soviet Union (see: **Russians**), it's hard to imagine a geographic area that has a worse image than the countries on the Balkan Peninsula.

To je hotový Balkán (That's the Balkan way of doing things) is a common exclamation when a Czech encounters unpleasant phenomena such as **corruption,** bulging **bureaucracy**, souring criminality, chaos, violence, religious intolerance or unacceptably temperamental behaviour (see: **Communication**). Jaroslav Hašek's soldier **Švejk** often refers to the wine cellar "Sarajevo" where people are fighting all the time. The name of a Bosnian city, Maglaj, has even become a frequently used expression in **Czech language** for anything that is wild and unpleasant. *V hospodě* *je maglajz* means that the pub is stuffed with people who very likely are beating the guts out of each other.

Not surprisingly, the Czechs' belittling attitude towards the Balkan has its roots in history. From the second half of the nineteenth century, the south-eastern part of Europe was more or less in constant turmoil. This affected the Czechs quite directly, since the Austro-**Hungarian** Empire, which they were a part of, occupied Bosnia in 1878.

Events like the "Bulgarian atrocities"; the "Maglaj butchery" and the "Balkan crises" had the same devastating impact on public opinion in **Bohemia** and **Moravia** as news from Iraq has in the West today. Then add a bloody Balkan war, where the south Slavs started fighting each other instead of fighting the Turks, and the Sarajevo assassination of Franz Ferdinand, the heir to the imperial throne in Vienna, and the Balkans' negative image among the Czechs was cemented for centuries. Needless to say, the horrible war in ex-Yugoslavia in the 1990s hasn't done much to change those old stereotypes.

The funny thing, however, is that Czech society itself can offer an abundance of exactly those phenomena that are so frequently associated with the much-cursed Balkan countries.

Most people in this country perceive bulging bureaucracy, souring criminality and corruption (the organisation Transparency International ranks the Czech Republic close to Romania) as serious problems. True, the Czechs have a better track record than, for instance, the Serbs when it comes to religious tolerance, but the 50,000 or so Muslims who live in the Czech Republic still don't have a single mosque in the classical style. And when some Saudi billionaire offered to sponsor the construction of a mosque in the city of Teplice, he was politely, but firmly rejected: such buildings don't belong to a Czech spa town!

Another Czech cliché is that people from the Balkan countries have some kind of inborn aptitude for violent behaviour. According to common wisdom, Czech women are strongly advised not to marry a man from ex-Yugoslavia, "because they are known to beat their wives".

Besides the fact that this is a silly generalisation, several non-governmental organizations have recently pointed out that physical mistreatment of women by their husbands is actually a widespread – and so far untargeted – problem in the Czech Republic.

So, should we agree right away with the writer Vlastimil Třešňák, who claims that the Balkans start outside Prague's Karlín district? The Czechs' obsession with wall-to-wall carpets, **sandals**, male-only *hospodas* and "Turkish coffee" (which under no circumstances should be confused with real Turkish coffee!) might indicate that there is something to this statement. On the other hand, the Czechs' laxity towards religion and military fighting (see: **National Identity**) suggest that the similarity should not be exaggerated.

Therefore, a quote from the Bible is probably the most appropriate way to summarise the Czechs' perception of the Balkans: It's easier to see the splinter in your brother's eye than the beam in your own!

Battle of White Mountain

Czech history is a virtual roller coaster, with both magnificent zeniths and incredible disasters. Two Czech kings, Charles IV (1346–1378) and Rudolf II (1576–1611), for instance, not only ruled **Bohemia**, **Moravia** and all of Silesia plus large chunks of the area which now is a part of Germany and Poland, but they were also elected Emperors of the Holy Roman Empire, making Prague a European centre of science and arts.

And then take a look at the Battle of White Mountain in 1620.

From a military point of view, the action that took place on the top of White Mountain (*Bílá hora*) – a 382-meter-high hilltop several kilometres to the west of Old Prague's city walls – probably didn't differ significantly from dozens of similar clashes at the time. Yet in the

Czechs' collective memory White Mountain has become a fetish of one of the biggest disasters in the country's history, widely regarded as "an event that triggered three centuries of darkness".

Although this term sounds a bit more dramatic than life in Bohemia and Moravia after 1620 actually was, it's still fair to say that the battle on that foggy November day in 1620 represented a major crossroads in this country's history. It also underpins the view that Czechs have revealed many talents throughout history (see: **Beauty Contests**; **Beer**; **Cimrman, Jára**; **Gott, Karel**; **Ice Hockey**), but they have never excelled in the military field.

The Czechs' most inglorious debacle was triggered when members of the mainly-Protestant Czech gentry and **nobility** broke into the royal quarters on the third floor in the Prague Castle in May 1618 and promptly treated the Catholic Emperor's governors to a full-fledged **defenestration**. The ruler in Vienna reacted with expected fury. The Czechs need to be taught a proper lesson once and for all! For the next two years, the imperial army fought numerous battles against the Czech forces without achieving any major victories.

However, the punitive expedition against the recalcitrant Czechs suddenly became more successful when the Catholic League, a union of South-German principalities that resisted Protestantism almost with the same fervour as they detested Islam, decided to support the Emperor's army. In the autumn of 1620, the two enemies fought brutal battles in several places in Southern and Central Bohemia. After one of these clashes, the armies of the Emperor and the Catholic League, numbering more than 30,000 men, sent some 13,000 soldiers from the Czech crown's army on the run towards Prague.

At one o'clock in the morning on the 8th of November, the Czech army arrived at White Mountain. Aware of the fact that his men were deadly tired, Commander-in-Chief Christian von Anhalt decided to pitch camp on the hilltop and prepare for a decisive battle against the enemy. Already at this point, contemporary eyewitnesses expressed grave doubts about the state of von Anhalt's soldiers.

Photo © Terje B. Englund

"Since the leaders of the Czech rebellion didn't wish to give ordinary people weapons in their hands, mostly **Germans** were hired. Thus, alongside a handful of our own men, the fateful battle for our national freedom was entrusted into the hands of paid mercenaries," the historian František Dvorský writes.

Widespread boozing (see: **Alcoholism**) was already a problem at that time. Early in the morning on the 8th of November, a huge number of the soldiers left, running off to Prague to get food, **beer** and women. "If Commander-in-Chief von Anhalt had not ordered all the city gates to be closed, at least every other soldier would have fled to the inns," Dvorský concludes.

Precisely at noon, when the fog had lifted, the Catholic League and the imperial army launched their attack. Except for a few displays of great bravery, namely by the Moravian Regiment, who fought almost to the last man (and, thus, laid the foundations for the commonly acknowledged theory that the inhabitants of Moravia generally possess more guts than their brethren in Bohemia), the Czech army's retaliation was, at best, disorganized and faint.

Less than one and a half hours after the battle started, the Czech army had been beaten into its boots. Most of the soldiers that the Catholic forces captured alive were mercilessly butchered. Historians disagree about the number of Czech army soldiers killed, but several estimates speak about 9,000 men – out of an army that originally numbered 13,000. Among the battle's victims were also a large number of **Hungarian** soldiers, who drowned when they tried to escape across the Vltava River in their combat gear. The Catholic League and the imperial army probably lost no more than 2,000 men.

So, what were the consequences of the disastrous Battle of White Mountain?

Early in the morning the day after the battle, King Bedřich – previously known as Prince Friedrich of Pfalz, whom the Czech nobility had elected their king a year earlier – fled the country with 300 members of his court and all the valuables they managed to stuff into their carriages. To many Prague burghers, who were eager to put up at least a symbolic fight against the Catholic forces, this was a tremendous disappointment.

"Now," the historian Dvorský reports, "they witnessed their king and his men, who were to defend the nation, preparing for a humiliating escape. They bid him a most bewildered farewell."

Unfortunately, this was not the last time in history when a leader of the Czech nation had to abandon his people at a moment when they were threatened from abroad. Just like unfortunate King Bedřich, President Edvard Beneš also fled the country after the tragic **Munich Agreement** in September 1938 (this time without the gold and jewels). Similarly, in 1968, when the **Russians** and their Warsaw Pact comrades crushed the Prague Spring (see: **Communism**), all but one brave member of the Czechoslovak Communist Party's *Politburo* signed the humiliating capitulation imposed by Moscow without grumbling.

Thus, the aftermath of the Battle of White Mountain was a symbolic preview of what some historians have described as the Czechs' long-lasting misfortune in picking their leaders. It also marked the end of the independent Czech kingdom, which from that day on was politically reduced to a province within the Austrian empire. Typically, when Czech

Euro-phobes in 2003 campaigned against membership in the EU, one of their slogans was "White Mountain – never again!"

The Emperor in Vienna, however, was not satisfied with only winning the battle. Half a year later, he decided to set a deterrent example by publicly executing 27 prominent Czechs in the Old Town Square. The rest of the population had to choose: either demonstrate loyalty to the Habsburg rulers by converting to Catholicism, or leave the country.

Here, too, exact figures are hard to obtain. Some estimates suggest that between 10 and 30 percent of the population, among them many of the Czech nation's best and brightest, chose to leave their country, thus laying the foundation for the Czechs' rich tradition as political **emigrants**.

The fact that the Catholic Church let itself be used by the Habsburgs in the aftermath of the Thirty Years' War as a tool to curb Czech patriotism didn't, of course, go unnoticed. So, while the **Poles**, for instance, regard the Catholic Church as a cornerstone of their nationhood, quite a few Czechs still perceive it as something that can't be fully trusted as loyal to their nation – a fact that might also explain why the Czechs in general harbour a rather chilly relationship to **religion**.

However, it's usually forgotten that the White Mountain battle, in a wider perspective, actually had some positive effects as well. The Catholic revival after 1648 resulted in a massive construction boom, particularly when it came to ecclesiastical buildings. Some of the most magnificent examples of baroque architecture in **Central Europe**, such as the St. Nicholas Cathedral at Prague's Malá Strana or the Klementinum library in Old Town, would probably never have been erected if the Protestant Czechs hadn't been defeated at White Mountain on that foggy November day in 1620.

And while thousands of Czechs were forced to leave the country, there were thousands of **foreigners** who settled in Bohemia and Moravia. Many of them were members of the imperial army and the Catholic League, who received confiscated castles and estates as a reward for participating in the crusade against the Czechs (see: **Nobility**), which quite understandably helped to ruin foreigners' image in this country for many centuries to come.

On the other hand, many artists and intellectuals also arrived, especially from Italy, where competition was strong. So paradoxically, what many Czechs still see as one of the biggest tragedies in the nation's turbulent history was simultaneously a significant contribution to this country's impressively rich cultural tradition.

Beauty Contests

When from time to time some daredevil tries to arrange a beauty contest in a Western European country, he or she can almost take it for granted that the arrangement will provoke wild protests. That's definitely not the case in the Czech Republic. Beauty contests are neither considered to be politically incorrect nor humiliating to women (see: **Feminism**). On the contrary, they seem to be an obsession not only for Czech males, but more surprisingly, for the females, too.

Each year there are probably more beauty contests arranged in **Bohemia** and **Moravia** than in all other European countries combined. The cultural highlight of every Czech region is the election of a local "Miss". When a new parliament is elected, media immediately pick an unofficial Miss among the fresh members. There is a Miss Deaf, Miss Internet, Miss IQ, Miss **Roma**, Miss Longhaired, Miss Under-Aged, Miss Czech Railways and even a Missis Mother. In short: picture any profession, company, ethnic minority, village, handicap or whatever, and you can bet your boots that the given group boasts a Miss.

Naturally, the ultimate contest is the election of Miss Czech Republic. The event – broadcast live on **TV Nova** and with more viewers than any other television program – is preceded by a series of similar contests

Photo © Jaroslav Fišer

at the regional level, so at least in theory, Miss Czech Republic can with some credibility claim to be the most beautiful woman in the country.

This is also reflected by the prestige that the title gives its holder. The new Miss, traditionally a 17-year old, scrawny blond who has learnt a poem by heart, is immediately catapulted into the nation's hottest jet set.

If she plays her cards skillfully, she'll stay there even after the title is handed over to another beauty.

A safe and frequently-used way to reach this position is to start a relationship with one of the Czech **ice hockey** stars playing in the NHL (according to some observers, an alliance between those without teeth and those without brains). If that doesn't work, the Miss title always makes a perfect stepping-stone for a career in business or politics. One Czech Miss even used her title to promote environmental issues.

But how can the Czechs be so out of step with Western Europe, where beauty contests are regarded as a relic from the political Stone Age?

The short answer is that the Czechs, because of their isolation under the communists (see: **Ocean, Absence of**), have not until now been confronted with the political correctness that has prevailed in the West for several decades. And since the communists so thoroughly discredited feminism, protests against low-browed beauty contests are not perceived as a defense of women's rights, but rather as a sullen roar coming from the Bolshevik past. Besides that, more or less every Czech is convinced that no other country on the planet can boast a higher density of beautiful women, so why not take pride in it?

Yet in the name of justice, shouldn't there also be contests for men? Isn't Czech society, after all, reputed for its **egalitarian** flair? Well, such contests do exist, even though most of them concentrate more on men's professional or intellectual abilities than their looks. But Czech chaps who love to dress up and strut on the catwalk needn't despair. They can always register for the very popular contest Miss Transvestite!

Beer

There are absolutely not many nice words to say about Vasil Bilak, the Husák regime's wily chief ideologist who, in 1968, begged Leonid Brezhnev to come and rape Czechoslovakia (see: **Communism**). Yet thanks to one of his statements, he is still widely remembered: "Beer is bread to the Czechs!"

The literary brilliance of this judgment can certainly be debated, but it undoubtedly belongs to the very few true-to-life comments the dogmatist ever uttered. In fact, it's still valid! No other nation on this planet drinks more beer – *pivo* to the natives – than the Czechs. Statistically, every single inhabitant in this country pours down 322 half-litres of beer annually. Considering that these inhabitants include babies, grandmothers and the evidently-not-too-many adult Czechs who never touch alcohol, the real consumption is by all estimates much more impressive – or depressive, if you happen to be a teetotaller (see: **Alcoholics**).

The Czechs' profound and long-lasting love for beer and their globally acknowledged tradition as brewers have convinced a lot of people in this country that the foaming comfort is actually a local invention. The legend even claims that the eleventh century Brabant Duke Jan I (Jan Primus = Gambrinus) was history's first brewer. This is indeed a slight exaggeration, as archaeological excavations prove that the Sumerians had already got in high spirits by the magic "barley water" some 5,000 years ago.

Still, the Czechs – accompanied by their Western neighbours in Bavaria – can claim the right to several inventions that changed the art of beer brewing forever.

Firstly, they understood sooner than anybody else that "barley water" (both the Czechs and the Bavarians resisted the temptation to experiment with grains other than the one prescribed by the original Sumerian recipe) could be mixed very successfully with hops. And second, thanks to Josef Groll, a Bavarian brewer who was head-hunted to Western

Bohemia in 1842, the city of Plzeň (in **German** Pilsen) was among the first to start mass production of beer using the "lower" fermentation method, resulting in a product which later has acquired worldwide reputation as *Pilsner*.

Yet it's fair to assume that the Czechs have been brewing beer more or less from the moment that the first tribes of Slavs settled in the area between the Elbe and the Vltava, sometime in the sixth century CE. The pan-Slavonic word for beer, *pivo*, is even closely linked to the word *píti* (to drink). According to the beer expert Antonín Kratochvíle, the first documentation of brewing in Bohemia is the Foundation Deed of the Vyšehrad Collegiate Church in Prague, dated 1088, which assigns a "tithe of hops" to be delivered to the canon regulars to enable them to brew.

During the following centuries, breweries popped up in several monasteries, where monks produced beer both for their own godly consumption, and for the probably-not-so-pious local noblemen. Beer brewing made considerable headway in the fourteenth century, when the Czech kings established new royal towns with amazing speed all over the country. To secure themselves as much public support as possible, the kings cleverly enough gave respected burghers the privilege to brew beer.

To start with, the burghers produced only for their own consumption, but this individualistic attitude soon proved inefficient. Therefore, they joined forces and employed brewers to make it for them. In other words, the basis of the first modern concessionary breweries was laid.

It was only with the nineteenth century's technological inventions that Czech beer brewing became a virtual industry and a business. In fact, all members of the current "Big Five" – *Prazdroj* and *Gambrinus* in Plzeň, *Staropramen* in Prague, *Budvar* in České Budějovice and the *Velké Popovice* brewery in Central Bohemia – were established around 1850. It's no coincidence that all of them are situated in Bohemia. In **Moravia,** people tend to compensate their less-excessive relationship to beer with a correspondingly excessive consumption of local wine.

Photo © Jaroslav Fišer

Now, you might object that several local breweries are marketing their products with the slogan "Brewed in this city from 1575". Well, they're certainly not speaking about the same type of beer as the one they produce today. In sixteenth century Bohemia it was, according to the Brewery Museum in Plzeň, not uncommon for brews to be "improved" with the bones of executed criminals, **dog's** faeces, sawdust from dug-up coffins, splinters from scaffolds or other delicacies. Therefore, the only thing a *Pilsner* beer brewed in, say, 1615, has in common with the light and delicious *Prazdroj* which is produced today, is the city of Plzeň as its place of origin, and barley and hops as its raw materials.

By the beginning of the twentieth century, the Czechs had emerged as the Austro-**Hungarian** Empire's ultimate beer nation. Of the 1,050 breweries that were operating in the entire empire in 1912, 666 were situated in Bohemia, Moravia or Silesia. After the founding of Czecho-slovakia, the number of breweries started to decrease (by 1937, there were 374 left), but, due to rapid modernization, production steadily increased. Obviously, not only thirsty Czechs benefited from the larger brewing capacity. In the 1920s, Czech beer exports skyrocketed, which hugely contributed to making the young republic visible on the global market.

There's not much to say about the unlucky combination of Czech beer brewing and **communism**. By 1948, all breweries were nationalized and the management centralized, which inevitably led to poorer quality. As late as in the 1980s, when people were shopping for beer in their local grocery, it was perfectly common to turn every bottle upside-down to check that it didn't contain deposits or other filthy things.

The Bolsheviks, however, by no means prevented the Czechs from flocking to their *hospodas* and drinking their beer as they always have. Actually, cheap and relatively tasty beer was one of the main enticements with which the communist regime bought support from the broad masses. Before 1989, some pundits even considered a dramatic hike in the price of beer to be among the few things that could make the Czechs revolt against the communists (see: **Velvet Revolution**).

As in almost all other fields of society, the fall of communism also had a positive impact on the breweries. With the exception of *Budvar* in České Budějovice, all members of the "Big Five" have been privatised (several of them, such as Prazdroj in Plzeň, by **foreigners**), and this also goes for the vast majority of the small- and medium-sized breweries. There have also been some new ones established, most of them microbreweries, so currently, the Czech Republic can boast about 84 breweries with total production approximating 19 million hectolitres. If this doesn't say anything to you, just try to imagine some 3.8 billion pints in a row…

Now, let's have a look at the practical part of this foamy subject.

If beer drinking is not a national sport, then at least it is a basic part both of the Czech lifestyle and traditional **Czech cuisine.** In fact, there are those natives who even consider beer to be a soft drink. A doctor, whom the author of this manual once visited, claimed in dead earnestness that fewer than four pints of beer does not count as alcohol. Some of his foreign colleagues might disagree about that, but he still had a point: about 60 percent of the beer consumed in the Czech Republic is of low gravity (ca. 3 percent alcohol), while stronger beer, popular, for instance, in Belgium, is more or less unknown.

This brings us to two basic terms from the Czech beer **world**: *desítka* and *dvanáctka*.

The first means *ten-degree* beer and the latter *twelve-degree* beer, and both correspond to the two main types that are consumed in this country. Many people, including lots of native Czechs, confuse this marking with the alcohol content, which is actually a big mistake. The term *desítka* means that the beer contains 10 percent (or degrees, as the brewers used to say) extract of the original young beer, while the *dvanáctka* has twelve percent.

Thus, the latter, containing about 5 percent alcohol, has a fuller taste and a stronger flavour of hops than the former, which normally has 3 percent alcohol. In other words, Czech beer, in both of its main versions, is relatively weak in alcohol, but is compensated by its rich flavour.

Beer is also an inexhaustible source of debates (and sometimes even black eyes) in this country. Questions such as, "Has *Plzeňský Prazdroj* reached at a higher level of beer evolution than *Budějovický Budvar?*" (it hasn't!), or "Should beer bottles (yes, bottles! Only stupid foreigners buy canned beer) be stored on the seventh or on the eighth stair in the cellar staircase?" are treated with the utmost seriousness by any true *pivař*. Most of them will even claim that beer is one of your health's best friends. Which, actually, is not all that untrue.

Most of us have already experienced that our hair gets shinier when we wash it in beer, and even the wildest hair-do can be tamed by a few drops of beer (famous as the *Pilsner Ur–gel*). You might have also noticed that beer is strongly diuretic, so it helps cleanse your kidneys and bladder of detritus. But did you know that beer also contains an incredible amount of minerals, ranging from potash and sodium to chloride, phosphorus, magnesium and silicon, plus all the most important substances in the vitamin B family? Or that some Czech spas even recommend a bottle of beer daily to fight coronary disease?

Perhaps there's no need to blow up the doctor's usual message that beer has a positive effect on your physiology only as long as it's consumed in "moderate" quantities. And you're probably aware of the fact that a *desítka* contains about 380 calories and a *dvanáctka* no less than 460 calories. Instead, remember **Jára Cimrman's** somewhat sexist, but still widely respected words of wisdom: *"Teplé pivo horší než studená ženská!"* – Warm beer is worse than a cold woman!

Blava

To a Czech ear, this frequently used slang abbreviation of "Bratislava" sounds very close to a combination of the two words *bláto* (mud) and *kráva* (cow). If this makes you believe that the Czechs tend to regard neighbouring Slovakia's capital as a somewhat dull and uninteresting place, you're exactly right. Small but romantic Bratislava on the Danube is a city most Czechs take great pride in not visiting.

One can, of course, perfectly understand that the Czechs after the **Velvet Revolution** and 40 years of isolation started exploring foreign countries instead of their own country, but the ostentatious ignorance and belittling of Bratislava is a quite evident expression of the Czech paternalism that enraged the **Slovaks** in the Czechoslovak era.

And it's also a bit comic, since the Slovak-**Hungarian-German-Jewish** city Pressburg (or Pozsony) in 1918 actually was renamed Bratislava (*brat'* – brother, *slava* – glory) as a tribute to the eternal brotherhood between the Czechs and Slovaks.

Bohemia

As the story goes, the Czechs descent from a Slavonic people who, in the sixth century, were led to the area of today's Bohemia by the legendary chief Čech and his younger brothers Lech and Mech. After having trudged thousands of kilometres from the Slav heartland somewhere by the Dnepr, old Čech commanded his exhausted tribesmen to climb Říp, a hilltop visibly resembling a woman's breast (see: **Sex**).

From this 500-meter high elevation not far from the Elbe River in Central Bohemia, indescribably beautiful scenery opened up in front of the newly-arrived Slavs. Not surprisingly, they immediately decided to stop roaming about, and to settle down on the gorgeous plains beneath them, which they called *Čechy* in honour of their wise chief.

Strictly speaking, it's more than dubious that great chief Čech ever lived (actually, there is also a chief called Čech in Croat mythology). The unromantic truth is that the name of the country is probably connected with the Polish word *czachy* (dry), which described the quality of the land between Labe (Elbe) and Vltava (Moldau) rivers.

However, what's not disputed at all is that the land that was settled by the Czech Slavs in the sixth century had earlier been inhabited by Celts. In the period 200–100 before Common Era Celtic tribes established numerous settlements, ritual buildings, burial sites and fortified villages, or *oppida*, all over the Czech lands. You can still find the remnants of one such magnificent *oppidum* only a few kilometres south of Prague, at Závist on the banks of the Vltava.

The Celts were kicked out of what are now the Czech lands by the Germanic Marcomannis several decades before Common Era, and if they had only left inventions such as the potter's wheel, the circular mill, some coins and an apparently eternal craze among the Czechs for everything Celtic, they wouldn't have deserved to be mentioned in this country's history with more than a couple of words.

Yet the Czechs can thank the Celtic *Boiohaemum* tribe for one basic contribution to their cultural history: the name *Bohemia* – the term most countries in the **world** use when speaking about the part of the country that the Czechs themselves call *Čechy*.

Needless to say, not all Czechs are too enthusiastic about this term. Ever since the French author Henri Murgers published his *Scenes from Life in Bohemia* in 1848, decent citizens have considered Bohemians to be painters, writers, poets and similar good-for-nothings, who don't feel bound by "ordinary" moral conventions. True, the Czech lands have certainly never lacked people in this category, but, still, isn't it a bit unfair to deem several million Czechs as morally devastated *Bohemians*?

To avoid this embarrassing confusion, some reputation-wary Czechs have come up with a sweet, pseudo-scientific explanation:

"Yes, it's correct that the Bohemians who came to France in the early nineteenth century drank and copulated far more and worked and went to church far less than they should have. But these people were actually not Czechs – they were **Roma**! In England they claimed to be of (E)gyptian origin, in Spain and the Czech lands, they claimed to be *Flamencos* (Flemings). Now, they use the same trick in France by saying they are *Bohemians*!"

But you know better: the original Bohemians were neither Czech Slavs nor Roma. They were Celts!

Bureaucracy

In **Bohemia** and **Moravia**, bureaucracy was booming already when the Czechs were a part of the Austro-**Hungarian** Empire (that's where they were originally infected by the disease). It got even worse under the communists, and notwithstanding all promises made by the **politicians** after 1989, the situation hasn't improved any much after the **Velvet Revolution** either.

The rule of the red tape is, admittedly, nothing exceptional in **Central Europe**. One might even say that this is perfectly normal in a country that has fostered both **Franz Kafka** and The Good Soldier **Švejk**. And indeed, Czech bureaucracy's tentacles can from time to time behave in a way that makes a poor citizen (not to mention a **foreigner**) a part of the same all-mighty and incomprehensible machinery as Kafka's **hero** Josef K.

In addition to its enormity, Czech bureaucracy is characterized by one basic feature: formal details are often much more important than substance.

This is very conspicuous in the judiciary system, where entire legal cases can be postponed because a form is not correctly filled out or an address has recently been changed. What's more, judges are often engaged in formal matters that other countries solve with a civil servant and a computer. As a result, operations, such as registering a new company, that take a couple of days in, say, Scandinavia, can take four to five months in the Czech Republic.

It's hard to say how many days (possibly years) of his or her life that the average Czech spends queuing up at different offices or running around gathering the necessary *razítka* (stamps). But more or less all of them have realized one crucial thing: you simply can't beat the system (well, you can grease it – see: **Corruption**). This goes double for a vulnerable foreigner. However legitimate your complaints are, loud outbursts or even frustrated yelling don't help you at all. On the contrary, the low-paid bureaucrat will be delighted to use his or her only privilege: i.e. the power to make the situation even worse for you, optimally causing you a nervous breakdown.

Consequently, there are only two ways of dealing with Czech bureaucracy. Either you pay somebody to fix the formalities and the queuing for you, or, if you decide to undergo the Calvary personally, you arm yourself with tons of patience, lots of phlegm, a half-witted smile – and a copy of Jaroslav Hašek's Good Soldier Švejk.

Carlsbad English Bitters

This somewhat exotic name refers to a brand of herbal liquor that is now sold under the name *Becherovka*. Although most Czechs praise it to the sky and revere it with the same intensity as the **Russians** worship their vodka or the French their Champagne, some (well, many) **foreigners** have problems swallowing this bitter mixture of aromatic oils and alcohol, delivered in its characteristic flat and green bottles.

Yet any foreigner who'd like to find friends in this country is strongly advised to conceal his or her potential dislike of *Becherovka*, as most Czechs would take it as an insult of their national pride. Miloš Zeman, the Czech Republic's Prime Minister until 2002, even cherished the national treasure so profoundly that the country's diplomacy still has to mitigate foreign governments whom Zeman offended while considerably animated by litres of herbal liqueur.

The widespread use of *Becherovka* as a fetish of Czech patriotism has, however, one slight drawback: it was invented by the pharmacist Josef Becher, and he was, like the vast majority of his fellow inhabitants in the West-**Bohemian** spa city of Carlsbad (now Karlovy Vary), actually a

German (obviously, this is also a detail that you are advised to keep to yourself). Still, *Becherovka* is a colourful part of Czech cultural history, and it certainly belongs to the well-oriented foreigner's basic knowledge of this country.

It all started in 1805, when the English doctor Frobig came to Carlsbad, where he found accommodations in the house where Josef

Becher had his pharmacy. Thanks to their common interests in mixing different fluids, the doctor and pharmacist soon got acquainted. In 1807, the two gentlemen presented the result of their long-lasting experiments: *Carlsbad English Bitters.*

It's known that Josef Becher sincerely considered the "gastric drops" to be a medicine. However, hordes of patients in the spa city rapidly discovered that Becher's Bitter not only improved digestion, but – thanks to the not insignificant alcohol content – also improved bad moods.

The production and marketing of Becher's *Gesundheits-Liqueur* (Health Liqueur) hit its stride when Josef's son Johann took over the management in 1841. It was also Johann (in Czech Jan) who registered the trademark – modestly enough, not in his father the inventor's name, but in his own.

For the next century, agile marketing combined with big chunks of luck helped Becher's liqueur to penetrate markets all over Europe, and it even became popular in Egypt. The company reached its zenith when Emperor **Franz Josef**, by coincidence, tasted the liqueur. The drops evidently pleased the imperial stomach, for after that day, Becher delivered 50 litres to the court in Vienna every month (His Imperial Highness probably didn't consume it all by himself).

The Becher family's success story came to a rather brutal end in 1945. As were nearly all the three million ethnic German citizens in Czechoslovakia, the Becher family was deported from the country (see: **Munich Agreement**). According to the Potsdam Conference's decisions on war reparations, all their property – including the distillery – fell to the Czechoslovak state as compensation for damages caused by the Germans during their more than six-year occupation of *Protektorat Böhmen und Mähren.*

During the 40 years of communist misrule, *Karlovarská Becherovka*, as both the company and the liqueur were renamed, scraped by without any significant investments or efforts to promote exports. Luckily for Czech *Becherovka* fetishists, the bad times ended with the **Velvet**

Revolution. In 1997, the distillery in Karlovy Vary – including the secret receipt of *Becherovka* – was sold to the Pernod-Ricard concern, which, after some wrangling with a Becher daughter company in Germany and a pirate distillery in Slovakia, has started the fight to regain the international position that was lost during the last half century.

That's the whole story. If you still think the beverage tastes more like the medicine it once was promoted as than an irresistible aperitif, try this trick: nonchalantly order a *beton* (concrete), which is the Czech slang expression for *Becherovka* mixed with tonic.

This method has two advantages. Firstly, it clearly demonstrates that you are a true connoisseur of Czech drinking culture. And secondly, thanks to the tonic, *beton* doesn't remind you of the gastric drops at all. Cheers!

Carp

The Czechs don't have access to the **ocean**, so they can hardly be blamed for not offering a wild variety of delicious seafood (see: **Czech Cuisine**). Nevertheless, a **foreigner** may be somewhat surprised by the fact that the Czechs' relations to fish can – with a slight exaggeration – be reduced to one single species: *Cyprinus carpio* – the carp.

Inhabitants of maritime nations often turn up their noses at this fat and thick-boned creature that revels in the mud and standing waters of fishponds. For a land-locked nation, though, the carp has its undisputed qualities.

First of all, the carp is an undemanding fellow, who is easily reared in artificial ponds. The Czechs discovered this practical advantage almost a millennium ago, when the country was christened. With the introduction of the new **religion**, a ban of eating meat in the time of fasting soon followed. Creative souls, however, got hold of the fleshy carp (how it found its way from China to the Czech lands is not documented) and the Lent problem was solved.

As in so many other fields of Czech economy and culture in the Middle Ages, also the rearing of carp took off under the reign of the dynamic Charles IV in the fourteenth century. Artificial ponds and lakes were constructed at big pace, especially in the Třeboň area, with the result that **Bohemia** and **Moravia** by the beginning of the seventeenth century could boast fish ponds covering a total of 160,000 hectares – almost three times the size of Balaton, **Central Europe**'s largest lake!

The Thirty Years' War (see: **Battle of White Mountain**) and the subsequent economic decline also affected the rearing of carp, and things changed for the better only in the 1860s. Today, artificial ponds and lakes cover about 51,000 hectares, which is rather bleak compared to their heyday four centuries ago. Modern breeding technologies, however, have worked miracles with productivity. Thus, the Czech Republic's fisheries annually deliver more than 21,000 tons – quite impressive for a land-locked country – of which carp represent nearly 90 percent.

One might, of course, ask whether there not are other and better-tasting species that can be successfully reared in ponds. Well, there definitely are. So why are the Czechs so fixated on the poor carp? Simply because of its almost mythical role in Czech culture.

This is not only based on the fact that the carp is a "cute" fish, whose marked lips, big eyes and fat belly make it an obvious **hero** in the illustrated fairy-tales which Czech children are raised with. The main reason is that the carp, ever since the Middle Ages, when people strictly observed Lent, has been the ultimate Christmas dish of the Czechs.

Neither centuries of **Austrian** rule, Nazi occupation or communist dictatorship managed to budge the carp's position. Just as stubbornly as the Czechs resisted the Moscow-promoted *Dyedushka Moroz* (Father Frost) and clung to their *Ježíšek* (Infant Jesus) as the holiday's main star, nothing can replace the carp, served fried with potato salad, at the Christmas table.

Thus, every December a fantastic show is performed all over the country. Large containers filled with water and wriggling carp pop up in streets and squares. Even if the thermometer falls to 20 degrees below zero, millions of Czechs queue up patiently for hours to buy their Christmas dinner. When they are finally served, the fishmonger, with clothes dramatically smeared with blood and guts, asks the classic question: to kill, or not to kill?

Most people tend to follow Pilate's example, and they give the fishmonger the go-ahead to smash the carp's noodle with a club, and thus promote the poor fellow directly to the frying pan. However, it often happens, especially when children have come with Mom or Dad to buy the Christmas delicacy, that the carp gets temporary mercy. Instead of being instantly dispatched to eternity, the fish is carried away in a plastic bag, and then allowed to swim in the family's bathtub until Christmas Eve.

Needless to say, there are those softhearted Czechs who can't bear to kill their new pets. This often leads to an even more fantastic spectacle than the carp-shows in the street. Every Christmas Eve, you can see people at the banks of Vltava and other big rivers. There, they are giving their fellow creature new life by putting it back into the water where it belongs. True, river water is usually far too cold for the carp, so they inevitably die, but probably not even Christ himself would have questioned the carp-owners' sincere motives.

Finally, a tip: if you are invited to celebrate Christmas with a Czech family, remember to take a look under your plate (preferably, without tipping the carp and potato salad onto the table cloth). If your hosts observe the old traditions, you'll find a carp's scale under it. Be sure to take it with you – it's bound to bring you good luck!

Central Europe

There are few things that enrage a Czech more than **foreigners** speaking about the Czech Republic as a part of Eastern Europe. Their indignation is quite understandable. Just because former Czechoslovakia spent some 40 years under Moscow's yoke and the Czech and **Russian** languages have common roots, it's pretty harsh to rub out the Czechs' almost 600 years of history as an independent principality and kingdom incorporated in the Holy Roman Empire, and later 300 years as a part of the Austro-**Hungarian** Empire.

In school, Czech children learn that their country has been in the very locus of European history since the Middle Ages. This might be considered slightly ethno-centric, but by and large, it's not that far out.

Take, for instance, the Reformation. Most people believe it started with the **German** Martin Luther. But actually, it was triggered by the Czech priest **Jan Hus**, who thundered so intensely against the Catholic Church's trade with indulgences that the Vatican found it most convenient to burn him on a stake, in 1415 – and thus provided the Czechs with the first of their many "heroic debacles".

The Thirty Years' War, in which more or less every state on the European continent became involved, started in 1618, when protestant Czechs threw the Catholic king's counsellors out of a window at the Prague Castle (see: **Battle of White Mountain**). Luckily for the counsellors, they both survived this **defenestration**, thanks to the latrine in which the gentlemen landed.

Two Czech kings, Charles IV (1316–1378) and Rudolf II (1552–1612) were even elected Emperors of the Holy Roman Empire. True, the title sounds quite impressive compared to the rather limited power that the Emperor exercised, and neither of them spoke Czech as their mother tongue (the former was from the Western German Luxembourg dynasty, the latter was an **Austrian** Habsburg). Still, for today's Czechs, they both represent indisputable evidence that this country, from a historical point of view, is an integrated part of Central Europe, and has no more in common with "Eastern Europe" than Austria, Germany or, say, Luxembourg.

Of course, this problem goes beyond religion and history. Take a look at the older buildings that surround you in any **Bohemian** and **Moravian** town. Read **Kafka**, **Švejk**, **Kundera** and Seifert (see: **First Republic**), listen to the music of Smetana, Dvořák and Martinů, or visit a gallery with the paintings of Josef Čapek, Emil Filla and Kamil Lhoták.

In short, there are thousands of examples within architecture, literature, music and the arts that prove beyond any doubt that Czech culture can be placed – literally speaking – in the middle of Europe. The renowned linguist R.G.A. de Bray puts it like this:

"Czech culture forms an ideal synthesis of East and West. Antonín Dvořák's opera *Rusalka* is a perfect example: an essentially Slavonic legend, with a Slav atmosphere of mystery and longing, set out against Dvořák's rich melodious music, Slav in spirit, if you will, but Western in technique and harmony."

And if this still shouldn't convince a sceptical foreigner, there is the ultimate argument at hand: geography. Prague is situated more to the West than Vienna, Stockholm and Helsinki. Does anybody speak about these cities as East European?

To outsiders, this may seem completely irrelevant; who cares about the difference between Central and Eastern Europe? Well, most Czechs do. Like it or not, it's a question about **national identity**. While the countries in Central Europe are regarded as countries that were "kidnapped from Europe by the Soviet Union", as Milan Kundera writes,

Eastern Europe is the mafia-infested, vodka-drinking part of Europe that still is mired in its communist past.

No matter how arbitrary and snobbish this border-line might occur to you, the essence of it is clear as crystal: in a Czech context, the nomenclature "Eastern Europe" should be used with the utmost care and only in a strictly geographical context.

Ultimately, this leads us to another, even more academic question. Where on earth is the border between Central and Eastern Europe? Certainly, the Czechs don't have the slightest doubt that they belong to Central Europe. As do the Hungarians, **Slovaks, Austrians**, Slovenes, Croatians (see: **Balkans**) and all the other nations in the former Austro-Hungarian empire.

But what about Poland, whose eastern part constituted the Russian empire's western-most province for more than a hundred years? And Galicia and Ruthenia, which for centuries belonged to the same monarchy as the Czechs, but now are a part of Ukraine. Where do the Baltic states belong?

The farther east you go, the more diffuse is the perception of the borderline between Central and Eastern Europe. The Polish writer Jacek Wozniakowski once got so frustrated by this vagueness that he decided to settle the question once and for all. The criterion he used was the frequency and the standard of public toilets in different European countries.

Not surprisingly, Wozniakowski found that his Polish motherland is clearly a part of Central Europe, while Belarus is not. Of course, if Wozniakowski's criterion is applied consequently, several states, which have always regarded themselves to be hard-core Western Europe, could risk ending up in its very Eastern part.

Charter 77

Czechoslovakia's president Gustav Husák was by all accounts convinced he had made a good deal when he solemnly signed the final act at the Conference on Security and Cooperation in Europe in August 1975.

The Helsinki Agreement, approved by the USA, the Soviet Union and 34 other Western states, finally confirmed the new borders that emerged in Europe after the Second World War, and formally cemented the control that the **Russians** (and their local vassals like Husák) had taken over Central and Eastern Europe.

Yet the Western countries didn't want to give the Russians the deal they so overtly longed for without anything in return. That's why the Helsinki Agreement also contained paragraphs that obliged all countries, regardless of their ideology, to respect basic human rights. But just like his Soviet protector Leonid Brezhnev, Czechoslovakia's Husák considered this to be liberal mumbo-jumbo without any practical relevance.

Surprisingly enough, it was not the rebellious **Poles** or the relatively liberal **Hungarians**, but the oppressed and resigned Czechs (see: **Communism**), who soon proved Husák completely wrong.

When a Prague court convicted a group of Frank Zappa clones called The Plastic People of the Universe of subversion (a term the Bolshevik regime used for any activity displaying the slightest expression of individual freedom), playwright **Václav Havel** and a group of his dissident friends published a document, in January 1977, titled Charter 77 (the name was inspired by the English *Magna Charta* of liberties from 1215) where they modestly reminded the regime of the human rights commitments it had solemnly signed a year and a half earlier in Helsinki.

This step formed the backdrop for one of the most amazing human rights movements in the former East Bloc. Contrary to Poland's Solidarity trade union, Charter 77 never became a mass movement. It was neither a proper organization, with leaders and rules, but rather a society of people, ranging from socialists to hard-line Catholics, united only by a common adversary – the Bolshevik tyrants.

The first Charter 77 document, which Havel, his playwright-colleague Pavel Kohout, philosopher Jan Patočka, journalist Jiří Dienstbier, Prague Spring's minister of **foreign** affairs Jiří Hájek and some 200 other people tried to publish via the national news agency ČTK (of course the agency rejected it, but Western media like Le Monde and The Times made it **world** famous overnight) caused wild panic among the Bolshevik leadership. Jaromír Obzina, Minister of Interior at that time, said in interviews after the **Velvet Revolution** that the comrades believed the Charter had great potential for becoming a mass movement, and therefore they immediately launched a hysterical counterattack.

Less than a month after Charter 77 was published in the West and broadcast to Czechoslovakia by Radio Free Europe, the regime summoned every actor, musician, composer, writer or painter in the country to a mass rally in the National Theatre.

After actress Jiřina Švorcová and a couple of other Bolshevik mascots had reeled off hair-raisingly pathetic proclamations condemning the Charter signatories as *samozvanci a ztroskotanci* (self-appointed [critics] and [morally] bankrupt people) who had willingly betrayed their "socialist mother country" to serve the Western imperialists, the entire cultural elite was marched in front of the television cameras to sign an "Anti-Charter" in defence of the regime. A week later, the depressing show was repeated with **Karel Gott** and hundreds of other pop music and television stars in the leading roles.

It's both a comic and a tragic expression of life in Bolshevik Czechoslovakia that more than 7,000 Czech and **Slovak** cultural celebrities signed the Anti-Charter without hesitation, and thus condemned a document they not even were allowed to read. And if they had read it, they would have seen that the "subversive authors" only referred to laws that the Bolsheviks themselves had promised to respect when they signed the Helsinki Agreement a year and a half earlier.

Eva Kantůrková, a writer and Charter 77 signatory, comments on this situation very aptly: "The Anti-Charter was a very effective weapon for the regime. The faithful had their faith strengthened, while the opportunists were assured that it paid to behave opportunistically." Needless to say, many of the celebrities who blindly signed the Anti-Charter in 1977 are still celebrities.

From the publication of its first document in January 1977 until the Velvet Revolution threw the Bolshevik regime into history's dustbin in 1989, fewer than 1,900 Czechs and Slovaks officially signed the Charter 77 document. Considering that the population numbered 15 million people, this is perhaps not such a dazzling a figure. Considering the constant police harassment, jail sentences (Havel himself served more than four years behind bars) and the loss of jobs and educational opportunities, combined with social excommunication and strong pressure to emigrate, it's impressive that at least 1,900 individuals were brave and unselfish enough to risk their very existence in the name of some abstract ideals.

Yet the Charter 77 signatories' courage and rare idealism have not automatically secured them common respect and eternal glory. True, the Civic Forum, which took political power after the Velvet Revolution, was totally dominated by Charter signatories, and hundreds of other Charter people were, quite deservedly, rewarded with official postings as ambassadors, mayors, professors and rectors. But as things usually go in Czech history, the number of opponents to a rotten regime quadruples at the moment the rotten regime is overturned. So as soon as the post-revolutionary euphoria had evaporated, wild discussions broke out about Charter 77's real impact on the Bolshevik regime.

One of the less creative and most common excuses for not supporting Charter 77 is that the movement "was dominated by reform communists". As Miroslav Kalousek, a Christian Democrat **politician** of the post 1989-generation puts it: "I had too little courage, while the Charter had too many Marxists."

This is, however, quite transparent demagogy. Even though some leading Charter 77 signatories never concealed that they had once been members of the Communist Party, the movement's official standpoints were always painstakingly formulated to defend human rights issues in general. Some of the Charter's most high-profile signatories, such as Václav Havel, the Catholic priest Václav Malý or actor Pavel Landovský could hardly be accused of communist sympathies, and in the trio that fronted the Charter as its spokespersons (every year, three new people were elected) there was never more than one ex-communist at a time.

Another objection is that Charter 77 was a social club reserved for Prague intellectuals with **personal connections** to Václav Havel and his theatre friends. This is also a rather handy excuse. Intellectuals were admittedly represented in large force, but on the list of signatories published after the Velvet Revolution there are surprisingly many railway workers, housewives, cooks and other completely ordinary people who simply saw the Charter as a way to react against the widespread moral **corruption** that characterized the Husák era.

Only the allegations about *Pragocentricism* can be said to have some substance. People in **Moravia** hate to admit it, but the Czech elite has always been based in the capital. So were the Charter signatories, who moreover found it easier to help and support each other in Czechoslovakia's only city with more than a million inhabitants. It's fair to say that the number of Charter people became smaller and smaller the farther away you got from Prague, and to find Slovak signatories, you almost needed a magnifying glass.

Today, Charter 77 definitely belongs to history. The movement was formally dissolved in the mid-1990s, and most of the signatories who entered politics in the wake of the Velvet Revolution, have left their offices. Symbolically, the most loaded change took place in the spring of 2003, when Charter 77's co-founder Václav Havel was replaced as the Czech Republic's president by **Václav Klaus**, a sly technocrat, who openly questions whether Charter had any political impact at all.

But that question is somewhat misplaced. The philosopher Jan Patočka, the Charter's spiritual guru who died from a heart attack during a 10-hour interrogation by the secret police, warned from the very beginning that Charter 77 had more to do with morality than politics. And that warning fits perfectly also as an epitaph:

To the millions of decent people who, for better or worse reasoning, never dared to protest openly against the Bolshevik regime, Charter 77 proved that the Czechs were not a nation of spineless **Švejks** who would support any rotten regime that happened to be in power (see: **National Identity**). Of course, there is also a not-insignificant part of the population who detest everything connected to the Charter 77, because it constantly reminds them of their own lack of courage.

Cimrman, Jára

Do you know who was the first to reach the North Pole? Who also projected the Panama canal, invented both yoghurt and the forerunner of Internet, made numerous revolutionary discoveries in chemistry and engineering, wrote several brilliant dramatic plays and symphonies and, in addition to that, inspired people such as Einstein, Chekhov and Zeppelin in their work? None other than the universal genius Jára Cimrman!

It has never been established exactly when the incredibly gifted Jaroslav (Jára among friends) was born. Since the priest responsible for the local church register was allegedly drunk, both 1853 and 1864 figure as his year of birth. However, it's undisputed that **Bohemia** and **Moravia**, at the time Cimrman was born were still a part of the Austro-**Hungarian** Empire.

It has also been established that his mother was an **Austrian** actress, Marlén Jelínková, while his father a Czech tailor named Leopold Zimmermann (quite typically for the ethnic and cultural mixture that prevailed in the Habsburg Empire, Cimrman's Germanic mother had a Slavonic name while his Czech father had a **German** one).

However, as it often goes in **Central Europe**, people with bi-national parentage tend to become bigger nationalists than those with both parents of the same nationality. In Jára's case, he became an ardent Czech patriot, who insisted that his über-German **surname** should be treated as a Slavonic one. But this is pretty much all we originally know about him, because in 1914, by the outbreak of the First World War, Cimrman disappeared from the surface of earth. Only in 1966 was a trunk with his belongings accidentally discovered in the village of Liptákov. Thus, the pantheon of Czech national **heroes** had suddenly been enlarged with one of human history's most extraordinary personalities.

As you might already have guessed, Jára Cimrman is a pure mystification, created by two journalists in Czechoslovak Broadcasting for a radio program that was released in 1966.

But contrary to all expectations, the listeners' response to the program about the unknown genius was so overwhelming that one of the radio journalists, Zdeněk Svěrák (also known as the author of the screenplay of the Oscar-winning film "Kolja"), decided to transform the gag into a theatre play. So in 1967, with assistance from his friend, the director Ladislav Smoljak, Svěrák staged *The Act* – "a play that was found among the unknown genius Jára Cimrman's belongings" – in a theatre in Prague's Malá Strana.

The Act was a tremendous success. People loved the wild exaggerations about the Czech giant-cum-patriot and all his crazy adventures from the days of the Austro-Hungarian Empire. Of course, it was no less fun that all the actors were clumsy and nervous amateurs, and that the play was opened by an ultra-scientific seminar about Cimrman and his life and adventures given by "Professor" Smoljak and "Docent" Svěrák (see: **Academic Titles**).

Four decades and 13 plays later, Jára Cimrman has become something like the quintessence of Czech humor and **national identity**. People queue up for hours to get tickets to his plays (like *The Act*, all of the others have also been written by Smoljak and Svěrák), which have been performed at the *Jára Cimrman Theatre* in Prague's Žižkov district for many years.

The most ardent fans have learnt entire passages from different Cimrman plays by heart, and "cimrmanologists" compete in reeling off the longest and funniest quotations from the 14 plays. To honour the great Czech, several cities have even installed plaques announcing that "Jára Cimrman once slept in this house" or "In this house, the Czech universal genius Jára Cimrman once had breakfast".

Foreigners may find the Czechs' Cimrman craze strange. When the ensemble turned up at a theatre festival in Austria some years ago, the festival's director immediately threw the Cimrman gang out, shouting that "these Czech dilettantes" were a disgrace to the performing arts. Yet the actors' profound amateurism is probably one of the reasons why the Czechs love the Cimrman figure. In fact, the very concept is a many-levelled parody: the actors are making fun of themselves and their lack of professionalism, the Cimrman figure is making fun of "great **heroes**", and the fact that the greatest – and also most unfortunate - of them all is actually Czech, is a parody of the nation's rather modest size and unfortunate destiny.

In other words, Jára Cimrman fully complies with the Czech tradition of not taking yourself too seriously. He also reflects the widespread tendency to regard the country's many historic debacles as something inflicted by others. In the same way that inexplicable mishaps prevented Cimrman from being awarded all of the Nobel Prizes he undoubtedly deserved, history, bigger countries or scheming neighbours (but under no circumstance the Czechs themselves!) have given the nation a harder fate than it really deserves.

In addition, Svěrák and Smoljak made a brilliant move by placing Cimrman in the Austro-Hungarian Empire (see: **Franz Josef**). On the one hand, it sated the nostalgia for an era that many Czechs regard as more innocent, lucky and even romantic than the grey normalization in which they lived. On the other hand, Cimrman could make jokes about politics without fearing reprisals from the Communist regime, because it "hadn't any relevance to the present".

Of course, the audience was more than capable of reading between the lines (see: **Communication**). Thus, in the dark years of normalization a Jára Cimrman performance became one of very few public media where the common Czech could roar with laughter from a half-hidden joke about the rulers without having to fear any consequences.

One should, of course, be careful to interpret Jára Cimrman's enormous popularity as a proof of some sense of humour common to all Czechs or even as a symbol of a "typical Czech mentality". But it may still be fair to draw one conclusion: the enthusiastic way in which millions of grown-up Czechs embrace a mythical, undiscovered genius suggests that there probably are more playful people in the Czech Republic than in most other countries.

Communication

Lots of **foreigners** who have come to the Czech Republic as managers of local companies tell the same story: after their first week in the job, they're all pleasantly surprised by how eagerly and quickly their Czech employees carry out their directions.

However, within a month or two, most of them have a surprising revelation. Their subordinates, who overtly accepted all orders from the boss without a single word of protest or disagreement, have in reality done something completely different.

Such troubles can't immediately be blamed on a language barrier. A foreigner and a Czech may both speak the same language flawlessly, but still have severe problems with communication. An extreme example is the **Austrian** military doctor who tried to diagnose The Good Soldier Švejk. After speaking with his patient for half an hour, he got so frustrated by the Czech's evasive and confusing answers that he uttered the now classical sentence: *"Das ganze tschechisches Volk ist eine Simmulantenbande"* – The entire Czech nation is a bunch of fakers!

This, of course, is both a coarse exaggeration and a literary generalization. Nevertheless, it's not entirely without an element of truth (see: **Jára Cimrman**), because the Czechs generally communicate in a far more indirect and understated way than Western Europeans usually do. To display strong emotions, for instance, be it raving anger or loud laughter, is often interpreted as proof of either mental instability or drunkenness (see: **Alcoholics**), and quite often, people say things that are only meant as an expression of courtesy.

A classic situation occurs when somebody invites you to his or her home and repeatedly insists that you don't need to take your shoes off. This must under no circumstances be interpreted literally! The Czech is not saying that you are free to ruin his wall-to-wall carpet (see: **Balkans**) with doggy turd. He or she only wants to indicate a willingness to go to great lengths just to please a guest. Which they actually very often do – the Czechs may not be the fastest in the **world** to invite foreigners to their homes, but when they finally do, they tend to be extremely hospitable. Consequently, you are supposed to smile in a friendly way, and immediately take your shoes off.

The importance many Czechs attach to demonstrations of modesty (which should by no means be confused with real modesty) may also bring the foreigner into confusing situations. When a Czech is offered something, it's considered blunt and ill-mannered to accept it without uttering something like *Oh no, that's too much,* or *Please, don't make any special arrangements just for me.* Again, this must not be interpreted literally. Afraid of being considered immodest or downright greedy, the Czech simply expects you to urge him or her to accept the offer with greater intensity.

This spectacle has been cultivated *ad absurdum* by Czech **politicians**. It's almost unthinkable that he (yes, bar a few bright and thick-skinned ladies, they are all men) will say something like *I am running for this or that position because I believe I'm the best*. Instead, they will modestly point out that their personal ambitions are very, very small indeed, but that a lot of supporters want them to candidate, and, of course, it's hard to let other people down, "so I'll take the burden on my shoulders".

How can a foreigner recognize that a Czech is doing or saying something just to express decorum? Unfortunately, there are no ironclad rules, but there are some clues – or rather patterns of accepted behaviour – you can cling to.

In addition to the widespread fear of giving an immodest impression, Czechs generally tend to avoid open confrontations. For instance, when somebody feels you have bothered him enough, he will – unless he's a friend of yours – probably avoid saying something like *Sorry, I have to go,* or even worse, *Sorry, I haven't time to talk to you.* Instead, he or she will use the fantastic Czech phrase *Nebudu Vás už zdržovat* (I don't want to detain you), which actually might mean *Bugger off; you're wasting my time!* Equally classic, when you ask a Czech something and the answer is *To je na dlouhé povídání* (That will be a long story), you are politely, but firmly, being asked to mind your own business.

Last, but not least: when communicating with a Czech, you should also remember that many people, because of their experience with the hard-hitting communist dictatorship, are still wary of sticking their necks out with a clear and unequivocal point of view. This, of course, doesn't mean they don't have strong opinions. There are few people on the planet who have such a rich history of anonymous denunciations as the Czechs, and local web debates are notoriously nasty.

The point is that many people tend to behave significantly differently when they're accountable for their actions, and when they're not. Admittedly, that's quite human. The surprising thing, though, is the formidable spread of this phenomenon in the Czech Republic.

Take, for instance, the Czech Parliament's election of **Václav Havel's** successor as president in February 2003. Prior to the voting, all Social Democrats in the Chamber of Deputies solemnly declared that they would certainly vote for their party's own candidate. But how did it turn out? Just to complicate life for the party's chairman, almost 30 Social Democrats used their secret ballots to vote for the opposition's candidate **Václav Klaus**, who subsequently won the presidential elections with a slight majority.

The Czechs are probably not more duplicitous than people elsewhere, but because of decorum, you should not take it for granted that a Czech really means yes when saying yes, or no when saying no. When it comes to **sex**, the old – and now pretty outdated – adage went that a woman, when answering no, actually meant maybe, and when saying maybe, indicated yes...

So, the only piece of advise that a foreigner can take is: look out for hints, don't expect people to support anything controversial in public, and tune your social antenna to a frequency considerably higher than what's used in Western Europe!

Communism

The Czechs' relationship to their totalitarian past is a pretty complicated affair. On one hand, they have taken stronger legal measures than the **Poles**, **Slovaks** and **Hungarians** against those who collaborated with the communists' secret police, the feared StB (see: **Lustration**).

When it comes to widespread collaboration with the Communist Party, though, the attitude is far more complex. At times, an outsider may even get the impression that the majority of those Czechs who have any personal experience from this era behave as if the 41-years long tyranny is a rather insignificant event that took place sometime around the **Battle of White Mountain**.

Then you have a smaller, but quite vociferous group of people, who vividly remember the communists – or the *Bolsheviks* or *Comanches* ("ideological redskins") as they are pejoratively called – but solely blame "Moscow" for all the horrors.

And finally, there is a small group of brave individuals who in the 1950s and 1960s served years in prison and forced labour camps for standing up against the regime, and now, legitimately, demand that their red tormentors should be punished. So far, the former political prisoners' claims have not met any particular success.

It's not hard to understand the broad masses' collective amnesia. Sometime in the beginning of the 1990s, then-Premier (and now, President) **Václav Klaus**, a gifted populist who has an amazing ability to always formulate things exactly as *Pepa Novák* – the common Czech – likes to hear them, put it like this: "It's impossible to drive forward with great speed if you constantly have to look in the mirror." This is undoubtedly a very handy piece of advice. Especially, a somewhat cynical observer might add, if the things you see in the mirror are not tremendously pretty.

Let's salt the wounds properly.

The Czechs themselves often say that the communists came to power through a coup d'état, which implies that it happened against most people's will. That's not entirely true. In the elections in 1946, the communists got 38 percent of the votes, which was more than any other party. Consequently, common parliamentarian rules determined that their chairman, Klement Gottwald, became Prime Minister in the "National Front government", a coalition of six parties.

True enough, in addition to being an **alcoholic** with syphilis, "Kléma" was an anti-democrat to the marrow of his bones who received his orders directly from Stalin. But the communists were able to take total control of the government in February 1948 simply because 12 of the non-communist government members resigned as a protest against the Minister of Interior's scheming, believing that President Edvard Beneš would not accept their resignation.

Well, he did. Silently admitting that Czechoslovakia had become a part of Moscow's sphere of power, Beneš concluded that the democratic forces didn't have much of a chance in the long run. Maybe he was right, but the "February Coup" nevertheless smacks of a tactical blunder committed by the non-communist parties. As Gottwald himself later commented with vulgar precision: "They bent forward in front of us, so we simply had to kick them in the ass!" And it's sad to say, but millions of Czechs were more than eager to help pave the way to disaster.

The Czechs' enthusiasm for communism didn't change much after the Bolsheviks came to power, either. When the brave democratic politician **Milada Horáková** was sentenced to death in a mock trial in 1950, people were signing petitions in support of her execution. True, the secret police's repression was strong. Thousands of Czechs fled the country (see: **Emigrants**), thousands were thrown into jail and labour camps, and almost 180 people were executed.

Some private farmers did actually protest against the forced collectivisation, and there were even signs of open demonstrations when the communists, in 1953, in complete contradiction to what they had promised, carried out a currency reform that rendered most people's savings worthless.

But for the most, the Czechs were content. So, when the Hungarians, in November 1956, were butchered in the streets of Budapest in their desperate uprising against Soviet-style communism, their neighbours in Czechoslovakia were busy buying presents and preparing for Christmas. The Czechs didn't even hesitate to erect the world's largest Stalin monument on the Letná Plain overlooking Prague. The atmosphere in totalitarian Czechoslovakia is well illustrated by the fact that the 30-metre-tall, 15,000 tons granite monster was only removed in 1962, nine years after the Soviet tyrant's death…

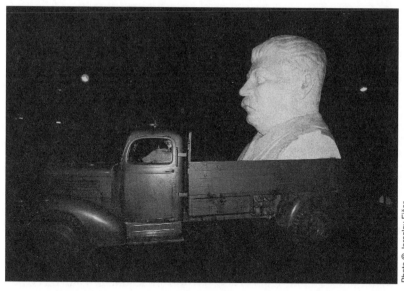

But didn't the Soviet invasion in 1968, which left dozens of civilians dead in the streets, crush far-reaching reforms? Wasn't the Prague Spring basically an anti-communist uprising? Not really. Alexander Dubček and the other supporters of "Socialism with a human face" definitely wanted to reform Czechoslovakia after 20 years of Stalinism and increasing economic problems. Some of their measures, for instance to remove censorship, represented a giant step towards liberalization, and secured the reformers massive popular support.

However, not even Dubček questioned the Communist Party's constitutional right to lead society. The Prague Spring reformers also worshipped Marxist-Leninist dogma, and they still believed in the command economy. Even worse, after the 1968 invasion, Alexander Dubček let himself be used as a puppet for the hard-liners by signing laws that were utterly un-democratic. That's why most Czechs today regard the Prague Spring basically as a battle between two factions of the Communist Party. Or, if you like, as a failed attempt to introduce *perestroika* and *glasnost* some 17 years before Gorbachov did.

The 20 years that followed the Soviet invasion are probably the main reason why so many Czechs are loath to look in the historic mirror. In its effort to "normalize" society back to Soviet-style communism, the new secretary general Gustav Husák and his fellow hard-liners kicked some 500,000 members out of the party, and then dissolved every single organization in the country that had shown even the slightest sympathy towards the Prague Spring reforms.

But simultaneously, the neo-Stalinist regime tried their best to secure the common Czech an agreeable standard of living. Their message could be interpreted as follows:

"If you just pretend to respect the fact that we're running this country, shut your mouth and show up at a pro-regime demonstration from time to time, we will guarantee you a (certainly not too exhausting) job, decent housing, the possibility of buying a Škoda car, a cottage in a beautiful place in the countryside, possibly a vacation at some Black Sea resort, plus, of course, the opportunity to fully exploit all life's carnal delights (see: **Hedonism**), starting with inexhaustible quantities of the world's probably best and definitely cheapest **beer**."

A vast majority of the population accepted the deal. Even though the Communist Party was thoroughly cleansed for "liberal" elements after the Prague Spring, it soon had about 1.8 million members, which was, compared to the size of the population, more than in any other East Bloc country, bar Romania (as an expression of their gratitude, the Kremlin made the Czechoslovak officer Vladimír Remek in 1978 the first non-Soviet *kosmonaut* ever). The human rights movement **Charter 77**, on the other hand, had about 1,800 signatories, so there were 1,000 Bolsheviks for every singly person who signed the document...

It may sound like a sweeping statement, but it's tempting to conclude that widespread collaboration with the neo-Stalinist regime, or at least a pragmatic tolerance of it, lasted to the very moment when the economic stagnation became evident to everyone, and it was clear that the Bolsheviks' days were numbered.

It's easy, especially for **foreigners** who never experienced communism, to poke fun of the Czechs for the way in which they kowtowed to a rotten regime. And yes, after the **Velvet Revolution** in 1989 it has undeniably been a bit comic to witness the veritable explosion of anti-communists in the Czech Republic. Even some of the country's most libertarian **politicians** are known to have been either former members of Husák's neo-Stalinist party, or at least to have flirted intensely with it (see: **Lustration**).

Yet there are some quite understandable arguments in the Czechs' defence. In the 1970s, most people really felt that the "*normalizors*" managed to raise the standard of living. Of course, ruthless exploitation of raw materials, such as coal, and total neglect of ecological measures were the other side of the picture. At the same time, they maintained a hard and repressive line towards any sign of opposition. As a result, the common Czech was markedly better off than the average Pole or Hungarian, while the punishment for openly disobeying the regime was far stronger than those imposed by the regimes in Warsaw or Budapest.

Another effective deterrent was the Bolsheviks' perverted take on the Bible's original sin: if you make any trouble, your children will be denied access to higher education and a decent job. So, from a human point of view, it was maybe not exactly heroic, but at least quite understandable that most Czech parents thought twice before stepping out of the line. In that respect, the playwright Arnošt Goldflam probably spoke for a majority of his countrymen when he stated after the Velvet Revolution that "the best thing with democracy is the freedom not to be brave".

What about those not-too-numerous Czechs who defied the widespread opportunism and put their health, family, future and even lives at stake by speaking out for freedom? For the former political prisoners, it's utterly disheartening that several known torturers (among them Alois Grebeníček, father of the Czech Bolsheviks' current boss) have not been taken to court, but are allowed to spend their last years living happily with their families.

So far, only one of the hard-liners who formally "invited" the Soviet Union to invade his country in 1968 has been tried and sentenced for sabotage. Among the younger generation of apparatchiks, Miroslav Štěpán, Prague's last and infamous party boss, is the only one who has served some time in jail.

This has both practical and morale-philosophical reasons.

Some of the former regime's worst henchmen have gotten off by claiming that their poor health doesn't allow them to stand trial. In other cases evidence have been destroyed, or witnesses have died. And then there was the urge to heal the nation's wounds as soon as possible; **Václav Havel** and the Charter 77 dissidents, who dominated the political leadership that emerged in late 1989, preached the gospel of reconciliation. "We are not like them" (i.e., the communists) and "Truth and Love shall prevail over Lies and Hate" were their main slogans. Consequently, this made anyone who was eager to punish the communists, look like either a communist himself, or an ardent supporter of lies and hate.

While the democratic political parties discuss whether to draw a thick line between the totalitarian past and the present, the Communist Party itself seems to have recovered from the giant blow it received in 1989. Contrary to their comrades in most other ex-East Bloc countries, the Czech Bolsheviks have not recycled themselves into a modern labour party (that space was taken by the Czech Social Democratic Party early in the 1990s), but only moved their ideological temple from Moscow to Havana and Peking.

Cleverly, the comrades have distanced themselves from all the "bad things" that happened prior to 1989, while they take full responsibility for all the "good things" that were done, such as securing everyone some kind of job.

Although party members have fled by the hundreds of thousands, the Communist Party unfortunately still has to be reckoned with in Czech politics. In the parliamentary elections in 2002 (where more than half the electorate decided to stay at home), they were supported by some 18 percent of voters. Yet the comrades have one serious problem. The vast majority of their supporters are pensioners nostalgic about the past, and only some 1,200 of their 101,000 members are under the age of 30.

The good news is therefore that hard-core communism as it is still practiced by most of the Czech comrades, will sooner or later meet the same end as the dinosaurs. The bad news, though, is that the Czech Republic even after their extinction will need time to cope with the legacy of their 41 year long tyranny.

Corruption

When a Czech, in the communist era, went to see the doctor it was not entirely unthinkable that he brought a bottle of liqueur with him discreetly hidden in his pocket. The booze was not necessarily meant as a means to shorten the dreadful waiting time. Instead, it was solemnly presented to the state-employed medicine man as an expression of good will. As a result, the chances that the doctor would brush aside your problems as being "mere nerves" were considerably reduced.

The tradition of knowing how to look after oneself has deep roots all over **Central Europe** and dates back to the days of the Austro-**Hungarian** Empire (see: **Bureaucracy**). As one might expect, the sleazy and basically Byzantine communist regime didn't exactly make things better. Corruption flourished at all levels of public life. In some instances – for example, when you wanted to rent a flat from the municipal authorities in your city – you wouldn't even be considered a serious candidate if you didn't hand over an envelope stuffed with *korunas.*

The Czechs are all too experienced and no-nonsense (see: **Scepticism**) to believe that the corruption problem would disappear with the communists. Therefore, nobody expected that the enormous privatisation of state industry that took place in the 1990s would come to pass without false steps. An American professor even joked that the best way, in which the Czechs could carry out the privatisation, was to put out all the lights in the country for half an hour...

Nevertheless, a decade and a half after the **Velvet Revolution**, millions of Czechs have an intense feeling that the country has utterly failed to cope with the communists' sleazy legacy. Not only because of the appalling irregularities that accompanied the privatisation process in the 1990s, or the secret donations to the ruling parties, which were revealed in 1997 (see: **Pepa from Hong Kong**). The problem is that everyday bribery is, according to surveys, perceived to be as widespread as it was before 1989.

This is hard to believe. Bottles are no longer handed over to doctors (at least not as a rule). Municipal flats can be obtained without money-stuffed envelopes, and yes, the police are investigating accusations of corruption and bribe-takers are being convicted. Yet the situation is far from satisfying. According to Transparency International (TI), a non-governmental organization which annually surveys how the spread of corruption among public officials and **politicians** is perceived in 91 countries, it's even grave.

Ranking the participants from countries where "corruption is non-existent" to countries where it is "widespread", TI deemed the Czech Republic to be the world's 54th least corrupt state in 2003. That result places the country between Bulgaria and Belarus, which most Czechs take as a deep offence (see: **Balkans**). And even worse: the Czech Republic has experienced a continuous slide downwards since 1997, when it finished in 27th place. While post-communist countries such as Hungary and Slovenia traditionally were considered to be more sleaze-prone than the Czech Republic, the situation is now the reverse.

There is, however, a light in the darkness. It may be that corruption is perceived as such a big problem in the Czech Republic partly because the media – rightfully – have been focusing heavily on it in recent years.

Although corruption represents an undeniable problem, its spread may, because of the media focus, seem bigger than it really is. And even better: after years of neglecting the problem, EU accession has prompted the government to take action to fight sleaze, for instance by introducing state provocateurs as a method to reveal corrupt civil servants.

Certainly, corruption can also be seen as a question of political culture. In that respect, many experts must admit that their prophecies from the early 1990s were wrong.

Post-communist Central Europe has not been threatened by a revival of nationalism, as they warned. Neither has any hard-line communist comeback happened. The major problem for these new democracies is corruption and its tentacles wrapped around politicians. In this respect, one can say that the Czechs, after the Velvet Revolution in 1989 made a historic leap out of Moscow's sphere of power. But when it comes to corruption, it might seem that they landed in Calabria...

Cursing

Just how foul-mouthed are the Czechs, and which weapons do they use? Generally speaking, most languages divide curse words into three groups: religious curses, expressions that relate to very private parts of the human body or its waste products, and those that describe all the peculiar things you can do with a close relative, most often your mother.

The **Czech language**, of course, is no exception. Blasphemy, as well as genitals and excrements, have traditionally been regarded as a taboo. However, the Czechs don't necessarily perceive the "strength" of a certain taboo in the same way as, for instance, the **Germans** or the **Russians**. Thus, a given language's register of curses and the focus of its obscenities reveal quite a lot about the mental hierarchy of its speakers.

As in English, religious curses are regarded as the mildest ones also in Czech. Exclamations such as *sakrament, Ježíš Maria, krucifix* and the originally German *herrgott* or *himmelherrgott* were once a safe way of evoking the wrath of the heavens – and the church – and therefore extremely well-suited as taboo words. But thanks to the declining role of **religion,** a phenomenon that has taken place all over Europe, but especially among the Czechs (see: **Battle of White Mountain**), these curse words have lost their force more or less completely.

Zatraceně (damned) is reduced to a literary expression, and some of the other religious taboo words have even been further trivialized into *sakra* and *krucinál*. It's also worth noticing that the Czech equivalents of devil – *ďábel* and *čert* – never became popular as curses (while they are very frequent in Russian). *Čert* is perceived as a rather nice figure from fairy tales, while *peklo* (hell) is not a place where a Czech would send people he or she doesn't like.

This may suggest two things: either that the Czechs think Earth is bad enough, or, in what may be the more plausible explanation, that they haven't found the Catholic Church even worthy of offence.

Same thing goes for the use of *fuck*. While vulgar (American) English uses it in every other sentence, it's almost totally absent in Czech (but widespread among Czech **Roma**!). There are, of course, several vulgar verbs for this activity (*mrdat, šukat, šoustat*), but they very seldom appear in a defaming or negative context. In other words, the Czechs take some activities really seriously…

On the other hand, the Czechs are extremely happy to fill this gap with the word *kurva* (whore). So expressions like: *Co to kurva má znamenat?* or *Šéf je zkurvenej hajzl* correspond fully to English *What the fuck/hell is this supposed to mean?*, and *The boss is a fucking ass-hole.*

Another remarkable Czech specialty is the term *debil* used instead of *idiot*. Actually, this might be interpreted as a demonstration of factual precision. While the statistical chance you'd bump into an idiot (IQ below 35) is relatively low, it's not so unlikely that you meet a person suffering from debility (IQ between 50 and 70). It might also prove the often-maintained hypothesis that the Czechs tend to avoid extremes (see: **Egalitarianism**)

However, there can't be any doubts whatsoever about the ultimate star among Czech curses: *prdel* (ass).

When a Czech drops a brick on his toe, he'll probably exclaim *do prdele!* Literally, it means *up the ass*, but in nuance and strength it corresponds fully to English *shit!* Similarly, a Czech will not tell somebody to go to hell, but *do prdele!* An even stronger variant is *vyliž/polib mi prdel!* (lick/kiss my ass), or if necessary the somewhat acrobatic *vyser si oko!* (shit your eye out!). A *vlezdoprdelka* or *prdelolez* is a slippery fellow who "creeps into somebody's ass", and if you have a really bad day, you'll probably feel that everything is *v prdeli* – i.e. in deep shit. The Czechs even make *prdel* – asses – of each other.

Logically, where English uses the adjectives "bloody" or "fucking", the Czechs go for an adjective closely linked to the body's rear end, namely variations of the verb *srát* (to shit). Your neighbour might be a *zasranej kretén* (a bloody cretin), your colleague *posral to* (fucked it up). An extraordinary stupid individual may be titled as *sráč* (a bloody fool), and anything of poor quality is a *sračka*. Needless to say, nouns such as *hovno* (shit), *prd* (fart) and *hajzl* (bog), also enrich this group.

Surprisingly enough, the Czechs are more modest with vulgarities connected to the genitals. True, an unsympathetic person may be described as a *čurák* (prick) or *píča* (cunt) – the latter is also used in the composition *do píči* (up the cunt, as a variant of *do prdele!*). But compared to related languages such as Russian and Polish, the rear part of the body so completely dominates over the genitals that it's tempting to conclude that the Czechs, in this respect, are utterly anal fixated.

What's more, the Russian obsession of referring to sexual intercourse with your mother is practically unknown among the Czechs (which, of course, doesn't mean they don't regard sex between parents and children to be a taboo).

So, what does all this tell us? If four-letter words can be seen as an authentic expression of popular culture, then the Czechs are definitely more influenced by their anal-fixated German and **Austrian** neighbours in the west and south than by their blasphemous and incestuous Slav relatives in the east and north. In other words, the tradition of cursing confirms the Czechs' deep roots in **Central Europe**.

Curtains

For more than 40 years, the Iron Curtain represented an almost impenetrable barrier that isolated the Czechs from everything coming from the West (see: **Ocean, Absence of**). Curiously enough, the stuff that the Czechs themselves put up in their windows and call curtains (*záclony*), are almost as penetrable as an open door.

Actually, they are a net, and are only meant to screen off the sunlight. A **Dane** or some other Scandinavian, for instance, who gazes at a block of flats from a distance, may get the impression that the Czechs don't bother to hang up curtains at all.

Well, they do. On each side of the net curtains, most households have what the Americans call drapes (*závěsy*) – fabric curtains. But the drapes can't be seen from outside when they're not drawn, which they usually are not, because it might evoke the impression that something really naughty and subversive is going on inside. So while the Iron Curtain is gone, the mental atmosphere from that period lingers on in windows all over the country.

Czech Cuisine

Czech culture has produced astonishing achievements in a wide range of disciplines, but in one field the result is more than depressing: the country's cuisine.

It's not that the average Czech is that bad at preparing food. Even many of the country's most image-conscious macho men (see: **Feminism**) love to portray themselves as affectionate cooks (according to a recent survey, 45 percent of Czech men claim they are capable of preparing a number of different dishes), and most Czechs make extreme efforts to please their dinner guests. The problem is only that the result, with a few exceptions, such as the **mushrooms**, is so, well, dull and fatty.

And that's quite strange, considering the diversity and imaginativeness that generally characterize Czech culture. Thanks to a location in the middle of Europe, Czech literature, architecture, theatre and arts in general have been influenced from all parts of the continent (see: **Central Europe**), and the result is a magnificent blend of domestic and **foreign** elements.

Unfortunately, that multitude of influences does not apply to Czech cuisine, which seems to be not only influenced but downright regurgitated from one single tradition: the **German**. And say what you want about the Czechs' great neighbours to the West, but their cuisine is definitely not their greatest contribution to mankind.

To start with the conclusion: Czechs are the ultimate meat-eaters. Cheap (and fatty) meat was one of the main carnal delights with which the former regime bought itself the people's acceptance (see: **Communism**). And the broad masses surely took full advantage of the offer. By 1990, the Czechs consumed more pork and beef per capita (50 kilos and 28 kilos respectively) than almost any other nation on the planet.

The only thing that seems to have changed after the **Velvet Revolution** is that vegetables have become somewhat more visible on the dinner plate. Before 1990, the Czechs shovelled down dishes of fatty meat with rawgrated cabbage. After 1990, they have been shovelling down dishes of fatty meat with rawgrated cabbage and some tomatoes and cucumbers. But the sauce's role in Czech cuisine is still the same. While other nations use it to stimulate the meat's taste, the Czechs drown the meat in loads of heavy sauce to make sure that the taste is killed completely.

This is not a militant vegetarian's personal opinion.

Surveys conducted by the Czech Statistics Office prove that consumption of red meat, thanks to extensive propaganda of healthy nutrition, went down in the first years after the Velvet Revolution, while the popularity of poultry grew. And, occasionally, a "mad cow" incident weakens the average Czech's taste for beef.

The problem, however, is that this healthy trend reversed by the end of the 1990s. Today, the Czechs' eating habits are only slightly healthier than in 1990. Their risk of dying from a cardio vascular disease is, according to official figures, still double the Western average. Their average level of cholesterol, which in the early 1990s dropped to Western standards, has rocketed back to its original heights and, eventually, with 16 percent of Czech men and 20 percent of women categorized as obese, this nation places itself in the forefront of Europe's lard league.

It's hard to point out one single reason for the Czechs' culinary impotence. Okay, they don't have access to the **ocean**, so you can't blame their cuisine for not offering a variety of delicious seafood (see: **Carp**). But that goes for the **Hungarians**, as well, and yet their *halaszlé* (fish-soup) is by all standards excellent.

A comparison with the world-famous Hungarian cuisine might seem unfair, but the fact is that the agricultural conditions that Mother Nature gives the Czechs don't differ all that much from their ex-neighbours'. Even the yodelling **Austrians** have come up with a more fiery cuisine. So why are the Czechs, in this respect, so drab?

One rather uncomplicated theory is at hand: the cuisine's character is to a large extent influenced by the beverage that is consumed to smooth its digestion. And in the Czech case, only one candidate can be taken into consideration: **beer**.

Indeed, this country's brewing traditions are as old, rich and various as the cuisine is dull, fatty and tasteless. It's simply impossible to imagine a genuine *hospoda* meal without a rosy glass – or three – of beer (statistically, every Czech consumes about 160 litres annually, which makes them the world leaders in this discipline). So, where the Hungarians, French and Italians swallow light and spicy food with sparkling wine, the Czechs use tasteful and high-calory beer to digest loads of fatty meat and heavy sauce.

To be fair, Czech cuisine also has some bright spots. The soups, for instance, which are an obligatory starter at any meal, can be delightful, and like all other nations in the former Austro-Hungarian Empire, also the Czechs revel in cakes and pastry. The ultimate Czech speciality, however, is the *knedlík* (dumpling).

You can find the same delicacy in Bavaria and Austria as well, but nobody serves this boiled savoury pudding with greater affection than the Czechs. There are even regular timed contests in stuffing down as many *knedlíks* as possible. In her now-cult-classic cookbook from the 1920s, Marie Janků-Sandtnerová listed 37 different ways of preparing the *knedlík*. Since then, some fifty more recipes have been published.

As a foreigner, you might mistake the *knedlík* for a soft-boiled **ice hockey** puck that moves through your intestines with the speed of a plasticine ball, but the locals treat it with sacred respect. Actually, no classic Czech dish can go without the *knedlík*.

To achieve the total Czech culinary experience, you should therefore find any ordinary *hospoda* and try the following combination: go for a glass of **Becherovka**, the traditional herbal liquor, as an aperitif, and then continue with one of the soups that are on the day's menu (if the *dršťková* is the only one left, consider whether you really wish to eat ground cow stomach). As for the main dish, there is no alternative other than the *vepřo-knedlo-zelo* (pork meat with dumplings and sauerkraut), which must be swallowed down by large quantities of beer.

The dessert can be a *palačinka* (a pancake) accompanied by a cup of what the Czechs dare to call Turkish coffee. If you're not used to filtering the coffee through your teeth to avoid swallowing the grounds, order a glass of *grog* (tea with rum) instead.

Finally, control that the waiter hasn't doctored your bill too heavily, leave a small tip – and be sure not to check your weight or measure your cholesterol for a couple of days. *Dobrou chuť!*

Czech Language

Let's start with the unambiguous verdict: Czech is the Rolls Royce of the Slavonic languages, and a star player in the Indo-European linguistic league. Czech is so rich, precise and, unfortunately, also complicated that a **foreigner** trying to learn the language may be driven to suicide. Either because he or she never manages to learn it, or because of the utter depression that follows when the foreigner realizes how primitive his or her own mother tongue is.

Linguistically speaking, Czech is – as are Slovak, Polish and the now nearly extinct Lusatian (Wendish) – a Western Slavonic language. Eastern Slavonic languages, such as **Russian** and **Ukrainian,** or members of the South Slavonic branch, as Serbian and Croatian, all belong to the same linguistic family. But because Czech, thanks in part to the unique vowel mutation it has undergone, is the most distinctive of all the Slavonic languages, its spoken version can be hard to understand even for other Slav peoples, bar the **Slovaks**.

The Czechs have traditionally been known as a book-loving people. Today, this can indeed be questioned (see: **TV Nova**), but one fact remains undisputed: no Slav people started to produce literature in their own language earlier than the Czechs. Within two centuries after the Macedonian missionary Cyril (ca. 827–869) and his brother Methodius arrived from Salonika to convert them to Christianity (see: **Religion**), the Czechs could boast an array of hymns, chronicles and ballads in their mother tongue.

Czech literature reached its first zenith under the reign of Charles IV (1346–1378), who made Prague the capital of the Holy Roman Empire (see: **Central Europe**). Among Charles' many bright ideas was the foundation of a university in Prague in 1348. Here, another Czech giant, **Jan Hus**, started to teach his students a version of Czech based not on literature, but on the language as it was actually spoken in Prague's streets at that time.

Hus not only chucked out tons of **German** and Latin loanwords, but he also introduced a "phonetic" spelling, which rendered every sound with a single letter. For those sounds that didn't exist in Latin, he invented diacritical signs (*ě, š, á, ř*). As a result, Czech school children have rejoiced ever since at an orthography that is extremely logical and perspicuous, at least compared to what their poor colleagues in Poland still must endure.

Some other landmarks should also be mentioned. When the German Johannes Gutenberg invented the "black magic" of printing books in 1445, the Czechs followed suit only 23 year later, when the Trojan Chronicle (*Kronika trojanská*) was published. In addition, the importance of the *Bible kralická*, a reformed translation of the Bible from Greek and Hebrew published in the **Moravian** town Kralice, should not be underestimated. The translation was finished in 1594, and the six volumes were completed with linguistic as well as factual and theological explanations.

The **Battle of White Mountain** in 1620 is often excessively portrayed as a national catastrophe of immense dimensions, but when it comes to the Czech language, it really was quite a disaster.

To the Jesuits, the Habsburg Emperor's storm troops, a book written in Czech (and not in Latin or German) was automatically treated as a demonstration of heresy. Thus, in the years that followed the Czechs' defeat, an entire literature was practically destroyed. A certain monk, named Koniáš, was said to have set a record when he, single-handedly, burned 30,000 books authored by Czechs in their own language.

The germanisation of the Czechs in the aftermath of the debacle in 1620 went so far that by the end of the seventeenth century, the Czech language had been more or less eradicated in the state administration, in literature, in schools, at Prague's university and among the upper classes. The language, which for centuries had produced literary works of sometimes amazing quality, was reduced to a means of communication among (often illiterate) peasants.

"Any person who wanted to be considered as well-bred and educated, was clinging with body and soul to German," the literary historian Jan Máchal writes. "And those who still cared about Czech were regarded as fools or even lunatics."

Things improved when the somewhat enlightened Josef II (see: **Jews**) replaced his mother Maria Theresia on the imperial throne in Vienna in 1780. Czech teachers were allowed to teach in their mother tongue, and a chair in Czech language and literature was established at the university in Prague. These rather modest reforms triggered what later became known as *České národní obrození* (the Czech National Revival).

Obviously, the revival of the language played a crucial role. Here, two persons have earned themselves immortality.

In 1809, Josef Dobrovský (1753–1829), a theologian by training, published an *Ausführliches Lehrgebäude der böhmische Sprache* (Comprehensive manual for the **Bohemian** language). Based on both old Slavonic and the language of Czech folk songs and tales, the stringent scientist Dobrovský formed the laws of modern Czech.

As Jan Hus had done four centuries earlier, Dobrovský also started to throw out loanwords of German origin, replacing them either with revived Czech words, or by creating completely new ones. So, while the rest of the Slavonic peoples go to the *teater* or borrow books in a *biblioteka*, the Czechs are still going to the *divadlo* ("lookery") and visiting the *knihovna* ("bookery").

The second revivalist, Josef Jungmann (1773–1847) used Dobrovský's work as a stepping-stone for further reforms. While the first regarded Czech mainly as a subject of scientific study, the latter struggled to put the grammatical laws into practice as a living language.

To achieve this, Jungmann first published a *History of Czech Literature*, then his master work, a Czech-German dictionary in five volumes (where he introduced Czech transformations of foreign loan-words with a creativity that even shocked good old Dobrovský), and finally a brilliant translation of Milton's *Paradise Lost*. When Jungmann put down his pencil, the foundations of a modern Czech literary language were laid.

Now, let's have a look at contemporary Czech.

Unfortunately for foreigners, no other Slavonic language has more cases (seven) or a more rigid grammar than Czech. Bar Slovak, Czech is the only Slavonic language where the accent always occurs on the first syllable of a word, which in some instances, for example when pronounced by an angry wife or a traffic constable, makes it sound like a burst from a machine gun. And finally, Czech is the only Slavonic language that allows its speakers to utter an entire sentence without using one single vocal. Try, for instance, this: *Strč prst skrz krk!* – Put a finger through your throat!

Czech also has another dimension, which is often ignored. It divides everything masculine from everything feminine with a downright sexist fervour!

The English sentence *I was tired and went to bed* does not reveal whether a man or a woman said it. When repeated in French, you get a hint: *j'étais **fatiguée** et je suis **allée** me coucher.* And now, take a look at the Czech version: ***Byla** jsem **unavená** a **šla** jsem spát.* Even the biggest ignoramus has to notice the speaker's gender! One should, of course, avoid jumping to conclusions, but it can't be completely ruled out that this linguistic sexism has had some consequences for the psychological relations between men and women (see: **Feminism**), and the natural way in which many Czech women demonstrate they are proud to be women.

The complexity of Czech may drive foreigners trying to learn it to utter despair. They can, however, take comfort in the fact that the language poses problems even for the Czechs themselves. In reality, there is not one Czech language, but three quite distinct versions of it: *Spisovná čeština* (Literary Czech), *Hovorová čeština* (Spoken Czech) and *Obecná čeština* (Common Czech).

Literary Czech is the official language as it is spoken on the radio and on television and at official occasions. However, only persons who want to be perceived as very educated or very important or both use the literary language in daily life. This leaves the Czechs with two possibilities: either to use Spoken Czech, which can be described as a light-version of Literary Czech, where the most bookish expressions are softened, either syntactically (*pracuju* instead of *pracuji*) or lexically (*kytka* instead of *květ*), or to embrace Common Czech, the language of the man in the street.

Naturally, every ambitious citizen aware of his or her social prestige despises Common Czech. But from a linguistic point of view, it might seem that Common Czech is the richest of the three versions. True, the grammar is a bit simplified compared to the standard language, but the wild array of slang expressions (often of German origin) and its immense capability of creating neologisms makes Common Czech extremely vigorous. It goes without saying that it functions as a continuous production plant for unbelievable obscenities (see: **Cursing**).

So, how do the foreigner cope with the fact that Czech comes *in triplo*? Basically, he or she doesn't have to care. The Czechs themselves know better than anybody else how difficult their language is. Even natives quite often make funny mistakes when they're trying to speak Literary Czech at some official occasion, and unwittingly mix Common Czech into their sober language.

Therefore, any foreigner who makes the most modest attempt to speak their mother tongue is usually greeted with boundless enthusiasm and support (see: **Communication**). But remember one crucial fact: the Czechs revel in self-flagellation, and often compete with each other to come up with the cruellest remarks about themselves and their country. If you, as a foreigner, do the same, even if your Czech is brilliant and your complaint is totally justified, you'll be hated forever!

Dancing Schools

Life in communist Czechoslovakia had more than its fair share of absurd elements, but few things could beat the dancing schools. Just think about it: a Stalinist country (after 1968 neo-Stalinist), which was ruled by the proletariat's dictatorship and officially worshipped Soviet culture, openly tolerated the existence of an institution so thoroughly *petit bourgeois* and reactionary as dancing schools. An American equivalent would probably be Joe McCarthy taking private lessons to learn to play the balalaika...

Yet due to a wholly unexplainable display of tolerance after their take-over in 1948 (see: **Communism**), the Bolsheviks decided not to replace the bourgeois dancing schools with something more progressive and Soviet-friendly, but let parents send their pubertal offspring to the courses, which they themselves had attended some decades earlier. Obviously, not even the **Velvet Revolution** did anything to change this. As a result, the traditional dancing schools from the heyday of the Austro-**Hungarian** Empire are still alive and kicking in the Czech Republic.

As the term itself indicates, the purpose of the dancing schools is to teach the youngsters the basic principles of a handful of the most common ballroom dances. But since the courses are attended by both young men and young women, the dancing school lessons also contain instructions about the basics of social manners according to long-established **Central European** protocol. In other words, they teach a young man not only how to lead a woman in a waltz, but also to behave gallantly and open the door for her, helping her with her coat or protecting her against any external danger.

Seen from a Western and politically correct standpoint, this represents a problem. In short: supporters of Western-style **feminism** will claim that the dancing schools cement gender roles, which they have tried to eradicate for several decades. Most Czech women, though, will probably claim that the ballroom dances are just another area of life where Czech men are allowed to behave like machos, while in reality they are totally controlled by their strong-willed women...

In any case, every October, when the dancing school season begins, the streets are filled with 15-16-year-old acne-pimpled boys and girls rushing to their lessons. Contrary to the **Germans** and **Austrians**, who have also kept this tradition, but in a laid-back and modernized version, the Czechs are painstakingly mindful of the formalities: the boys are obligatorily dressed in dark suits (usually too big and borrowed from dad) and bowtie or smoking, and their sweaty hands are covered with white gloves when dancing.

Indeed, the formalities are enforced with such vigour that dancing schools are probably the only place in the entire Czech Republic where a man can't be seen wearing **sandals and socks**. The girls are expected to wear frocks, but due to the peculiarities of the Czech dress code, also mini-skirts are tolerated. More rarely these days, mom accompanies her daughter as a chaperone.

One of the reasons why hordes of youngsters are still signing up (or rather, their parents are signing them up) for the dancing schools is utterly practical. From November to March, every thinkable Czech organization, from the government to the Union of Fire Fighters down to the village's Stamp Collectors Club, organizes a ball.

This is an event of huge social importance, where any image-conscious person should turn up, and it is widely recognized as a perfect place for a man to make advances towards a woman. Just keep one thing in mind: while you are allowed to be as drunk as you please (see: **Alcoholics**), and can probably also have **sex** in the cloakroom with your colleague's wife without causing any locomotion, you will completely discredit yourself if you don't master at least the basics of ballroom dancing!

Danes

Denmark is one of those few European nations that have never in history done a single bad thing to the Czechs (see: **Austrians**; **Germans**; **Hungarians**; **Poles**; **Russians**). Yet this small and peaceful nation has got the dubious honour of starring in a well-known Czech saying: *pít jako Dán* (to drink like a Dane), which actually means to drink yourself dead-drunk, or respectively, that you have a serious drinking problem (see: **Alcoholics**).

This is by all means unjust to the Danes. True, Shakespeare already concluded long ago that there was something rotten in their country. And it's also true that the Danes have a more relaxed attitude towards alcoholic beverages than other Nordic countries. Yet to most of the **world** their civilized drinking culture may serve as a model, and not to be made an example of. So why have the Czechs stigmatised them in this cruel way?

One explanation might be that the Czechs invented "drink like a Dane" just to avoid "drink like a Czech", which would have taken its toll on their **national identity**. Of course, they could, with great justification, have tried "drink like a Russian", but in that case they would have risked provoking a much bigger and often touchy country. Small and distant Denmark, on the contrary, represented the ideal scapegoat.

However intriguing these theories might sound, the actual explanation is to be found in the **Czech language**, or, to be more precise, in its impressive creativity.

In the beginning of the twentieth century, the Czechs started to import a blotting paper from Denmark. The sales were formidable, because the Danish blotting paper was more effective than any other in use at that time (see: **Bureaucracy**). In Czech, this product is called *sací papír* (literally "sucking paper"). Now, take a look at the verb *sát/nasávat* (to suck), which in slang means to drink heavily. Thus, the link is clear: a person who boozes as thoroughly as the Danish paper blotted ink, was simply called a Dane.

So, while the Danes' blotting paper has long been obsolete, their unjustified reputation as heavy drinkers is still alive and kicking. Poor Danes…

Defenestration

A dictionary will tell you that the word *defenestration* is of Latin origin, and that *de fenestra* can be translated as *out of a window*. Thus, *defenestration* describes an action, where something – or rather, somebody – is thrown out of a window.

This might occur to you as a totally irrelevant piece of information – as long as you're not in the Czech Republic. In this country's history, defenestration plays a very significant part. It's still a bit unclear how many of them deserve the label "historic" (were they two or three?). What's undisputed, though, is that all of them took place in Prague, and all of them had a tremendous impact on political developments in **Bohemia** and **Moravia**.

The first and indeed historic defenestration happened on July 30, 1419, four years after **Jan Hus**, the Czech cleric who thundered so intensely against the trade with indulgences that the Catholic Church (see: **Religion**) chose to burn him at the stake. Hus' Protestant supporters – the Hussites – immediately started to revolt against the Catholic Church and its royal protector, King Václav IV. While the Hussites soon gained support from the reformist counsellors of Prague's Old Town, their colleagues in Prague's New Town had absolutely no sympathy for the rebels.

That attitude cost them their lives. On a bright summer day in 1419, a group of Hussites, led by the former monk Jan Želivský, stormed New Prague's town hall (on the square that is today known as Charles Square). Furious about the counsellors' unwillingness to negotiate with them, the Hussites drove 14 municipal **bureaucrats**, including the burgomaster himself, up to the gallery on the top of the Town Hall's tower, which was more than 70 meters tall.

There, the poor Catholics were mercilessly thrown out. To make sure they would cause no more trouble, the Hussites had even erected lances and spears at the spot where the poor fellows landed. "The enemies of truth were seized by great fear," a chronicler wrote, and King Václav had no other choice than to accept the new counsellors, chosen by the Hussite rebels. As a result, Prague was totally controlled by anti-Catholic rebels, and defenestration had proved to be an effective political weapon.

In September 1483, another defenestration took place. Except for the scene – the tower of the Old Town's city hall replaced the tower in the New Town – this was basically a repetition of the first one (Catholics hurled into the air by furious Hussites), so it's usually not counted as a real defenestration. The incident that has earned itself the title "Second Historic Defenestration" happened only 199 years after the first, but its political impact was so strong that it practically changed the course of history in Bohemia and Moravia.

The Second defenestration was actually triggered in 1526, when Archduke Ferdinand of Austria was elected Czech king. Considering that the majority of the Czech **nobility** and gentry were Protestants (the Vatican would probably have used the term "extremist troublemakers" here), it might seem strange that they chose a member of the super-Catholic Habsburg dynasty as the head of their state, but, unfortunately, they were not the last Czech elites to suffer from a lack of political providence (see: **Communism**).

As expected, the relations between the Catholic king and the Czech nobility steadily grew more and more embittered. In May 1618, the Czechs had had enough.

Just as the Hussite rebels 199 years earlier had stormed New Prague's town hall, the members of the Czech gentry and nobility now broke into the royal quarters on third floor of the Prague Castle's Ludvík wing. There, the governors Jaroslav Bořita and Vilém Slavata were quickly overpowered, and then mercilessly slung out of the window. Historians differ when it comes to the exact spot where the two imperial bureaucrats actually landed (was it on a shack over the latrine, or in the moat?), but in any case, both fellows survived the assault.

Photo © Terje B. Englund

However, the Second Defenestration was so successful that it encouraged the Czech gentry to go a step further: to kick the **Austrian** Ferdinand II from the Czech throne and elect the Protestant prince Friedrich of Pfalz as king instead. This shuffle was, as one might expect, met with extremely little sympathy at the imperial court in Vienna. Furious about the rebellion, Ferdinand sent a huge army to Prague to teach the impudent Czechs a lesson. On November 8, 1620, the Protestants were beaten into their boots in the disastrous **Battle of White Mountain**.

The Second Defenestration, in other words, heralded one of the most significant political changes in Czech history. Bohemia and Moravia were essentially downgraded to provinces in the Habsburg Empire, a situation that lasted, under varying pressure from Vienna, right up until 1918, when Czechoslovakia's **First Republic** was founded.

The fact that the third and last defenestration was a proper defenestration, and not a tragic suicide, was established only in March 2002, precisely 54 years after Minister of Foreign Affairs, Jan Masaryk, was found dead early one morning in the courtyard of the Černín Palace, the imposing baroque palace where the Foreign Office resides. Nearly 14 meters above the dead minister, in Masaryk's private apartment, investigators found an open window and wild disorder.

Half-empty liquor bottles and boxes with tranquillizers were strewn about the floor, and on the minister's night table, there were two books – a closed Bible, and an open **Švejk**. The subsequent autopsy confirmed that Masaryk was killed instantly by the impact, and that both of his heels were crushed. To the investigators from StB – the secret police (see: **Lustration**) – the conclusion was unambiguous: Jan Masaryk had committed suicide.

The verdict was immediately met with massive disbelief among common Czechs. How could "Honza" Masaryk, son of Czechoslovakia's first president **Tomáš G. Masaryk** and, thanks to his witty and biting radio speeches from London during the war, the country's most popular **politician**, leave his people when they needed him most?

Two weeks earlier, the communists had taken power in Czechoslovakia. Fear and uncertainty about the future prevailed. Thousands of democratically-minded Czechs had fled the country (see: **Emigrants**), and Masaryk, as the single non-communist member of Klement Gottwald's government, was the last hope for those who had decided to stay. True, people close to Masaryk later recounted that he had been very depressed in the days prior to his death, but still: in this fateful hour, Masaryk could not have died by his own will. He must have been killed!

The mysterious death of Jan Masaryk was thoroughly re-investigated both during the Prague spring's thaw and after the **Velvet Revolution**. The conclusion remained unchanged: suicide. In the middle of the 1990s, however, things started to happen. The special police commission established to document crimes committed by the communist regime ascertained two important facts: on the night when Masaryk died, a group of unknown persons forced themselves into his apartment in the Černín

Palace. And secondly, Masaryk had not fallen from the window, but from the cornice, several feet away from the window. Could Masaryk have tried to escape the intruders by climbing out on the cornice, where he slipped and fell to an accidental death?

A fairly convincing answer to this question was presented in March 2002 by a professor in the somewhat obscure discipline of biomechanics. After several months of experiments, the renowned scientist concluded unambiguously that Masaryk had been killed – or defenestrated.

Why? If Masaryk – at 61, somewhat corpulent, soggy and out of shape – had jumped consciously and of his own free will, he would allegedly have landed about 70 centimetres from the building wall. The distance between the wall and the place where the body was found measured about 2.2 meters. Add the fact that the body didn't rotate during the fall, and the only explanation, according to the professor, is that one, or more likely, two persons pushed Masaryk to his death.

This explains *how* Masaryk died, but it's not very likely, that we will learn any time soon *who* committed the crime. The Czechoslovak communists are probably innocent. To them, Masaryk's presence in the government was an enormous political victory, and they had no reason to liquidate their one and only democratic alibi. There are, though, some signs pointing to Moscow and the NKVD – the forerunner of the KGB – but it's foolish to expect that institution to open its archives.

Yet it's tempting to draw some historical parallels. While the First Defenestration in 1419 marked the start of the Hussite Revolution, and the Second Defenestration in 1618 heralded the Thirty Years' War, the Third Defenestration – Jan Masaryk's tragic death – symbolized the start of a 41-year communist tyranny. Hopefully, it was the Czechs' last experience with a totalitarian regime, and also the last time that defenestration was used as a political *modus operandi.*

Dogs

To some people, four-legged, barking creatures are a delight and a blessing. Others hate them like poison. Irrespective of which of these two groups you belong to, prepare for the reality: the Czech Republic is the ultimate dog country.

The exact number of hounds running around in **Bohemia** and **Moravia** is hard to come by, since owners do not always bother to register their pets with the Czech Canine Association. But anyone who has spent a day or two in this country will probably conclude that it must be close to the number of inhabitants.

Some **foreigners** have compared the Czechs' relationship to dogs with the Hindus' worship of cows. That's by all standards a bit exaggerated – the Hindus don't eat their cows, while dog meat is considered a delicacy in Valachia in Moravia. What we can say for sure, though, is that dogs are serious business to many Czechs.

However, it would be more speculative to explain why they have become such passionate dog-lovers. One might have understood it if the Czech Republic had been a typically rural country, where people traditionally used dogs to tend cattle or sheep. But it's not, as nearly 70 percent of the population live in cities. Maybe the explanation is that most of today's city-dwellers are children or grandchildren of rural Czechs who moved to find work in the cities after the Second World War, so they are subconsciously more attracted to dogs than people in countries with longer urban traditions?

A psychologist would likely see the Czechs' dog craze in a broader perspective. When the Bolsheviks were in power, the shrink would say, the average Czech always had to be on the alert (see: **Communism**). You constantly had to watch your mouth, and you never really knew whom to trust. In such circumstances, what could be a better friend than a dog?

True, its **communication** capabilities are somewhat limited, but that shortcoming is abundantly compensated for by the affection, loyalty and love it offers. Moreover, a dog would never squeal on you, which is a big asset in a country where the StB – the secret police – had some 80,000 informers (see: **Lustration**). Subsequently, the more disgusted the Czechs were by their communist surroundings, the more they loved their dogs.

Or perhaps it worked the other way round? When the regime constantly bossed people about, the people got themselves dogs just to boss somebody about too?

In any event, the Czechs' doggy passion has its bright and dark sides. The bright side (that is, if you share this passion) is that you can run into dogs of all thinkable races and sizes in any thinkable place. For instance, in a cinema. And a dog can almost always be used as a pretext to strike up a conversation. If you see an attractive woman walking her pet in a park (see: **Sex**), some nice words about her dog ("Is this beautiful creature a poodle or a pit-bull?") will increase your chances far more than if you were to approach her in a bar with some "Hi baby, haven't I seen you somewhere before?"

The dark side is that absolutely every person in this country regards it as his or her human right to keep a husky or a St. Bernhard's hound in a flat of 20 square meters. This anarchy is also reflected by the country's legislation. Even though people – sadly enough, often children – are regularly killed by fighter dogs, every attempt to prohibit the rearing of aggressive races has been firmly and so far very successfully blocked by the vociferous Canine Association as "violations of the individual's freedom".

And most annoying: while having a dog is considered every person's natural right, cleaning up its waste is, putting it mildly, rarely considered to be a duty. In Prague, for instance, some pavements are so densely decorated with doggy droppings that you'd better put on rubber boots before taking a stroll.

True, this goes for lots of other European cities as well, but hardly any of them has such a lethal mix of magnificent architecture and lovely ladies (see: **Beauty Contests**). One moment you're admiring the facade of a baroque palace or a local sex bomb passing by, and the next moment you slip on a big, fat, smelly......

Driving a Car

All nations have their strange sides. The Scandinavians, for instance, loudly praise their potato brandy, *aquavit*, even though every sane **foreigner** knows it tastes like an **alcoholic** blend of wolf urine and enriched uranium.

The Czechs, of course, have their peculiarities, too. One of the most amazing ones occurs every time the otherwise jovial and polite *Pepa Novák* – the Czech Everyman – becomes a car driver. Just as Řehoř

Samsa, the protagonist in one of **Franz Kafka's** short stories, woke up one morning and discovered he had metamorphosed into an enormous beetle, the power of the engine seems to convert most of the *Pepas* into ruthless maniacs.

Unfortunately, this view is not the personal prejudice of some militant ecologist. In 2003, nearly 1,300 people were killed on **Bohemian** and **Moravian** roads (victims under the age of 30 made up an alarming majority), and another 5,000 were severely injured. Measured in number of accidents in relation to the number of cars, the Czechs rank among the most dangerous drivers in Europe.

To paint an even gloomier picture: while fatal accidents in OECD countries during recent years have decreased by an annual average of 2 percent, in the Czech Republic they increased by almost 10 percent. Currently, you are eight times more likely to be killed by a Czech car driver than by a Czech criminal (see: **Kajínek**) – if that can be of any comfort.

Let's be fair to *Pepa*: this is definitely not only a question of venting suppressed aggression behind the steering wheel or downright ruthlessness.

During the first ten years after the **Velvet Revolution**, the number of vehicles on Czech roads – mainly thanks to enormous imports of used cars of dubious quality from Germany – grew more than it did during the entire century before 1989. Today, auto density in areas like Prague is one of the highest in Europe, while the average car is older than modern safety inventions such as airbags or ABS brakes.

And then there's the issue of money, of course. With all those tunnelled banks to save, the state simply lacks the funds to pay for improved road quality, roundabouts, more police controls (some 10 percent of the people who annually die in traffic accidents are killed by drunken drivers) and even such basic safety measures as traffic lights. And finally, it's a question of education. But *Pepa* can hardly be blamed for the fact that Czech auto schools are somewhat outdated.

What can be done to curb the grim death toll? Abolishing the speed limit on highways or raising it to 70 km/h at night in inhabited areas, as a group of right-wing politicians (see: **Pepa from Hong Kong**) suggested some years ago, might not be the correct answer.

The Ministry of Transport, on the other hand, came up with a somewhat better idea when it presented a new traffic law, introducing such revolutionary novelties as pedestrian priority on zebra crossings, the obligatory use of children's safety seats and helmets on motorcycles, cars using lights in the day-time, the banning of speaking on mobile phones whilst driving and the abolition of anti-radar devices. The draft law triggered a heated debate in the Parliament, but eventually, it was adopted with some minor adjustments.

So, will it work? Václav Špička, of the Czech Auto Club, believes it will. But not without some help. "We won't achieve a radical improvement until driving safely becomes a social convention," he told Czech media right after the new law was adopted. "Just as it's not accepted to spit on the floor, it must be conventional that you don't behave like a hooligan behind the wheel."

This certainly sounds nice, but, unfortunately, there are few signs that an improvement is imminent. In October 2003, Czech traffic police carried out the largest crackdown in its history. The effort had, unfortunately, a minimal effect. During the following weekend, 25 persons – including three police officers – were killed in accidents, and the death toll on Czech roads had set yet another dark record.

Egalitarianism

If you happen to meet a Czech acquaintance on the street, he or she will probably greet you with the obligatory *Jak se máš?* (How are you?).

As in most other places on earth, this question does not necessarily reveal any deep interest in your person, but should rather be considered a common expression of social convention. And after all, the Czechs are apparently more polite than most people in Western Europe, taking extreme care to greet even the most distant acquaintance with an obligatory phrase (they are also extremely good at being rude – see: **Cursing**).

Yet this seemingly innocent *Jak se máš?* may represent a dangerous pitfall for the unsuspecting **foreigner**. In most Western countries, and especially in the US, you would try not to be too negative, stating something that makes you look successful and happy even though you've just been kicked out of your job or your wife has left you for your oldest pal.

With the Czechs, however, the problem is the opposite. If you don't want to bother people with your personal problems and therefore answer something like *Thanks, I'm really fine – life is just marvellous!* your friend will probably reward you with a compassionate smile, and inwardly snort *Jesus Christ, what a swaggering idiot!*

This reaction is obviously a remnant of the communist era, when no sane person had any reason to be very happy or satisfied. Consequently, revealing a negative and pessimistic attitude towards life (see: **Scepticism**) only meant that you were a completely normal person. And even though the communist regime, thank God, now belongs to history, lots of Czechs are apparently still anxious not to be perceived as too positive or satisfied (see: **Service-mindedness**).

Some pundits will say that the main reason for this behaviour is envy. And as "evidence", they'll tell you the old anecdote about a global survey where sociologists tried to establish what people in a number of different countries wished for the future. To the French, nothing was more important than peace on earth, the **German** longed to solve the problems of the Third World, while the Czech respondent wished of all his heart that his neighbour's goats would kick the bucket.

There are those foreigners who don't consider this as a bad joke, but as a cruel reality. Try to buy a new and impressive car, they'll say. Park it on any public space in the Czech Republic, and then wait and see how long it will take until somebody, just out of pure envy, will make a long and ugly scratch in the enamel with a one-*koruna* coin. Maximum half an hour, the most pessimistic will say, adding that for the common Czech, envy is an even stronger urge than the sexual instinct.

Of course, this phenomenon can be explained with greater leniency towards the Czechs. Actually, it may seem that they are having a long-lasting and passionate love affair with the *zlatá střední cesta* (the golden, middle of the road). And the reason for this can probably be found in Czech history. Since most of the local **nobility** fled the country after the **Battle of White Mountain** in 1620, the remaining Czechs became a socially and economically very homogenous lot.

So, while other nations got their elite from the nobility, the Czechs made farmers and townspeople or even artists (see: **Mácha, Karel Hynek**) their aristocracy. This process was fuelled by industrialization, which in **Bohemia** started earlier and on a far more massive scale than in any other part of the Austro-**Hungarian** Empire.

As a result, a vast proletariat, where everyone was equally rich (or, if you'd like, equally poor) as his neighbour, was created. Needless to say, the communists' attempt to build a classless society didn't exactly make the average Czech more tolerant towards people being better off.

One shouldn't, of course, take this middle-of-the-road theory too far, but it's tempting to make one more point: it may seem that the strong fixation on equality and the corresponding aversion to everything that goes beyond the average (i.e., what's not commonly accepted as main stream) have led to a certain timidity towards the new and unknown (see: **Foreigners**).

Radical changes, be it in politics, fashion, architecture or whatever, are not good. "*The status quo* may have its bad sides," the saying goes. "But at least we know what we have, and things could always be far worse." Considering the Czechs' turbulent history, this attitude seems if not extremely brave, at least understandable.

Call it a deeply rooted sense of egalitarianism; call it envy or aversion against extremes or even a combination of all three. In any case, foreigners should learn a basic lesson. If you ostentatiously present yourself as better, richer, more successful or even different than the common herd, you're not only making a fool of yourself, but also provoking your surroundings.

Certainly, nothing prevents you from actually being better, richer and more successful – as long as you don't show off! Logically, the expected and non-provoking answer to *Jak se máš?* fully corresponds to the Czechs' aversion of extremes: *Ujde to* – I'm doing fairly good.

Emigrants

When the **Poles** or **Hungarians**, not to mention the **Russians**, speak about their nation's greatest daughters and sons, they usually don't care if the persons concerned actually lived in the country their whole lives, or if she or he gained fame as a citizen of another state. The **Slovaks** go even further, by operating with long lists of "**world** famous" countrymen who nobody outside Slovakia has ever heard of.

With the Czechs, the situation is, as usual, somewhat less straightforward. Not that emigration, be it for political or economic reasons, is something new to them. The reform theologian and pedagogue Jan Amos Komenský is probably the most famous of the earliest Czech emigrants. Like thousands of other prominent Czechs who fled the country after the **Battle of White Mountain** in 1620, Komenský spent the rest of his learned life roaming about Europe.

In the middle of the nineteenth century, the Emperor in Vienna once more made Czechs leave their mother country, this time by encouraging **Bohemian** and **Moravian** farmers to settle in the Banat region in today's Romania and in the northern parts of former Yugoslavia. In both areas, there are still Czech minority communities who vivaciously care for their cultural heritage, and you can thank industrious Czechs for founding the brewery that still produces ex-Yugoslavia's only decent **beer**. There were even daredevils who settled in places like Volhynia in Western Ukraine and Kazakhstan.

The descendants of the nineteenth century emigrants don't bother anybody today. The Czech minority in Romania, for instance, has even aroused widespread sympathy for the way they cling to their old traditions, including a charmingly archaic version of the **Czech language**, amidst the dreariness of the Banat. Similarly, when the remaining Volhynia Czechs – the majority of whom had already re-emigrated in the 1920s – settled in the Czech Republic early after the **Velvet Revolution**, they were mainly met with understanding and sympathy. Who would, after all, like to live in the vicinity of the Chernobyl nuclear power plant?

The "problems" start with those who emigrated from totalitarian Czechoslovakia in two big waves – in 1948, after the communist takeover (see: **Albright, Madeleine**), and then 20 years later, following the Warsaw Pact's brotherly invasion of the country. Today, it's hard to imagine a place on this planet where there isn't a Czech immigrant community. The largest groups are in Canada, Australia, Germany and the United States, but individual Czechs are reported in such incredible places as the rain forest of Costa Rica.

Sure, most Czechs are proud of countrymen who have made the American National **Ice Hockey** League look more or less like a competition between Czech clubs. When a **foreigner** mentions film director Miloš Forman, a Czech will almost certainly remind you that this respected artist was actually born in Czechoslovakia, and of course it's not insignificant that people like Chicago's mayor Antonin Cermak or Brazil's president Juscelino Kubitschek were of Czech origin.

But what about the thousands of ordinary Czechs (according to some estimates approximately half a million people) who chose to leave the country instead of putting up with the Bolshevik regime? What were the real reasons for their decision to emigrate? Are the emigrants better than us, since they didn't collaborate with the communists? Do they now have any moral right to criticize developments after 1989? And, most importantly, are these people still Czechs?

It's easy to understand the feelings of both sides. Take the average emigrant, who had to build up a new existence practically from scratch. Most of them have been amazingly successful. In Sweden, for instance, several surveys show that the approximately 20,000 Czech immigrants, from an economic point of view, belong to the most successful of all ethnic groups represented in the country – including the Swedes themselves. The think-tank in Stockholm that conducted one of the surveys concluded that those who chose to emigrate represented the most active, ambitious and well-educated layer of the Czech population.

When these industrious people started to return to the old country after 1989, either as **tourists** or on a permanent basis, they were often disappointed with what they found: a country mired in **bureaucracy** and **corruption**, **politicians** wasting their time and energy in petty quarrels, and people still more prone to complain passively about all their problems (see: **Hospoda**) than to do something to solve them. Some emigrants even found that the houses they once owned were now inhabited by former communist big-shots, who were allowed to buy the properties for a song.

Nevertheless, when emigrants have dared to criticize – no matter how legitimately – the country's state of affairs, they usually arouse wild and negative reactions. "It's easy for you to fault us for being backward and incompetent," the saying goes, "when you for the past twenty years have enjoyed all the advantages of a modern Western society!"

There might be something to this reaction. Under the rigid *normalization* of the 1970s and 1980s, emigration was a tempting option. But many ambitious and competent people, however fed up with the communists, resisted it for entirely unselfish reasons. Some could not bear the thought of leaving old and feeble relatives behind. Others felt so devoted to the Czech **national identity** and the country's long-lasting struggle for cultural emancipation that they never wanted their children to grow up in a foreign country. And to many members of the political opposition (see: **Charter 77**), resisting the pressure to emigrate was a matter of principle: what makes the Bolsheviks believe they have more right to live in this country than I have?

In addition, the Czechs' obsession with **egalitarianism** (some people would probably prefer the term envy here) also plays a certain role. Most of the emigrants, who have returned to the old country, are economically far better off than those who stayed. Being wealthy and smart – and moreover eager to demonstrate it – has never been a good way of making friends in this country.

The Czechs' somewhat cold relations towards emigrants can also be explained in a more scientific way. The social anthropologist Ladislav Holý, himself a Czech who settled in Great Britain in the 1970s, claims that his former countrymen perceive emigration in a different way than is common in the West.

In the ideology of Western liberalism, Holý maintains, emigration is considered a personal matter, which is of no interest to the rest of the society. In a cultural ideology, as in Czech society, which, on the contrary, underlines collectivism, emigration is seen as a moral problem. One of the key concepts in Czech national identity is, according to the social anthropologist, the birth and the re-birth of the nation. In other words, the term "mother country" is to be interpreted literally; i.e., as a mother. Thus, those who leave their country for a longer period have in practice renounced their nationality forever.

Ladislav Holý's views on emigration in a Czech cultural context were undoubtedly coloured by his own experiences with former colleagues, who did not exactly greet "the British smartass" with open arms when he returned to Czechoslovakia shortly after the Velvet Revolution. Today, however, his views on emigration may sound a bit categorical.

During the last decade, emigrants have gradually lost their diabolical reputation, and emigration as such has been treated less and less as a touchy issue.

As a result, it stirred only minor commotion when two returned emigrants (both of them with double citizenships) took places in the government that was appointed in 1998. Another important milestone was reached three years later, when some 80,000 Czech citizens living outside the country's borders got the right to participate in elections. It's a less important fact that just a minority of them actually used their formal rights to vote.

Feminism

Ask any modern, educated Czech woman whether she thinks it's acceptable for a man in the same professional position to earn 15–20 percent more than her. Then ask if she shares the view that women don't belong in the Parliament or in the management of big companies. Or if she believes that a young woman's natural career is that of a mother and housewife. Most likely, she will answer "no" to all three questions. But if you then, logically, conclude, "So you are a feminist", consider yourself lucky if she only smashes your face.

Why? To the great majority of Czech women, the word "feminism" is automatically associated with an ugly, militant, man-hating creature with unshaved legs, greasy hair and a nasty personality; in short, a hag who will never ever get a husband, which she doesn't want anyway, because in this country it's commonly known that all feminists are, in reality, lesbians.

One obvious reason for this somewhat eccentric attitude is to be found in the recent era of **communism**. To the Bolsheviks, women's liberation and feminism – in its Marxist interpretation – were important political topics. True, the Czech communists didn't go so far as their **Russian** comrades, who took great pride in putting women at building railroads or **driving** cranes and heavy machinery, but also their method of "liberating" women from the capitalist order was based on forcing them to work. As a result, in no other country on the planet, except in the former **German** "Democratic" Republic, did women represent a larger part of the working force than in communist Czechoslovakia.

This, however, definitely did not mean that women were treated as equals with men. On the contrary, the propaganda spoke loudly about equal opportunities for both genders, but women were in fact systematically discriminated against, both in terms of wages and career opportunities. When it came to higher education, the communists even revealed themselves as far more conservative than most capitalists: as late as in the 1980s, young men were almost automatically preferred in natural sciences, whereas their female counterparts ended up studying humanities.

The political dimension of the communists' mock fight for "equal rights" made it even more inedible. To show how progressive the regime was, many political organs had quotas that fixed an obligatory number of female members. Of course, in most cases these women were only assigned to walk-on roles as political alibis, but thanks to female comrades such as the infamous Marie Kabrhelová, a red version of Margaret Thatcher who preached the Party's equal-rights gospel with downright religious intensity, feminism's credibility was ruined for generations.

So are Czech women today generally oppressed? Compared to some Western countries, there are still few women in top politics (among the 200 members of the Parliament's House of Deputies elected in 2002, there were 34 women) and business managements. And those who have fought their way up must often endure extreme chauvinism (a newspaper cartoonist once portrayed the Social Democrats' former vice chair Petra Buzková as a prostitute with the party chairman as her pimp). Moreover, Czech women are still paid less than men for doing the same job, even though the labour law strictly prohibits such discrimination.

Unfortunately, this goes for a lot of other developed countries too. In fact, when you compare this country with the rest of post-communist

Central Europe, Czech women, measured by their level of education, which on average is higher than Czech men's, their legal protection and their participation in decision-making bodies (more than half of the country's judges are women), fare better than in any other state.

Generally, their situation doesn't differ significantly from that in Austria, which, admittedly, isn't exactly a feminist heaven on earth, but at least this comparison indicates that the need for urgent intervention is not as acute as several international activist groups in the beginning of the 1990s believed. Seen in a historic context, one can even, with some artistic liberty, claim that the first Czech state was established by a woman.

According to *Staré Pověsti České* (Old Czech Tales), a collection of historic myths published by the writer Alois Jirásek in 1894, the Přemyslíd Dynasty of princes, who were later to become Czech kings, was founded when the strong-willed Princess Libuše ordered her guards to find her a man. The guards set off, and when they ran into a plain farmer who was ploughing his fields, they brought him back to the princess. Thus, Přemysl the hard-working ploughman became the fabled Libuše's husband and head of the Czech principality.

But the story about Libuše and Přemysl can also be seen from another perspective. Thanks to her position as princess, there's no doubt that Libuše was the boss, and poor Přemysl was only used as a convenient cover and sperm donor. In other words, it was an undercover matriarchy. A millennium and a half later, the Czech tradition of women letting their husbands officially act as tough macho men while, in reality, they are totally controlled by their bossy wives, is still alive and kicking. The famous comic Jan Werich once defined this balance of power very precisely: *In my family, I decide all the important things, such as our relationship with Taiwan. My wife is only responsible for the rest...*

Božena Němcová is another female monument in Czech history. Born in 1820 to poor parents, she lived a desperately unglamorous life caring for her children and hiding from her drunk and abusive husband. Nevertheless, when she finally managed to publish her novel *Babička* (Grandmother) shortly before she died, at 42, she became a national star overnight.

A somewhat cynical observer may find the novel utterly sentimental, and grandmother herself hopelessly bigoted. But the point is that not one single chauvinist stood up and brushed Němcová off for "just being a stupid woman", and nobody complained that the novel's grey-haired **hero** was as anti-masculine as it is possible to get. The probable explanation is that the novel, whether written by a man or woman, was first and foremost seen as a literary victory for the Czechs, who felt dwarfed by German cultural suppression.

Actually, this nationalistic aspect might have a wider importance for the relationship between Czech men and women. Jiřina Šiklová, professor of sociology and founder of gender studies at Charles University in Prague, points out that because of the Czechs' long-lasting experience with **foreign** domination – be it by the **Austrians,** Germans or Russians – most Czech women don't feel oppressed by men. On the contrary, they feel solidarity with them as compatriots.

Maybe professor Šiklová has a too positive attitude, but, on the other hand, she definitely knows what she is talking about. As a supporter of the **Charter 77** movement**,** Šiklová and many other women resisted the communists with great courage and in total solidarity with their male fellow-dissidents.

That also goes for Charlotte and Alice Masaryk, wife and eldest daughter of **Tomáš G. Masaryk**, Czechoslovakia's "founder". During the First World War, when the later president's struggle for national independence brought his family great suffering and himself exile, they stood by his side. And after 1918, both Masaryk and his family used their influence to promote equal rights for women, who were secured the vote by the independent Czechoslovakia's constitution (see: **First Republic**). The president himself stressed the importance of women's emancipation so intensely ("Women are often more valuable humans than men") that he has been called the first Czech feminist. He even took his American wife's maiden name Garrigue as his second **surname** to demonstrate that he considered her his equal.

Neither should one forget that the Catholic Church, which hardly can be accused of having a tremendously progressive stance towards women's emancipation, has never enjoyed really massive support in **Bohemia**, traditionally the Czech state's centre of political gravity. The Hussite Church, on the other hand, which emerged as a "national" church shortly after Czechoslovakia was established, took an overtly liberal stance on the issue of women's liberation. Today, a clear majority of its approximately 100,000 registered members are females (see: **Religion**).

So, what will the future bring? By now, an entire generation of women who never had any personal contact with the communist regime have come of age. Unlike their elder sisters, they don't automatically consider feminism to be a downright dirty word, and not few of them nourish ambitions of having a professional career.

Yet (early) marriage and subsequent motherhood still seem to be a more obvious and unambiguous goal for young Czech women than is common in Western and Northern Europe. And still, most Czech women expect to be treated as women (see: **Dancing Schools**). Okay, unlike Polish women they don't fancy a chivalric kiss on their hand, but any well-mannered man is supposed to open the door for a woman, let her enter before him and, on some occasions, help her with her coat. In the Czech Republic, a man can even risk praising a woman's beauty in public without being called a sexist monkey, or, as in Scandinavia, being knocked down on the spot.

In short: it seems that young Czech women are trying harder and harder to combine the cool self-confidence of a Western feminist with the proud womanliness of a South European **sex** bomb (see: **Sandals and Socks**). And – just to be a bit chauvinistic – it's amazing how they succeed in doing it!

First Republic

Most countries have a certain period that they romantically cherish as their golden era. Thanks to their roller coaster history, the Czechs have more of these ups and downs than most other nations, but if there is one period which a vast majority of contemporary Czechs, right or wrong, would consider an indisputable golden era, then it is the First Republic – Czechoslovakia from its foundation in October 1918 to the tragic **Munich Agreement** almost precisely 20 years later.

It's not hard to understand why. When the founding of Czechoslovakia was announced and the enthusiastic masses started to tear down any symbol of their former **Austrian** masters (or oppressors, as Czech nationalists would put it) a dream almost 300 years old had come true. But more than that: the creation of Czechoslovakia and the collapse of Austria-**Hungary** marked the end of the then-most-bloody war in man's history. The monuments you can still see in almost any **Bohemian** and **Moravian** village are a reminder of the 210,000 young Czechs who lost their lives in the First World War's meaningless slaughter.

The new state got off to a flying start, at least compared to the other countries that emerged from the ruins of the Danube monarchy. Hungary was demoted from a great power to a bankrupt "royal republic" that tumbled between economic crises and political turmoil, and Poland was soon thrown into a new war and a subsequent military dictatorship. The Czechs, on the other hand, had not only received national sovereignty after three centuries under the Austrians. They also expanded geopolitically, as both Slovakia and Trans-Carpathian Ruthenia (see: **Ukrainians**) were incorporated into their state.

The economy was another bright spot. Over 60 percent of the industry in the Austro-**Hungarian** Empire was located in Bohemia, and now it churned out goods to war-torn countries in the East and the West. In addition, new and visionary entrepreneurs, such as the Moravian shoe-manufacturer Tomáš Baťa or the inventor and engineer Emil Kolben (actually a colleague of Thomas A. Edison), emerged on the scene. As a result, Czechoslovakia's economy grew to become what common Czech wisdom stubbornly refers to as "the world's tenth-largest economy".

In reality, Czechoslovakia's economy in the 1920s, broken down, in terms of GDP per head, was, according to the respected historian Vlastislav Lacina, the world's seventeenth largest, placing itself right in front of Austria. But it was, thanks to extensive coal mining, the world's seventh biggest exporter. Nevertheless, for most Czechs the First Republic is still associated with an economic boom that dwarfed most of the other countries in Europe.

Be that as it may, one fact remains undisputed: the end of the First World War's carnage and the Czechs' and **Slovaks'** subsequent independence brought about a tremendous eruption of creativity, which recalls the atmosphere of Western Europe in the 1960s.

Take, for instance, the architect Josef Gočár, who redefined French cubism into the peculiarly Czech rondo-cubism. Or the poets Jaroslav Seifert (in 1984 awarded the Nobel prize) and Vítězslav Nezval, who worked out the basis of modern Poetism. In only a few years after 1918, the Barrandov studios right outside Prague (established by ex-president **Václav Havel's** uncle Miloš) grew into one of the leading studios in the European film industry, with an average production of 80 movies annually.

The Čapek brothers' *R.U.R.* (where the word *robot* was introduced) and *The Insect Play* gave European drama a virtual vitamin injection; the artist Alfons Mucha, who founded the graphic poster art as we know it today, further developed the unique symbioses between art noveau and Czech folklore; and Jaroslav Hašek in 1924 revolutionized the history of literature with his flap-jawed, **beer**-drinking anti-hero **Švejk**.

Even more impressive is the fact that this eruption of creativity seethed with a spirit of relative tolerance. Certainly, the Czechs tend to exaggerate the harmony during this period, especially so in the dark years under the grossly intolerant Bolsheviks. It remains a fact that

Czechoslovakia's 3.2 million ethnic **Germans,** who clearly outnumbered the 2 million Slovaks, were not regarded as constitutionally equal to their Slav compatriots. But it's a telling sign of the tolerance that a vast majority of the country's **Jews** rapidly assimilated themselves.

In the end, however, neither prosperity, nor relative tolerance, blooming arts nor a liberal president **Tomáš G. Masaryk** helped Czechoslovakia very much. The First Republic survived its founder by a mere year and a half. Yet the nostalgic memories of this golden era and its cruel end have made their mark on modern Czechs.

First, the treason committed against Czechoslovakia in 1938, when Great Britain and France signed the Munich Agreement with Hitler and thus threw the country to the Nazi wolves, made many Czechs wary about the West, and, after the war, adequately enthusiastic about the East (see: **Communism**).

Second, the stabbing of the First Republic is seen as a classic example of the destiny which history has reserved for the Czechs: there is always some nasty **foreigner**, be it a militant aggressor or a football referee, who eagerly uses dirty tricks to muck things up for them (see: **National Identity**). In other words, the Czechs themselves are not to be blamed for their many national disasters.

And third, thanks to 20 years with something that resembled modern parliamentary democracy, many Czechs are firmly convinced that they, after the fall of the Iron **Curtain** in 1989, had a much shorter path to Western political standards than other nations in the former East Bloc.

Foreigners

Generalizations are always dangerous, and especially when speaking about an entire nation, so let's put it a bit cautiously: even though

Bohemia and Moravia have a 700-year long history as a multicultural society (see: **Germans**; **Jews**), there are plenty of other countries where a foreigner probably will feel more welcomed than in the Czech Republic.

This, unfortunately, seems to go double if the foreigner's complexion is darker than what's common in **Central Europe** – or at least it did in the 1990s, when not only Czech **Roma**, but also numerous black and coloured foreigners were physically attacked just because of the pigmentaction of their skin.

Except for the intolerable demonstrations of violent racism (which is on the retreat, thanks to firmer reactions from the police), it's not totally impossible to understand why many Czechs are a bit **sceptical** towards foreigners.

Just take a short look at their history: the **Battle of White Mountain**, in 1620, where a coalition of (Catholic) foreigners beat the Czech army into its boots, led to 300 years of **Austrian** rule. In 1938, Czechoslovakia was – after only 20 years as an independent state – sacrificed to the Nazi wolves (see: **Munich Agreement**) and then submitted to six years of German occupation that cost more than 120,000 Czechs (78,000 of whom were of Jewish origin) their lives. And finally, in 40 years of **communism**, the Czechs were in reality governed by dictators based in Moscow. Such traumatic experiences would have marked any nation.

In the Czech instance, it has resulted in what some people regard as a rather inward-looking mentality. Which is quite logical. Every culture can be seen as a defence system; the more you try to change it, the more defensive it becomes. This has not made the Czechs overt nationalists in the ludicrous Scandinavian way ("We are simply the best!") or in the militant **Balkan** manner. Instead, the Czechs have, as the Danish **communication** expert Claus Munck Birch points out, "learned to live with this pressure without really being influenced by it". Thus, on the surface, many Czechs will accept things imposed on them by their foreign master, but eventually, they'll do whatever suits them (see: **Švejk, The Good Soldier**).

In the Czechs' relations to the approximately 250,000 foreigners officially registered (at least another 250,000 are living here illegally), this has found expression in a somewhat duplicitous attitude.

On the surface, most Czechs are polite and often even obliging towards foreigners. Yet their inner feelings, it seems, often tell them to be cautious and regard them as **intruders**, just as those scumbags who came in 1620 and 1938 and 1968. As a result, it may be hard to get to know them on a more personal level – especially if the foreigner lacks a command of the **Czech language**.

The fact that Czechs have to speak a foreign language (which many of them still don't) and thus risk making fools of themselves seems to be very, very scary. This language problem, however, applies even more the other way around. Many foreigners have lived for years in this country without mastering more than a few phrases in Czech. Learning Czech (of course, nobody expects you to speak it fluently) is therefore a fundamental requirement for breaking the ice.

In addition to the historic traumas and the language troubles, there is a social barrier. To many Czechs, only two types of foreigners exist: either those from a Third World country who have come to the Czech Republic to learn how to become a civilized human being, or "businessmen and managers" from Western Europe or America, who have come to exploit the country's economic wealth. While the members of the first group are tolerated as long as they express their admiration for Czech culture and, not least, leave the country as soon as they have been "civilized", the Western foreigners are more enigmatic and troublesome.

According to the widespread cliché, Western businesspeople and managers (who were, in a survey in late 2003 elected the most detested professional group in the country, alongside members of the Czech **nobility**) behave like colonizers in some Third World country. The typical businessman – more seldom a businesswoman – lives in a luxury flat that ordinary Czechs only can dream of, or in Disney land-inspired villaghettos where most natives never set foot. The foreigners don't drive Škodas or Zhiguliks, but rather fancy cars – which are even singled out by

blue number plates. And, most importantly, they earn in a month what a Czech earns in half a year, which is not a great advantage in a nation obsessed by **egalitarianism**.

But then, one might ask, hasn't the freedom that followed after 1989 managed to curb xenophobic sentiments and stereotypical thinking?

In some aspects, the answer is definitely yes. Open borders and free access to information have done miracles to the atmosphere of musty provincialism that reigned under the communists (see: **Ocean, Absence of**). During the last decade, millions of Czechs have travelled abroad and acquired personal experiences from international surroundings. And even more importantly: by now, a new generation of young Czechs not traumatized by the Bolshevik regime's cheap propaganda, have grown up. Yet one unexpected setback has appeared.

The separation of Czechoslovakia, in 1993, had an impact that is often ignored. After centuries of multicultural co-habitation with Sudeten

Germans (who were kicked out in 1945), Jews (who were, largely, killed during the war) and **Slovaks** (who now had their own state), the Czechs could finally say they were living in a more or less mono-ethnic state (typically, Czech Roma tend not to be counted).

In addition, after the collapse of the Soviet Empire, the Czechs were finally masters of their own house. So why should they now greet foreigners with open arms? Well, for economic reasons, foreign investors had to be tolerated, but as late as in 2003, more than 50 percent of the Czech population, according to a survey, said that they regarded the inflow of foreigners as a negative phenomenon, especially so when it comes to people from Asia and the former Soviet Union. The survey suggested that two thirds of the Czech population would prefer to live in a closed society where they "could solve their problems themselves".

Does this attitude explain why the "right-wing" government in the first half of the 1990s was so hesitant to sell state industry to foreign investors, as the **Hungarians** had done, but instead launched an unsuccessful voucher privatisation program for the country's citizens? Or was it rather an expression of the **golden hands** formula – the notion that the Czechs have a God-given talent for creative improvisation (see: **Cimrman, Jára**)?

In any case, the xenophobic revival in the 1990s has by now, to all appearances, passed its peak. Besides that, the Czechs have, during their turbulent history, demonstrated an amazing capability to adapt to new regimes, so there's no reason to paint the devil on the wall. The historian Dušan Třeštík probably hit the nail on the head when he stated that the Czechs have already become completely normal Europeans. "The only problem is that they're not yet aware of it."

Franz Josef

To the citizens of the Habsburg empire, Franz Josef I – who ruled his multi-national subjects with a firm hand for an incredible period stretching from 1848 to 1916 – was something like Queen Victoria to the British: a seemingly immortal symbol of the empire's stability, the predictability of its conservative politics and the moral **values** preached by the Catholic Church (see: **Religion**).

However, when the First World War ended in late 1918 and the Danube Empire fell apart, Franz Josef was soon forgotten by his former Slavonic subjects, not least by the Czechs, who had lost more than two hundred thousand young men in a meaningless war they never supported. Neither had they forgotten that the Emperor, or *Mister Procházka*, as they spitefully called him (a newspaper once printed a photo of the Emperor in Prague with the caption *Procházka na mostě*, or "A Walk on the Bridge"), for letting himself, in 1867, be crowned as king of the **Hungarians**, while he didn't take the trouble to go to Prague to be crowned as the king of the Czechs.

And when his nephew, Franz Ferdinand – the unlucky fellow in Sarajevo – married a lady from the Czech gentry, Žofie Chotková, both the Emperor and his court reacted with unconcealed horror. Franz Ferdinand was even pressed to accept the condition that the children of such an "unequal" marriage would have no rights to ascend to the imperial throne.

Small wonder, then, that the citizens of newly-established Czechoslovakia exceeded one another in smashing statues of the former Emperor. Jaroslav Hašek, the author of the tales about the good soldier **Švejk**, uses one episode to pinpoint the Czechs' aversion towards Franz Josef: when flies "decorate" the Emperor's portrait in a *hospoda* with their waste products, the Czech innkeeper (and millions of readers with him) hardly manages to hide his pleasure, while the **Austrian** undercover agent goes bananas and arrests the poor guy.

Yet Franz Josef has left one tradition that still characterizes the Czechs' daily life. One of Franz Josef's allegedly numerous virtues was his great diligence. Thus, in all the 68 years he ruled, the Emperor went to bed early (okay, often with his mistress), and – even more importantly – woke up and started working at an almost ungodly early hour.

Some pundits claim that the real reason was not diligence, but rather the Emperor's long-lasting problems with insomnia. Be this as it may, the consequence was inevitable: when Franz Josef was busily working at six o'clock in the morning, his staff and administration were also busily working at six o'clock. And when state bureaucrats all over the empire jumped out of bed before the sun rose, private industry, trade and transport couldn't be far behind. In short: the Austro-Hungarian empire must have been hell for all of us late sleepers.

Almost a century after Franz Josef was promoted to eternity, this awful tradition is still frightfully alive and kicking in the Czech Republic. In most hospitals, for instance, patients are woken up at six o'clock, even if the doctor's visit is scheduled only at nine. In schools, lessons start at eight o'clock, while at the universities, lectures might begin even earlier. Also, in many Czech factories, production starts at least one hour earlier than is common in Western and Northern Europe. The government of Vladimír Špidla, which was installed in 2002, took this perversion so literally that it started some of its meetings at six o'clock in the morning!

To be fair, this tradition certainly doesn't represent a serious problem, but it affects one, not insignificant, layer of the Czech society: **beer** drinkers. To give the millions of Czechs who spend the evening in a local *hospoda* a chance to sober up before work starts at six o'clock the next morning, most pubs mercilessly close at ten o'clock in the evening – i.e., at a time when people in other parts of Europe have just started the evening.

So, next time you are being kicked out of your local *hospoda* just in the middle of a spirited discussion about everything from football to quantum physics, don't blame it on the poor innkeeper, but on His Imperial Highness Franz Josef!

Fridays

As you might have already noticed, the Czech Republic is not an Islamic country (see: **Religion**), and, therefore, Fridays should be an ordinary working day when business goes on as usual. However, anyone who has tried to sort out a problem at a public office in this country on a Friday afternoon has probably discovered that this day is not an ordinary day at all.

After noon on Friday, most Czech public offices tend to work with even bigger delays and troubles than earlier in the week. This, of course, is not a Czech speciality – public officials all over the Western **world** count down to the weekend. There are, however, few countries where the countdown is performed with greater fervency and matter of course than in the Czech Republic.

If you think this is a legacy of the former communist era, you're right. During the former regime, it was commonly acknowledged that those who didn't steal from their (state) employer stole from their families. In practise, this meant that everyone felt entitled to "borrow" bricks, machines, spare parts or whatever his or her company produced, for private use (by the way, how could this be deemed stealing, when everything belonged to the state, which equalled the people?) Subsequently, those who worked in public offices could, without greater pangs of conscience, snatch pens and pencils – but most of all time.

The private sector, which emerged after the **Velvet Revolution**, has put a more or less effective stop to this deep-rooted tradition. But the public sector, to put it mildly, has not been as successful. Czech state **bureaucracy** is almost as over-grown as it was under the communists. Symptomatically, some years ago, an elderly fellow was discovered in a dusty room at the Ministry of Interior, and nobody knew that he had been vegetating in the office for several decades.

When **Václav Klaus'** government started its fight against **bureaucracy** in the middle of the 1990s, its first step was to establish a committee

(which, after all, doesn't seem all that illogical in the country of **Franz Kafka**). And still, the army of bureaucrats have lousy wages compared to the private sector, so who can blame them for compensating for a miserable salary by cutting out early on Fridays?

What's more, the Czechs have quite a good reason for starting the weekend early. Outside Scandinavia, there's probably no other European nation with more cottage- and cabin-owners than the Czech Republic. Some estimates suggest that there are 1.2 million of these holiday houses (see: **Munich Agreement**) and that every other Czech family has access to a second home in the countryside. During the communists, it was not uncommon for people to live out a kind of "inner exile" at their cabins, which were their private property. Therefore, all the physical efforts, money and time spent on maintenance were not wasted, because people were investing it in their own property.

Since the Czechs' passionate love of their country houses hasn't weakened much after the fall of **communism**, a **foreigner** is advised to take one necessary precaution: if you need to sort out an urgent matter in a public office, pray to God it's not Friday afternoon.

Germans

„Fate has left us to clash and to co-operate with the Germans." This is how František Palacký, the founder of history as a scientific discipline in **Bohemia** and one of the spiritual leaders of the nineteenth century Czech national revival once characterized the Czechs' relations with their great Western neighbour.

However contradictory and ambivalent this may sound, it's actually a very apt description. On the one hand, the Germans have played a totally irreplaceable part in the cultural and economic development of the Czech nation. On the other, no other country has caused the Czechs greater trauma.

Take a look at a map of **Central Europe**, and you'll immediately understand what Palacký had in mind. Today, the Czech Republic's border with Germany accounts for about 800 kilometres of its 2,300 kilometres of borders. But when you also remember that most of Polish Silesia until 1945 was a part of Germany (Prussia before 1918), and then recall that the Czechs' southern neighbours, the **Austrians**, also belong to the Germanic culture, you realize that the Czechs have formed a Slavonic wedge in German territory for almost a millennium.

As some Czech cynics prefer to depict the situation: "We are like the birds that sit in the crocodile's open jaws!" However wild this parallel might occur to you, it pinpoints some significant differences between the two nations.

Firstly, while the Germans are Central Europe's largest ethnic group and by far its largest economy, one of the basic ingredients in the Czechs' **national identity** is their self-perception as one of the continent's smaller nations. To use Biblical terms, this is a story about a David who for one thousand years has been living next door to Goliath, and who, at times, has problems with curbing his feeling of inferiority.

Secondly, there is the language barrier, which originally was so insurmountable that the Czech word denoting a German – *Němec* – derives from the adjective *němý*, which actually means mute. Thirdly, the justified fear of being politically dominated – and during Second Word War liquidated – by the Germans has repeatedly driven Czech **politicians** to seek support and comfort from the **Russians**. The last attempt to team up with their big Slavonic fellows in the East cost the Czechs 40 years of stagnation, decay and thousands of lost lives (see: **Communism**).

Yet it would be wrong to describe the Czechs' relations to the Germans merely as a somewhat troubled neighbourliness. Actually, this is a story about co-habitation. From the thirteenth century onwards, Bohemia and **Moravia** saw a constant influx of German settlers. Some of them were merchants invited by the Czech kings, while others were craftsmen offering their services. After the **Battle of White Mountain**, in 1620, there was also a significant influx of farmers, who took over estates left by exiled Czech Protestants (see: **Foreigners**). Even an invention as ultra-Czech as *Pilsner* **beer** should in reality be credited to Josef Groll, a Bavarian brewer who was headhunted to Western Bohemian Plzeň in 1842.

By 1918, when Czechoslovakia was founded, approximately three million ethnic Germans – more than one third of the population in Bohemia, Moravia and Silesia – were living in the country's Sudeten region. The capital Prague had at that time approximately 30,000 German inhabitants, most of them living in the area near Old Town Square. In addition to the Sudeten Germans, the majority of pre-war Bohemia and Moravia's 100,000 **Jews** were either German speaking or bi-lingual, thus forming a natural bridge between Czech and German culture.

Take, for instance, Max Brod. This Prague-born, German-speaking Jew didn't only do **world** literature a tremendous favour by saving and publishing his friend **Franz Kafka's** manuscripts. Thanks to his German contacts and personal influence, Brod persuaded the Berliner Opera to stage the composer Leoš Janáček's *Jenufa,* and he was also instrumental in presenting Jaroslav Hašek's Good Soldier **Švejk** to German readers. In both instances, a smashing success in Germany paved the way to global fame.

During their 700 year presence in Bohemia and Moravia, the Germans have left so many traces that it's hard today to say what's originally Czech and what's German.

Just look at Bohemia's cities. Nobody doubts that Prague and the Hussite stronghold Tábor were founded by Slavs. But names like Nymburg (Neuenburg), Šumperk (Schönberg), Kolín (Köln) and Varnsdorf reveal that these cities' first inhabitants almost certainly were of Germanic origin. It's not that clear who the first settlers in Karlovy Vary (Carlsbad), Liberec (Reichenberg), Cheb (Eger) and Domažlice (Tauss) was, but it's unquestionable that these cities were completely dominated by Germans right up until 1945 (see: **Munich Agreement**).

As one might expect in nationalism-ridden Central Europe, several Bohemian cities that were originally dominated by Germans were in 1918 given not only Czech-sounding names (Budweis became Budějovice), but were also equipped with the adjective Czech – as in

Český Krumlov. Is this an attempt to falsify history? No, it's a verbatim translation of the original German name – *Böhmisch Krumau*.

The interesting thing, though, is that *Böhmisch* in German only refers to geography, i.e. the city is located in Bohemia and not Bavaria, and does not say anything about the inhabitants' ethnic origin. Similarly, the German term *Böhme* means simply a person who lives in Bohemia, and might ethnically be a Czech, a German or even a person who didn't care about his nationality. However, *Český* and *Čech*, the equivalent terms, do not leave any room for a German element.

The German influence on Czech culture is expressed even more strongly by the nearly half million people with **surnames** like Müller, Bauer and Töpfer, or with Germanic surnames masked by Czech orthography (Šubrt). Peculiarly enough, *Honza*, the most Czech of all Czech Christian names, is actually German *Hans*. True, a German-sounding surname is not necessarily an airtight proof that a person has German ancestors. The priests who kept the church registry were often zealous servants of the Emperor in Vienna (see: **Religion**) or heavy boozers (see: **Cimrman, Jára**), and germanised names by whim or by mistake.

Still, human passion has always been stronger than language barriers and cultural differences. If the colonizers who settled in Bohemia and Moravia were only half as interested in Slavonic women as the hordes of Germans who nowadays visit Czech brothels (see: **Sex**), it's fair to assume that a pretty slice of the Czech population is the product of a fleshy Slavonic-German clash that once took place.

Neither has the **Czech language** gone untouched. While *spisovná čeština* (the official, literary version of the language) has been so thoroughly cleansed of foreign elements that Czech can compete with modern Icelandic for the title of Europe's most purified language, *hovorová čeština* (spoken Czech as you can hear it in the streets) bursts and bubbles with Germanic loan words. Indeed, some of the most frequent and expressive slang phrases in modern Czech (see: **Cursing**) are of German origin. (Just to name a few: *Je mi šoufl* – I feel sick, *Jsem švorc* – I'm broke, *Ksicht* – face, *Fotr* – father, *Hajzl* – bog.)

Paradoxically enough, **Karel Hynek Mácha**, author of the poem "May" and the most brilliant Czech poet who has ever lived, felt more confident when speaking German than Czech. Josef Dobrovský, the father of the modern Czech language, wrote to himself in German, and his no less famous colleague Josef Jungmann even used a German dictionary as a model for his revolutionary Czech dictionary. In other words, *Němčina se vybíjela němčinou* – German was driven out by German.

Obviously, the Germans have also left numerous robust traces of their seven-century-long presence in Bohemia.

It's hard to imagine a more loaded symbol of Czech statehood than Prague's Charles Bridge and St. Vitus' Cathedral, but both of them, and the St. Barbora Cathedral in Kutná Hora as well, were actually designed by the German builder Peter Parler (1332–1399). Several magnificent examples of Czech baroque, most notably St. Nicholas Cathedral at Prague's Malá Strana, were built by the Bavarian architect Christopher Dientzenhofer (1655–1722) and his son Kilian (1689–1751) in the aftermath of the Battle of White Mountain. And the Charles Bridge would definitely look naked without the sculptures created by the German artist Ferdinand Brokoff (1688–1731).

Now, add hundreds of synagogues spread all over Bohemia and Moravia plus numerous functionalistic gems erected by ethnic German architects during the **First Republic's** boom, and you'll realize that a decent part of the elements that make Prague and other Bohemian cities extraordinary should actually be credited to German-speakers. In other words, Prague would never have become a "magic city", to use a somewhat pathetic term introduced by the Italian literate Angelo Maria Ripellino, had it not been for the Czech-German-Jewish cultural symbiosis.

It wouldn't, of course, be correct to present the Germans' 700-year-long co-habitation with the Czechs in Bohemia and Moravia as a wholly harmonious affair. True, until 1939, they never waged war against one another, and mixed Czech-German marriages were not totally uncommon during the First Republic. But the sole fact that these two peoples lived side by side for seven centuries without becoming one people proves that the relations were perhaps peaceful, but rather distant.

During the nineteenth century, when modern nationalism emerged, Prague's Germans took their Sunday promenades exclusively *Am Graben* (today's Na Příkopě), they visited only German theatres and restaurants, read only German newspapers and sent their children to German-speaking schools (and, after 1882, a German university), while the Czech upper classes strolled only on Ferdinand Avenue (now Národní Třída), visited Czech theatres (after 1883 the National Theatre) and restaurants, read Czech newspapers and educated their offspring in Czech schools. At one time Prague even had one Czech and one German botanical garden, and Czech hotheads regularly clashed with like-minded Germans in veritable mass brawls.

Still, it's foolish to pretend (as some nationalists do) that the Germans' long-lasting presence in Bohemia and Moravia and the close distance to Germany itself didn't have a tremendous impact on the Czechs' cultural and economic development in the eighteenth and nineteenth centuries.

Prague's Germans have a theatre, you say? Well, then we will certainly have one, too! Have the Germans codified their language by producing a large dictionary? Then we must do the same for the Czech language, and, in addition, develop an encyclopaedia that dwarfs any German lexicon! The Germans are establishing tourist clubs and erecting lookout towers on the peaks of the Krkonoše (Giant) Mountains? Just wait and see – our Czech tourist clubs will get far more members who'll erect even taller lookout towers!

How did the northern parts of Bohemia and Moravia become one of the most heavily industrialized areas in Central Europe? Because these regions were densely populated with Germans, who "imported" mining technology, textile industries, mechanical factories and glass blowers from their kinsmen on the other side of the border in Saxony and Silesia.

The Czechs' correct, although not too hearty relationship with their German compatriots received an almost fatal blow with the Munich Agreement in 1938 and the subsequent Second World War, during which a vast majority of Czechoslovakia's Germans (but not all of them!) proved more loyal to Hitler's Nazi regime than to Masaryk's democratic ideals.

It's easy to understand how this treason embittered the Czechs. First, they suffered the humiliation of being pressed to cede a large chunk of the country to Nazi Germany, and then they endured six years of occupation, which cost 120,000 Czechs – 78,000 of them of Jewish origin – their lives. In the Nazi retaliation against Reinhard Heydrich's assassination in 1942 alone, more than 3,000 people, including all male inhabitants of the village of Lidice, were murdered.

Then add immense material damages and a population boiling with hatred (within the end of 1945, more than 700 collaborators had been executed), and mix it with 40 years of Cold War, when the communist propaganda portrayed Czechoslovakia's Western neighbours as irreparable militarists, and you can with some tolerance understand why *nácek* (Nazi) and *vepř* (pig) still are among the slang words used for a German.

Yet the end of the Cold War has undeniably warmed most Czechs' relationships to the Germans. After the **Velvet Revolution** in 1989, Germany has become by far the largest foreign investor in the Czech Republic and there was, quite surprising, only sporadic grumbling (see: **Klaus, Václav**) when the German icon Volkswagen took over the Czech national treasure, Škoda Auto, in 1993. Today, German-owned Škoda accounts for almost 10 percent of the Czech Republic's total exports.

"Our mutual relations have definitely stabilized," Václav Houžvička, leader of the Czech-German Forum for Discussion, recently told the *Mladá fronta Dnes* daily. "But unfortunately, there are still certain barriers that hamper the co-operations."

What Houžvička calls "barrier" is what less diplomatic people would probably call plain Germanophobia. There is a widespread conviction among Czechs that the German government will someday officially support the evicted Sudeten Germans' demand that Prague must compensate them for property that was confiscated by Czechoslovakia in 1945 (see: **Carlsbad English Bitters**). However wild and exaggerated this fear of revisionism might be (only one organization, the militant Wittiko Bund, has publicly demanded compensation), the "Sudeten ghost" wakes up every time there is an election in either Germany or the Czech Republic.

The Germans' unpopularity is, almost inevitably, also a question of good old envy (see: **Egalitarianism**). The Eastern German tourists, who until 1989 were happy to buy toothpaste during their visits in Czechoslovakia, have suddenly, thanks to a financial injection from the Western part of Germany, become real *Zápaďáci* – Westerners. When they now come on swift shopping trips to the Czech Republic, they splash *korunas* about as if they were Monopoly money (some, well, quite a few pay a substantial contribution to the Czech prostitution industry as well), drive fancy cars or even lapse into parvenu behaviour – which is not exactly the recommended way of winning friends among the Czechs.

This feeling of economic inferiority grows even bigger when the common Czech visits Germany. At home, a Czech's purchasing power is, thanks to the moderate price level, about half that of the common German's (in 2003). But once over the border, Czechs discover that their purchasing power has shrunk to one fourth of their neighbours'. In Germany, the average welfare recipient is a Rockefeller compared to a Czech teacher with five years university education.

Luckily, the economic differences are slowly but steadily diminishing, but the mental pattern – "poor and humble Czech" vs. "fat and rich German" – has started living its own life. Consequently, "ambivalence" is probably the most apt description of the Czechs' stance towards Germany and the Germans today.

This is also reflected by a survey published by the Czech Academy of Science's Sociological Institute in December 2003. When asked whether it was possible to live in peace and harmony with Germany, only 15 percent said it was impossible. But when asked if Germany might represent a threat to the Czech Republic, 40 percent of those Czechs questioned more or less agreed. The percentage skyrocketed to almost 70 when asked whether the Czechs should always be on guard against the Germans, and when it came to the justification of the expulsion of the German minority from Czechoslovakia after the Second World War, a staggering 80 percent of those surveyed had no qualms about it at all.

Does this sound very depressing? Actually, the situation could have been even worse. According to the renowned Dutch Clingendael Institute of International Relations, the **Danes** and the Dutch have an even more negative stance towards the Germans. And contrary to the Czechs neither country has been ideologically brainwashed and financially ruined by 40 years of communist misrule.

Golden Hands

As soon as you get to know some Czechs, you'll discover that many of them don't hesitate in the slightest to reel off different qualities that they consider very typical of their fellow countrymen (see: **National Identity**). Thus, according to common wisdom, the Czechs are an educated, cultivated and broad-minded lot, with a natural flair for democracy (see: **Hospoda**) and keen sense of humour (see: **Švejk, The Good Soldier**).

There is, however, one "typical Czech feature" which most people would regard as even more typical than the others: the Czechs are so handy and nimble-fingered and good at improvisation that one might believe they are equipped with golden hands.

Like many other stereotypes, also this one is not entirely without a grain of truth. Just take a look at the magnificent buildings that surround you. Forget that many of the architects were of Italian or **German** origin – the craftsmen were definitely Czechs! Who built the main part of "new" Vienna in the last part of the nineteenth century? Correct, Czech and **Slovak** workers. And which country on this planet has the highest number of engineers per capita? Right again, the Czech Republic.

Actually, the ability to be handy, i.e., mend things in your flat or cottage, fix your car or even build pieces of furniture (a double bed is a safe winner) are all basic elements of the ordeal that divides an average Czech *Pepa* from *a real male*. Even though you are two meters tall and a regional champion in boxing, you'll probably still be considered a sissy if you're unable to change a leaking seal in your bathroom.

Have you ever wondered why many Czech house-owners keep a shack stuffed with scrap and rubbish in their gardens? Simply because it works as an inexhaustible stock of materials and spare parts when dad needs to get something fixed. *Kutilství* ("do-it-yourselfism") also explains the tremendous density of ironmongers and the virtual invasion of **foreign** chains such as OBI, Hornbach and Baumax in the Czech Republic after 1989.

To be fair, nobody can dispute that there really are lots of handy people in this country. And many a Czech craftsman demonstrates an ability to improvise that dwarfs the qualities of his average Western colleague. The reason for this, however, is not because the Czechs have any natural talents which people of other nations lack (as many people in this country apparently believe). Instead, it seems to be based on two quite obvious facts.

Firstly, since *kutilství* is commonly regarded as the primary male-creating rite of passage, the mental pressure to become a *kutil* is strongly felt by most Czech boys. Secondly (and more importantly), the communist era was infamous for its large-scale absence of both decent services and modern consumer goods. When something broke down (which happened all the time), the simplest – and often only – way of fixing it, was to do it yourself. And since the necessary spare parts could usually not be obtained, you had to improvise and find something else.

Photo © Jaroslav Fišer

Thus, the communists quite unwillingly contributed more to the development of ordinary people's handiness, creativity and ingenious improvisation than any other rulers in their turbulent history.

However, the widespread conviction that all (male) Czechs are equipped with golden hands has led to one rather unfortunate phenomenon: this country boasts an incredible number of self-proclaimed experts. For instance, when **Austrian** specialists some years ago warned that the cooling system of the newly erected Temelín nuclear power plant might be unsafe, thousands of Czech *kutils* brushed the warnings off angrily, because they had all installed "something similar" in their kitchens, and it had worked perfectly!

The author Ondřej Sekora aptly describes this feature in his immensely popular children's books about Ferdinand the Ant, whose clumsy companion, Pytlík the Beetle, "knows everything and understands everything, because he has seen it all in cinema" (see: **Klaus, Václav**). In the real Czech **world**, however, millions of *kutils* know everything and understand everything because they have managed to fix a leaking sink.

Gott, Karel

Take Tom Jones and mix him with Enrico Caruso, the Italian tenor-cum-castrato singer. Then add tons of pathetic love songs, faked **sex** appeal and musical kleptomania focusing on Western hits from the 1970s. Spice it up with a political flexibility rare even for **Central European** standards and a personal status close to that of the Pope. What do you get? Karel Gott, Czech pop music's most mega-super, long-lasting and brightest star.

As his very name (which is not faked!) indicates, Gott was predestined to become a god from his birth in 1939.

His unique career as a singer started in the early 1960s when Gott still was a pimpled electrician's apprentice at Prague's ČKD engineering factory. After surprisingly winning several talent competitions, he made an astonishing breakthrough at the legendary Semafor Theatre in 1963. Virtually overnight, an unknown, 24-year-old electrician from Plzeň had become Czechoslovakia's leading pop star, who later also performed in some of Czech cinema's most popular films ever.

So far, so good – nobody has ever disputed Gott's talents or his hard work, and in the 1960s, he definitely deserved the people's admiration, which reached a peak during the Prague Spring's euphoria (see: **Communism**).

A bit more disputed, though, is his behaviour after Czechoslovakia was invaded, in 1968, and the **Russian**-backed Husák regime launched its neo-Stalinist *normalization*. Gott's first reaction was to emigrate, but after a few months in German exile, he returned to the mother country, where he energetically pursued his career further. After all, life went on for bus-drivers, plumbers and doctors, so why shouldn't it also go on for pop stars?

The price Gott paid for his success, however, was a very cosy relationship with the Bolsheviks. Too cosy, lots of critics would say. When the Husák regime, in 1977, launched its rabid attack on **Charter 77** in the form of the infamous Anti-Charter petition that cried for the protection of "socialist law and order", Karel Gott was the very man for the job of reading the proclamation when it was broadcast live on TV. As expected, Gott was soon thereafter awarded with the state title "National Artist", the Communist equivalent of a knighthood from the Queen, and the official media presented photos of a pop star who smiled so sweetly at Comrade President that one almost got the impression that the two of them were registered partners.

There seems to have existed an unwritten contract between Karel Gott and the communist regime. Its essence can be described as follows: by churning out millions of records with "optimistic" and "positive" music, the pop star helped to cement the shameful lie that the neo-Stalinist comrades were normal rulers just as in any other normal country. The communists, for their part, could finally boast a pop star with the same reputation and calibre as those in the West, from where he, without any inhibitions, "borrowed" many of his biggest hits.

Thanks to this pragmatic symbiosis, Karel Gott managed to defend his position as the very icon of Czechoslovak pop culture for an incredible period of 30 years. Not that people seemed to mind. In a society as stagnant as Czechoslovakia in the 1970s and 1980s, time went so slowly that one could get the impression that it almost had stopped.

The truly amazing thing, however, is that Karel Gott managed to survive the **Velvet Revolution**. More than that, on Wenceslas Square in November 1989, thousands of Czechs heard him sing the National anthem together with artists who had been banned for almost 20 years. Karel the collaborationist had suddenly been transformed into Karel the convinced democrat! Those who found this miracle a bit too stiff were quickly silenced. The new democratic leaders were also eager to use the pop-star's popularity to promote national unity and, not to be forgotten, their own political goals.

So, instead of applying for retirement together with his Bolshevik protectors, Karel Gott is still, 40 years after his breakthrough, the unrivalled king of Czech pop music.

True, neither dyed hair, an imposing number of face-lifts, nor an army of young mistresses can hide the fact that the Maestro, Elvis Presley's junior by only four years, is getting older. And even though his repertoire has been slightly refreshed (his former *svazácko-vekslácké hity* – tunes that were politically correct enough to please the regime, but rough enough to please the baddies from the black money market – have been replaced by a Tom Jones-like sound), music critics still accuse him of degenerating common people's taste.

Yet no show at the immensely popular **TV Nova**, no gala-concert or national **beauty contest** is imaginable without Karel Gott's participation. Otherwise serious newspapers present interviews with him every other week, and the pop star is happy to demonstrate his newly-discovered talents as painter and political commentator ("**Jews** and freemasons are ruling the **world**").

Logically, when Maestro Gott some years ago, after an especially cruel critic had compared him to "a zombie who causes acute depression to innocent radio listeners", decided to stop performing in protest, the situation was considered so grave that the Minister of Culture himself went to console the deeply insulted star.

Could this have happened in another country? Hardly. Both Tom Jones and Julio Iglesias have, admittedly, accomplished a kind of comeback, but neither of them would be voted their countries' most popular singer, as Gott is almost every year. Old stars such as Uriah Heep or Alla Pugachova are still worshipped by fans in their home countries, but most people consider them to be marginal acts or living fossils. So what's the explanation for Karel Gott's indestructible popularity?

Clever marketing undoubtedly plays an important role. Take, for instance, Maestro Karel's habit of kicking out a blond, 19-year-old mistress a couple of weeks before his latest CD is to be launched. Usually, the media instantly swallow the bait, with the result that the often-negative reviews of his mediocre music are completely drowned in the bombastic gossip about his sexual escapades. What's more, it's no secret that Gott is

closely connected to the small group of people who have run the Czech music business for the last 35 years (he has himself been called the "Gott-father"). As any other local businessman, Gott takes the advantage of a combination of lowbrow media and an un-transparent business climate (see: **Balkans**; **Personal Connections**).

The ultimate explanation, however, of the Czechs' worshipping of Gott might lie in the tendency to prefer the familiar and safe to the unknown and challenging (see: **National Identity**; **Ocean, Absence of**). This goes double at times when the nation is experiencing large and far-reaching changes. However provincial and musically outdated, Karel Gott has become one of the few fixed and unalterable points the common Czech can cling to in a crazy world.

Besides that, during the communist regime, he made the same humi-liating compromises as most other people, but he has still sold more than

30 million records and CD's during his 40-year career. Can a former electrician in any other country beat that?

Havel, Václav

As is customary for internationally famous and admired persons hailing from smaller countries, Václav Havel arouses far more controversy at home than abroad.

True, most Czechs will agree that he was uncommonly brave during the communist era, and they were proud that their president was received with fanfares and standing ovations all over the **world** during the 13 turbulent years that followed the **Velvet Revolution**. Yet there are plenty of people who simply can't hide the fact that they are overjoyed that he has finally left the Prague Castle.

Czechs can be sorted into roughly four groups, according to their views on the ex-president.

Probably the largest and definitely the least vocal group is comprised of all those ordinary people who deeply respect Havel and don't question anything he has ever done or said (a majority of them are women, in whom the physically extremely clumsy Havel apparently aroused a strong maternal instinct). Here, of course, you also find liberals and **Charter 77** fellows who share the former president's political views on human rights, consideration for the environment and the importance of non-materialistic **values**. Havel's opponents often use the sarcastic nickname "Brotherhood of Love and Truth" when speaking about this group.

Then there is a closely related group of Havel-fans, many of them artists, actors or people working in the culture sector, who basically agree with him but don't hesitate to criticise him for various shortcomings.

Photo © Jaroslav Fišer

Some of his former friends got childishly offended when their old pal "Vašek" didn't have time to see them any longer, while others (once again, mainly women) were outraged that he married his mistress, the actress Dagmar Veškrnová (17 years his junior) less than one year after his first wife, the widely admired Olga Havlová, died from cancer in 1997. Another frequent complaint from Havel-fans is that "he could have done more" to prevent the break-up of Czechoslovakia. However, exactly what he should have done when both the Czech and the **Slovak** leadership had decided to divorce is not that clear.

The Havel-bashers can also be divided into two major groups (those in between don't seem to exist).

The less important group consists of quite ordinary people who just are fed up with what they perceive as "Havel's constant moralizing" against consumerism, cheap architecture and widespread atheism. "A person who was born into wealth and has inherited millions hasn't any right to criticize us," their mantra goes. Havel's amnesty of thousands of criminals in 1990 was grist for their mill. Although this act was quite understandable in light of the four years he spent behind the bars himself, the deeds of the released convicts didn't help to save his image among grouchy Czechs. Needless to say, Bolsheviks of every conceivable category are well represented in this group (see: **Communism**).

And finally, there is the group of extremely vociferous, hard-hitting and well-connected Havel-haters. The spiritual standard-bearer of these alleged right-wingers is **Václav Klaus**, and their main mouthpiece is the lowbrow but extremely popular **TV Nova**.

It's hard to give a single reason for their almost irrational loathing of Havel. Klaus was obviously upset when, in 1998, Havel publicly called the result of his economic reforms Mafia capitalism, and his personal envy of Havel's international fame also seems to play a significant role ("While I'm concerned about the Czech Republic, Havel was for 13 years solely and only concerned about himself"). Many Klaus-clones hate Havel out of servility or gratitude to their great master, others because the Charter 77 founder made their newly minted anti-communism seem ridiculous.

By and large, the Czech media must also be counted in the anti-Havel group. In the early 1990s, most of the country's journalists believed uncritically in Klaus' reform miracle, and they often sided with him in his regular brawls with Havel. As a result, Havel granted more interviews to **foreign** media than to local ones, which provoked the locals to sling more mud with even greater enthusiasm.

Not that Václav Havel seemed to care what the media wrote about him. After swiftly establishing an office in Prague's Voršilská Street, he spent his first year as an ex-president jetting all over the globe to pick up doctorates and prizes of honour. In a rare public appearance in early 2004, he said that he intends, if his health allows him, to use his energy and international prestige to focus on the violation of human rights in dictatorships like Belarus, Burma and Cuba, and he also hinted that he might write yet another book.

Havel's personal account from the political kitchen in the 1990s, stripped of political cautiousness and diplomatic concerns, would certainly be interesting. But if he finally decides to dedicate the rest of his life to gardening at his villa in Prague's Střešovice or to drinking wine under a palm at his country house by Portugal's Atlantic coast, most Czechs would find that perfectly well-deserved. And his petty critics will, sooner or later, have to admit that Havel has earned himself a place right beside **Tomáš G. Masaryk** in Czech history.

Hedonism

Take a look at the following statistical data: with an average consumption of 161 litres per capita, the Czechs drink more **beer** than any other nation on this planet. The relative frequency of Czech **alcoholics** is one of Europe's highest, and although their love of meat has slightly weakened after the **Velvet Revolution** (in 1990, the common Czech gulped down 50 kilos of pork and 28 kilos of beef), the Czechs still belong among the **world's** most gutsy meat-eaters.

Then add information from the national census in 2001, which showed that almost 60 percent of the population describe themselves as atheists or non-believers, while tolerance towards **sex** in general and marital infidelity in particular is notoriously high. Don't forget either that there are more owners of cabins and cottages where you can hide away from work and stress (see: **Fridays**), than in most other countries on the European continent.

What is the inevitable conclusion of these data? That the incomparably largest religious society in the Czech Republic is that of the hedonists!

Homosexuals

Sadly enough, the Czechs have a pretty bad track record when it comes to discrimination against their fellow **Roma** citizens, and they cannot be said to be exceedingly warm towards **foreigners** either. However, when it comes to sexual minorities, they display a broadmindedness that is downright amazing.

True, there are still some lunatic Parliamentarians who believe that gays can be cured (see: **Academic Titles**; **Moravia**) and therefore have succeeded in blocking a draft law on registered partnerships. But this medieval stance strongly contrasts with that of the Czech mainstream.

According to the researcher Peter Weiss, only six percent of the population say that they don't accept homosexuals, a result that places the Czechs among Europe's most tolerant nations. During the first years after the Second World War, Jaroslav Foglar's homoerotic serial about the Fast Arrows, a group of boy scouts, even became some of the best-selling books in Czech literary history.

One obvious reason for this sexual tolerance (perhaps indifference is a better word) is the relatively weak position that **religion** occupies in the average Czech's life. Contrary to the neighbouring **Poles** and **Slovaks**, where the Catholic Church is a national cornerstone and homosexuals are openly discriminated against, the largest "religious" society in the Czech Republic is that of people without any affiliation (6.1 millions according to the 2001 census).

Another, although more speculative explanation, is that the Czech-speaking elite, which emerged under the national revival in the middle of the eighteenth century (see: **Czech Language**), focused more or less entirely on one object: the Czech cause. Thus, categories like male-female (see: **Feminism**) or sexual preferences were treated as completely inferior to the crucial issue – to be a good and loyal Czech.

The Bolshevik regime also turned out to be less rigid against gays than their comrades in other East Bloc states. In 1961, homosexual acts, which during the Stalinist era of the 1950s were punished by up to five years imprisonment, were decriminalized, and, in the 1980s, they were completely deleted from the official list of illnesses. Still, to a regime so profoundly intolerant and suspicious of any signs of inconformity as the Czechoslovak communists, a citizen's sexual orientation was of great interest.

StB, the secret police, meticulously registered every person who might be suspected of not being entirely heterosexual – not least if they also happened to be political dissidents – and frequently tried to blackmail them into co-operation (see: **Lustration**). Needless to say, when being an open homosexual represented a possible threat to your professional and social existence, lots of gays and lesbians preferred to hide their sexual orientation. And plenty of those who were not protected by the anonymity of a big city chose to cover up by getting married and having children.

Luckily, this has changed profoundly with the liberalisation that followed the **Velvet Revolution** in 1989. After decades on the fringes of society, gays and lesbians have "come out" without risking, at least in Prague and **Bohemia**, more badgering than in, say, Holland, although most of them prefer to do it in a more low-key and less proclaiming manner than in the West (see: **Communication**). Homosexuality, in any case, is no longer considered a social stigma, which was clearly demonstrated by Václav Fischer, a successful businessman who ran some years ago as a candidate for the Czech Senate.

In an attempt to ruin his chances of being elected, Fischer's political opponents put up lots of billboards announcing that he belonged to "a four-percent minority". The trick backfired completely. Not only because the voters found it utterly cheap, but also because most Czechs apparently consider a politician's sexual orientation to be totally irrelevant. Fischer was elected by one of the biggest landslides in the Czech Senate's history.

So, if the **German** philosopher Theodor Adorno was right when stating that a society's relation to its sexual minorities is the best indicator of its tendencies towards fascism, it's fair to conclude that Czech society is admirably non-fascist (and also caring about its relatively few HIV and AIDS victims). If we also add its great tolerance to **sex** in general, the conclusion must be that the Czech Republic, in some matters, is one of Europe's most liberal countries (see: **Values**).

But, just to avoid confusing and perhaps also disappointing potential admirers, English speakers are still strongly advised to pay attention to one lingual detail: in the Czech language, the sentence "I'm warm" can be translated in two ways. And semantically, there is a profound difference between *Jsem teplý* and *Je mi teplo*!

Horáková, Milada

During its 41-year dictatorship, the communist regime executed almost 180 political opponents. Most of these court-sanctioned murders took place in the late 1940s and early 1950s, and the scenario was very often the same:

Party bigwigs commissioned the courts to manufacture "evidence" that a person who the communists (or their masters in Moscow) considered to represent a threat to their autocracy, in reality was spying for CIA, Israel, Tito's Yugoslavia or even the successors of Gestapo. The unlucky victims were without exception found guilty and then expedited to a swift death in Prague's Pankrác prison.

Most of the accused reacted like the much-admired general Heliodor Píka, who knew he had absolutely no chance to escape the gallows and did practically nothing to reject the insane charges that were filed against him. Others, such as former party boss Rudolf Slánský and ten of his top *apparatchiks* (by "coincidence" all of **Jewish** origin), were tortured to reel off long and tear-dripping confessions about the crimes they had allegedly committed that ultimately didn't help them at all.

And then, there was the tiny and seemingly defenceless Milada Horáková, who rejected the constructed charges with a vengeance, and then went bravely into death without a word of grief. The cold-blooded murder of the 49-year old lawyer, mother of an under-aged daughter, represents one of the darkest spots on the communist regime's ugly record. Few other communist crimes caused stronger reactions in the Western **world**. And few of the Bolsheviks' many victims displayed more civil courage.

Born in 1901 when **Bohemia** and **Moravia** still were a part of the Austro-**Hungarian** Empire, Milada Horáková grew up to become a typical proponent of the **First Republic** and the liberal ideals set forward by its president, **Tomáš G. Masaryk.** As one of Czechoslovakia's first women, Horáková graduated from Prague's Law Academy and started her career as a lawyer in the Central Social Office. Two years later, she became a full-time official of the National Socialist Party (no connection to Germany's later NSDAP!), which was popular among workers and members of the lower middle class.

Ever since the party's establishment in 1897, its members had promoted the Czech cause and struggled against what they regarded as **Austrian** militarism. When Czechoslovakia emerged in 1918, the focus shifted to social matters. To Milada Horáková, this meant not only the fight for social justice, but also for women's emancipation (see: **Feminism**).

As one might expect from a committed democrat, Horáková had only contempt for the Nazis who occupied Czechoslovakia in March 1939 (see: **Munich Agreement**) and immediately engaged herself in the Czech resistance movement. The Gestapo arrested her a year later. Miraculously escaping a death sentence, she spent the rest of the war in a **German** concentration camp.

The communists, however, were not that complaisant. As a protest against their take-over in February 1948 (see: **Communism**), Horáková, who by now had become not only a member of the Parliament, but also the head of the Czech Women's Council and one of the leaders of the National Socialist Party, withdraw from all her functions and left politics. The communists were still not satisfied. Assuming (probably correctly) that a democrat with Horáková's moral integrity and broad popularity wouldn't silently tolerate their appalling abuse of human rights, they fabricated evidence and charged her with treason and espionage.

Horáková fought like a tiger to the bitter end, but didn't have a chance against the Bolshevik machinery. She was executed on June 27, 1950.

It's tempting to claim that Milada Horáková didn't die in vain. Like **Jan Palach**, she certainly represented a bright light in the dictatorship's darkness. After the **Velvet Revolution**, a monument in Horáková's honour was erected at Prague's Slavín Cemetery, where the nation's most prominent daughters and sons are buried. The location of Horáková's monument, in front of the others, even indicates that she is a **hero** among the heroes.

Yet the brave politician's death more than half a century ago still evokes some painful thoughts. Notwithstanding the posthumous honour she has rightfully been awarded, it's often forgotten that Horáková was not killed by Soviet advisers, as some Czechs like to believe, but by her own countrymen. Not a single person has been charged for staging the murder.

Even worse, during the mock trial, hordes of brainwashed Czechs signed a petition that demanded her death. One can only pray that those who still might be alive are tormented by a guilty conscience. And one should also keep in mind that the bravest and most hard-balled **politician** in modern Czech history actually was a woman.

Hospoda

"Today, all parts of the Czech lands are as a big inn or shelter, where one can, not just for a few days, but for the entirety of one's life, heartily enjoy all delights and riches."

These enthusiastic words were written by the Jesuit priest and historian Josef Balbín in the 1680s and seem as apt today as they were three and a half centuries ago. The **beer** house – *hospoda* – is still the cornerstone of Czech popular culture (see: **Švejk, The Good Soldier**), and their sheer number is downright amazing. At one time, Prague's Žižkov area alone had more pubs and beer houses than the entire Norwegian capital of Oslo.

To a **foreigner** not familiar with the **Czech language**, the word *hospoda* might seem reminiscent of the English *hospital*. Linguistically speaking, there actually is a distant connection. *Hospoda* derives from old-Slavonic *gospoda*, composed of *gost* (guest) and *potis* (master), and the latter of the two elements is the same word that occurs in Latin *hospes*. But also semantically the comparison with *hospital* makes perfect sense, since the *hospoda* from time immemorial has been the place where the Czech man (see: **Feminism**) has healed his soul.

To undergo the classic *hospoda* therapy, there are only three things you need: beer (the larger quantity, the better result), a problem that really bothers you, and the company of a friend or acquaintance (if you don't have any, you'll find some in the *hospoda*). Now, all you have to do is to pour down hectolitres of the foaming potion while intensely complaining about your hysterical wife, greedy mistress, imbecilic boss, incompetent government, unlucky national football team or whatever. After three or four hours of thorough therapy, your soul will be filled with total relief.

A foreigner may perhaps doubt the mental effects of *hospoda* therapy, but it's hardly a coincidence that the Czech Republic has fewer psychiatric patients than all its neighbouring countries (however, they also have more **alcoholics**).

Theoretically, you don't even need a *hospoda* to carry out this therapy, as an incident in the city of Mladá Boleslav some years ago illustrates.

Fed up with the drunkards who constantly gathered for beer parties in the main city park, the mayor decided to prohibit consumption of alcoholic beverages in all public places, thus confining the beer-drinkers to local *hospodas*. The drunkards, however, reacted stoically. Pointing to the *Listina základních práv a svobod* – The Charter of Basic Rights and Liberties – adopted by the then Czechoslovak Parliament in 1991, they argued that drinking beer in the city park was one of their human rights. And guess what? The mayor admitted that the drunkards were right, and backed down!

Yet the fuss was rather wasted energy, because any Czech town with some self-respect boasts at least one *hospoda* where a pint of beer costs less than a bottle of soft drink. But even in the humblest establishment you have to respect a set of *hospoda* rules.

Firstly, every *hospoda* has its *štamgasts* – regular guests. This is a group of local drunkards, who enjoy certain privileges, such as keeping their personal tankards on the shelf over the bar, a reserved chair at a table far from the door to the toilet, and – most importantly – the right to be served prior to other guests. This is one of the few areas where Czech society still respect **nobility**, and there is no way you can escape this "beer-apartheid". If your ego is too provoked by this discrimination, you have two options: either switch to wine and start frequenting *vinárnas*, or visit your local *hospoda* so often that you acquire the *štamgast* status yourself.

Secondly, the *hospoda* is a profoundly democratic institution, where (at least theoretically) people of all layers of society meet to drink and discuss. Consequently, you can sit down by any table where there are unoccupied seats as long as you formally ask the people that already are sitting there if it's okay! Similarly, if you are sitting in a *hospoda* and there are unoccupied seats next to you, be prepared for a group of stran-

gers to suddenly clump down next to you and start a heated discussion about academic subjects such as football referees, female anatomy or the latest trends in modern Mongolian poetry. This is the charm and the intention of the *hospoda*. If you want quiet contemplation, try a walk in the forest!

Thirdly, the *hospodas* have always been a man's **world.** True, the number of women frequenting *hospodas*, especially the new and trendy establishments where beer is served in 33 centilitres glasses with stems, has been growing after the **Velvet Revolution.** But the real *hospodas*, dives where drinking beer from glasses with stems would be considered something between heresy and a perversion, are still a male dominion and a sanctuary where men can seek refuge and understanding. Logically, many *hospodas* have introduced at least one day in the week when the waitresses are serving beer topless.

The atmosphere of male solidarity has even been ritualised: after pouring down four-five half litres, all the men sitting round the same table may suddenly march off to the toilet to perform a collective **urination**. To the diehard beer drinkers, this is the ultimate expression of brother-hood. To most other people, it's an unambiguous sign that the *hospodas* make fertile soil for hidden **homosexuality**.

Needless to say, not all Czechs are fans of the *hospoda* culture. To a disgusted minority of the population, the *hospodas* represent everything that's vulgar, smelly, loud and lazy. This view is hard to reject completely. The army of Czech alcoholics (according to some estimates, 10 percent of the male population!) would no doubt have had a more troubled life without a watering hole on every other corner. And yes, the common *hospoda* humour tends to smell of armpits. Yet nobody can deny that some of Czech literature's greatest names, be it **Karel Hynek Mácha**, **Jaroslav Hašek**, Bohumil Hrabal or Jaroslav Seifert, all were closely linked to the *hospoda*, and some of them even worked there.

In essence, the *hospoda* reflects both the best and the worst sides of Czech society. On the one hand, they offer an abundance of joviality, friendliness, creativity, communicativeness, playfulness and a flair for grotesque humour and egalitarianism. On the other, they richly nourish the habit of complaining about everything and everybody without making the slightest practical effort to change things for the better.

However, nobody can dispute that the *hospoda* is a uniquely Czech institution. In what other country can you pop in at a pub with a large mug, have it filled with foaming beer and then carry it happily home to dinner?

Hungarians

The sapper Vodička, one of the colourful characters in the book about The Good Soldier **Švejk**, has earned himself eternal fame among the Czechs for one single remark: "Every Hungarian can be blamed for being a Hungarian!" Despite its chauvinistic punch, it quite adequately reflects the way in which many Czechs still regard their Hungarian ex-neighbours. **Czech language** even operates with the unbelievable expression *Seš Maďar?* (Are you Hungarian?) meaning "Are you a complete idiot?"

At first glance, this seems rather strange. Throughout history, the Czechs and Hungarians (today, both countries have 10 million inhabitants) have been allies against common adversaries and even subjects of the same king. Budapest looks like an over-sized, albeit dirtier, version of Prague, the Hungarian language is full of Slavonic loan words (see: **Cursing**) and both nations are culturally deeply marked by centuries when they where a part of the Danube Empire; for instance, by a common flair for committing suicides.

Yet the Czechs and the Hungarians, in contradiction to the traditionally hearty relations between the **Poles** and the Hungarians, have never become close. Bar a quite natural reaction against the communist regime's forced friendship with other "socialist brother countries", it's hard to point out a single reason for the lack of common sympathy. Plain rivalry, though, appears to be a big part of the explanation.

First of all, the Czechs are one of many Slav peoples, while the Hungarians (or *Magyars*, as they say themselves) are a small lot of Finno-Ugric origin. The antagonism between the numerous Slavs and the linguistically and ethnically unique Hungarians profoundly deepened during the 250 years the two nations spent as subjects of the Danube Empire.

While the power apparatus in Vienna clearly distrusted the Czechs and the other Slav peoples in the Empire, the Hungarians were treated with somewhat greater consideration. Not because the Emperor had any specific love for the Hungarians, but, as the author Zsigmond Kémény points out, because Hungary was given the role of protecting the Empire's multi-national character by dividing its Slavonic and **German** elements, and thus preventing any of them from becoming the top **dog**.

Hungary's position as more equal than the other equal nations was formalized in 1867, when the Empire was split into two parts – the **Austrian** and the Hungarian – with the river Leitha, near Vienna, as a symbolic border. The fact that Emperor **Franz Josef** let himself be crowned Hungarian king, but forgot about the Czechs, didn't make him more popular in **Bohemia** and **Moravia**. The magnificent Spanish Hall at Prague's Hradčany castle, which was refurbished for the crowning ceremony that never took place, became a symbol of Czech jealousy towards the Hungarians.

What's more, the Hungarians, who had now become full-fledged bosses of the Empire's eastern part, didn't waste any time in starting a rather tough *magyarization* of their Slavonic subjects. This didn't directly affect the Czechs, who were ruled from Vienna. However, the **Slovaks** in *Felvidék* – Upper Hungary – were hit quite discernibly when Budapest decided to abolish the use of Slovak language in schools. Ultimately, the Hungarians backed down, but the way they badgered their Slovak subjects didn't earn them much praise among the victims' Czech brethren.

The mischief reached a climax in 1918, when the whole of Slovakia – including the Southern part, which for nine centuries had been densely populated by ethnic Hungarians – was declared a part of the newly-established Czechoslovak republic. When the communist government that seized power in Budapest in the spring of 1919 refused to abandon *Felvidék* Czechoslovakia launched a military attack on Hungary.

The Czechoslovak armed forces managed to kick the Hungarians out of Slovakia after the Western powers helped them diplomatically, but a three-month-long war was not an ideal starting point for friendly relations between Czechoslovakia and Hungary. Twenty years later, the two countries clashed again when Hungary, after the **Munich Agreement**, occupied the eastern-most tip of Czechoslovakia (see: **Ukrainians**), and then the southern part of Slovakia. Hungary had to turn most of the territory back in 1945, but ever since then, the Czechs have shared the Slovaks' suspicion that the Hungarians are suffering from latent irredentism.

There is also a social aspect that divides the Czechs and the Hungarians. Czech society has traditionally been pronounced **egalitarian**, with a rather limited **nobility** and upper class, but with a relatively broad middle class. Hungarian society, on the contrary, was until 1945 characterized by deep class divisions, and the local aristocracy was heavily involved in politics.

This has led to a comical situation. The Czechs, based on the fact that the average standard of living for the last centuries has been higher in industrialized Bohemia than in strongly agricultural Hungary, have regarded the Hungarians as poorer and more backward. The Hungarians, on their side, have regarded the Czechs as poorer and more backward, because their upper classes have been wealthier and more influential than those in Bohemia and Moravia.

The communists didn't smooth out the animosity, but they at least managed to suppress open demonstrations of it. Yet certain wounds have never healed. As a part of the settlement after the Second World War, more than 12,000 ethnic Hungarians were forcefully moved from Southern Slovakia to Bohemia, where they replaced Sudeten Germans that were kicked out. Even though most of them by now are fully assimilated into their Czech surroundings, they are still aware – and proud – of their Hungarian origin.

It's fair to say that the relations between the Czechs and Hungarians took a large step towards improvement after Czechoslovakia split into two parts. While the Slovaks then had to cope with all of the unsolved bilateral problems (the Hungarian minority's demand for cultural autonomy in Southern Slovakia, the ecological consequences of the hydroelectric power plant in Gabčíkovo on the Danube), the Czechs, who no longer had any common border with their former neighbours, could regard Hungary as just another country in the region.

Yet the old rivalry is still alive and kicking. Hungary started its economic transformation even before the communist regime fell, and has often been perceived as the most Western and progressive country in post-communist Europe. As expected, this view was not acceptable to **Václav Klaus** and the other protagonists of Prague's short-lived "Reform Miracle", who saw the Czech Republic as the unquestioned frontrunner. As a result of this rivalry, the attempt to coordinate the two countries' integration into the EU – together with the Poles and Slovaks – in the so-called Visegrad Group utterly failed.

In the future, however, the Hungarians and Czechs seem destined for closer cooperation. NATO membership in March 1999 made them close military allies, which was strengthened further, after both countries acceded to the EU. Thus, it's fair to assume that the two relatively small Central European countries will find far more pragmatic reasons for cooperating than petty-minded excuses for competing with each other.

Hus, Jan

Recently, *Mladá fronta Dnes*, the country's leading daily, conducted a large-scale survey to find out who the Czechs consider to be their greatest national **hero** of all times. As expected, **Tomáš G. Masaryk**, Czechoslovakia's "founder", and king Charles IV, who doubled as Emperor of the entire Holy Roman Empire (see: **Central Europe**), topped the ranking list. More surprising, though, was that these two giants were closely trailed by a priest who only managed to produce a handful of books during his 44-year-long life: Jan Hus.

Yet the Czechs' admiration of Hus is not that strange. In a European perspective, it's even fair to say that his importance overshadows that of both Masaryk and King Charles.

One of the reasons for Hus' popularity probably lies in his utterly unglamorous heritage. His mother was a country lass who lived in the village of Husinec near Prachatice in Southern **Bohemia** around 1371. Since his father was unknown, young Jan got his funny **surname** (*husa* means goose) after his birthplace. All that is known about his childhood is that he liked to play chess and that his mother wanted him to become a priest. After studies at Prague's newly-established university, Jan fulfilled her wish in 1400, when he was ordained.

Only two years later, Hus' career as a spiritual shepherd took a major leap upwards. The young country priest was appointed preacher in the Bethlehem Chapel in Prague's Old Town. Contrary to most of his colleagues, Hus was deadly serious about his job. Like the English theologian John Wycliff, who in many ways was the role model to the young Czech priest, Hus was obsessed by the idea that the Church must get out of the moral mess in which it had landed because of its ostentatious greed. And the only way out, Hus argued, was to behave in greater accordance with the New Testament.

At a time when most Catholic clergymen behaved like the Chicago mafia in the 1930s (it was, for example, quite common for well-connected good-for-nothings to buy a lucrative priesthood and then employ a substitute to do the job), ordinary people welcomed the Bethlehem preacher's sincerity with open arms. Besides preaching in the **Czech language**, Hus relentlessly thundered that the church would improve its shabby reputation only if it abandoned its sinful striving for worldly goods and, most importantly, did not allow the country's rich and mighty to buy forgiveness for their sins!

As time went by, Hus' clean-hands gospel gained the support of Prague's **nobility** and even of King Václav IV and his court. By 1409, the Bethlehem preacher had become so popular that the king appointed him rector of Charles University, at that time Central Europe's most important educational establishment. However, the majority of the Catholic clergy, for obvious reasons, hated him, and so did the university's **German** professors.

In 1412, after Hus and his followers had raged especially hard against indulgences, the Pope himself got so furious that he laid the entire city of Prague under interdiction. Frightened by the political consequences of Hus' activities, King Václav realized that he could no longer support the hard-hitting and rebellious preacher. For the next two years, Hus lived as an outlaw, hiding at the fortresses of local noblemen who still supported him.

At this stage, Hus had already secured himself a decent place in Czech history books. During the last year of his life, he earned himself an entire chapter.

In 1414, the Czech preacher was called to the city of Constance (now near Germany's border with Switzerland) to explain his teaching to the Catholic Church's top leaders, the Synod. To make sure that he accepted the invitation, both the Roman Emperor and the Pope promised Hus safe conduct. But soon after he appeared in Constance, Hus was arrested and subsequently charged with heresy.

On July 6,1415 – a date every true Czech bears in his memory – the brave preacher was burned to death at the stake as a heretic. Less than a year later, the Synod gave Hus' friend and fellow reformer, the philosopher Jeroným Pražský, the same treatment. This, the Catholic Church reasoned, would certainly convince the Czech troublemakers that enough was enough.

As history later proved, it didn't. The murder of Jan Hus triggered wars (see: **Defenestration**) and long-lasting upheaval. What's more, many Czechs still claim that Hus' death on the martyr's stake in Constance bears a clear resemblance to that of Christ himself: like Jesus, Hus was subjected to a mock trial that had sentenced him to death even before the trial started. While Judas betrayed Jesus, several of Hus' earlier friends turned against him in Constance. And just like Jesus, Hus could easily have saved his neck by renouncing his teaching as wrong and heretical. Instead, he voluntarily chose death after having uttered the golden words:

"Search for truth, listen to truth, learn the truth, speak the truth, keep to the truth, defend the truth until you die, for at last, truth will redeem you!"

Seen with modern eyes, the life and death of Jan Hus occurs as a perfect screenplay in an action film where good fights evil. And indeed, to thousands of Czechs Jan Hus still has the halo of a religious Rambo, who put up a fight for true and clean Christianity against a degenerated and corrupt church. This view might be a bit simplifying, but it's well documented that Hus' central work *De ecclesia* made a striking impact on the reformer Martin Luther. "Without being aware of it, I had preached and written everything Jan Hus taught," Luther later acknowledged. "Instinctively, we are all Hussites."

Therefore, the Czechs can with some rights boost their **national identity** with the fact that Reformation didn't actually start with the German Martin Luther, but with their own Jan Hus. Quite symbolically, both Tomáš G. Masaryk (in 1918) and **Václav Havel** (in 1989) took up Hus' slogan *Veritas Vincit* – truth prevails – when they spearheaded the reformation of the Czech nation. The nationalist *Sokol* movement is clearly inspired by the Hussites, and it's even tempting to claim that it was no coincidence that **Jan Palach** chose to *burn himself* to death to protest against the Soviet occupation of Czechoslovakia.

Yet Jan Hus' legacy still manages to divide the Czechs. Even though Cardinal Miloslav Vlk, the current head of the Catholic Church in the Czech Republic, has made great efforts to reconcile with the Hussites, many Czech Catholics still regard Master Jan as a fanatic, the Hussite warriors as a medieval Taliban and their leader Jan Žižka as the predecessor of Osama bin Laden (see: **Religion**).

"What's so great with a movement that threw Bohemia and **Moravia** into two centuries of economic depression and cultural isolation from the rest of Central Europe?" they spit.

Obviously, to the communists, Jan Hus was a natural hero: a peasant's son who fought for the common people ("proletariat") against the weal-thy clergy ("greedy capitalists") and German professors ("vengeful nazis") at the university, simply had to be abused. Even though nobody can accuse the communists of nourishing exaggerated sympathies towards religion, from 1948 to 1954 the totalitarian regime handed out millions of *korunas* to restore the derelict Bethlehem Chapel. Later in the 1950s, they willingly financed a lavish film trilogy about Master Hus.

Needless to say, the Bolsheviks' clammy embrace of Jan Hus (curiously enough, the Italian dictator Benito Mussolini was also a great fan of him) backfired and made people either confused about his real historical importance, or even more indifferent to religion as such. And while the Bolshevik regime luckily belongs to history, the antagonism between Czech Catholics and Hussites is still alive and kicking, as a quite entertaining quarrel about the monuments on Prague's Old Town Square demonstrates.

Ever since the **Velvet Revolution,** Czech Catholics have struggled to reinstall the magnificent Mary column that was torn down in 1918. Money has been raised through a collection campaign, a suitable stone has been transported all the way from India, and a copy of the column has even been finished. But the Catholics are still waiting. To a majority of Prague's inhabitants, it's simply unacceptable that a symbol of "Hus' murderers" is erected next to the statue of the Martyr himself.

So, how may the Czech state pay respect to Hus' historic importance without offending the country's Catholics and their *Svatý Václav* (Saint Wenceslas), who for centuries has been the national patron?

The first Czech Parliament that emerged after Czechoslovakia split in 1993 found a truly Solomonic compromise: to honour the legacy of Jan Hus and please his contemporary followers, the 6th of July remained a national holiday. To please the Catholics, the 28th of September, Saint Wenceslas Day, was named a holiday as well. And just to be on the safe side, Parliament decided to tolerate Cyril and Methodius Day, the 5th of July, so the country's Orthodox believers didn't get mad.

Say what you want, but three days free from work every year thanks to saints and martyrs is not bad for a nation that can boast probably more atheists than any other country in Europe.

Ice Hockey

❖

Take a look around you in any public place in this country, and you'll immediately understand why the relatively small Czech Republic has become a superpower in fields such as **beer** drinking, beautiful models or heart diseases caused by obesity (see: **Czech Cuisine**). However, there is actually no logical reason why the country has also become a superpower in ice hockey.

The winters are usually so mild that the **Bohemian** and **Moravian** fishing ponds only freeze to ice for a week or two, and totally, this nation of 10 million people doesn't contain more than some 150 ice hockey halls. Nevertheless, the Czechs have – bar Russia (who has an abundance of ice) and Canada (who invented the game) – won more **world** ice hockey championships than any other nation on the planet. In 2004, the Czech National Theatre even staged an opera – *Nagano* – about the national team's smashing victory in the winter Olympics in 1998.

To an outsider, the Czech hockey miracle seems to be based on two pillars: the urge to make the nation visible on the international arena, and – today – money. The Czechs themselves will probably also add factors such as "natural talent for improvisation", "good team players" and "typical Czech cleverness", but these arguments seem to be more closely linked to the common perception of their **national identity** than to reality.

Hockey fever arrived in Bohemia from England at the end of the nineteenth century. As in all other parts of the Austro-**Hungarian** Empire, the new game aroused great enthusiasm also among the Czechs, who already had discovered the delight of sports through the *Sokol* movement. However, to the Czechs, ice hockey soon became something more than a sweaty fight for a rubber puck. It was, according to Tomáš Čechtický, a writer and expert on Czech ice hockey, "a way in which they could beat their **Austrian** masters in public".

The urge to humiliate Vienna was so strong that the Czechs even found it more important to be recognized by the International Ice Hockey Federation before the Austrians were (in November 1908) than to establish their own national hockey federation (in January 1909).

The first time ice hockey boosted the Czechs' national pride internationally was in 1909, when their team won the European Championship. Naturally, the thirst for hockey victories didn't weaken after Czechoslovakia was established. At the World Championship in Prague in 1938, for instance, on exactly the same day that Adolf Hitler threatened to crush Czechoslovakia with all conceivable means, the Czechoslovak team crushed Germany 3:0 in the fight for the bronze medal.

"Those hockey sticks can be transformed into rifles," the popular poet and later Nobel Prize laureate Jaroslav Seifert (see: **First Republic**) exulted after the fantastic victory over the **Germans**. Well, they could not. But as Czechoslovakia suffered one devastating humiliation after the other in the arena of international politics, its triumphs in the arena of international ice hockey were at times the only source of national pride.

Ice hockey's political impact became, according to Čechtický, even more evident under the communists. In 1949, the Czechoslovak national team won the World Championship for the second time. The next championship was scheduled in London, and the Czech and **Slovak** players prepared thoroughly to repeat the success. The communist regime, however, had other plans.

First, party bigwigs told the players they were not allowed to travel to capitalist Western Europe. Then secret police agents provoked the frustrated players, who in the classic Czech manner were drowning their sorrows in a *hospoda*, to start a fight. The *hospoda* brawl was subsequently used as a pretext to arrest the sportsmen. Shortly after, 11 members of the Czechoslovak national hockey team were sentenced to long prison terms on different fabricated charges.

It's hard to say whether the rotten attack on the hockey **heroes** was initiated by the Czechoslovak communists or by their masters in Moscow.

In any case, it's obvious that the Bolsheviks regarded the national hockey team's enormous popularity as a political threat.

By an odd twist of fate, the national hockey team was once more to humiliate a detested occupant on the ice. In 1969, only half a year after the Soviet Union "brotherly" invaded the country, Czechoslovakia's national team beat the **Russian** team 2:0 in the World Championship in Stockholm.

As expected, the victory was greeted with tremendous joy by millions of Czechs and Slovaks, who, on their television screens, noticed that several of the players had even pasted tape over the red star that disgraced the Czech lion on their shirts. In fair play, the apparently all-mighty Russians didn't stand a chance against little Czechoslovakia! The spirit of the *Prague Spring* (see: **Communism**) was not crushed!

Paradoxically enough, it was precisely that hockey triumph in Stockholm that marked the end of Czechoslovakia's reform experiment in the late 1960s.

As soon as the referee blew his whistle, thousands of exhilarated Czechs and Slovaks filled the streets of towns and cities all over the country in boundless transports of joy. But once more, the secret police staged a provocation. When an agent disguised as hockey fan started demolishing the office of the Soviet airliner Aeroflot on Prague's Wenceslas Square, he was immediately joined by hordes of enthusiastic citizens who had no idea that their actions would have tragic consequences.

But they had. To the orthodox wing of the communist party, the incident clearly proved one thing: Alexander Dubček, the party's reformist general secretary, didn't have the "anti-Soviet elements" under control, and therefore had to be sacked. Thus, the elation after the ice hockey victory over the Russians was soon replaced by 20 years of *normalization*.

Ice hockey's political and nation-creating role has definitely not diminished in the post-communist Czech Republic. Thanks to the recent successes in World Championships (gold medals in 1996, 1999, 2000 and 2001) and in the Olympic games in Nagano in 1998 it still is an inexhaustible source of national pride. In addition, a career as a professional hockey player with a million-dollar salary has become a far more realistic goal than it used to be.

In the aftermath of 1968, nearly 100 hockey players emigrated to the West. After the **Velvet Revolution**, they have been followed by hordes of others. Today, the US-Canadian National Hockey League would probably cease to exist if all the star players of Czech origin disappeared. But only for a couple of days, for hundreds of young and talented Czechs would be more than willing to replace them.

Jews

When the BBC and a number of other public broadcasters joined forces several decades ago to produce a large-scale documentary about the history of European Jewry, the opening sequence was quite telling: Abba Eban, the formidable Israeli statesman who appeared as the documentary's narrator, was sitting in front of a *maceva*, a tomb at the Jewish cemetery in Prague's Josefov ghetto.

Thus, Prague, and in a wider context **Bohemia** and **Moravia**, were rightfully acknowledged as one of the Ashkenazi diaspora's major cultural centres in Europe.

The Jews' history in what's now the Czech Republic began almost 1,000 years ago. Actually, one of the oldest documents about Prague that is preserved was written by the Jewish merchant Abraham ben Jakob, who travelled from Spain to Bohemia sometime around 966. "The city named Fraga is built of stone, and it is the largest trading place in the whole region," ben Jakob wrote to attract his compatriots.

Some years after ben Jakob's visit, a Jewish settlement (which in the mid-1200s turned into a regular ghetto behind walls) was established in the Old Town's northern part, right at the Vltava's bend. In the following centuries similar settlements-cum-ghettos popped up nearly all over Bohemia and Moravia. Still, more than 150 Jewish cemeteries, many of them devastated by a half century of neglect, and numerous dilapidated synagogues that are slowly being reconstructed (the Bolsheviks, with their usual sensitivity, let local collective farms use some of them as warehouses) give solid evidence of the Jews' millennium-long presence in cities and towns throughout this country.

As it has everywhere else in Europe, also the Czech Ashkenazi diaspora has witnessed times of both prosperity and persecution.

In the ghettos, the Jews had self-government, but since they were regarded as "direct subjects" of the king, he was allowed in practice to do what he wanted with them. Emperor Rudolf II (1552–1612), for instance, constantly pressed the wealthy Jewish banker Mordechai Maizel to lend him money, which the emperor never returned. Maizel, however, discreetly used the debt to make life easier for his fellow believers, among them Rabbi Löw, the famous Talmudist who, according to the legend, created the clay robot Golem.

Twice, in 1541 and 1744, the entire Jewish population was expelled from Bohemia and Moravia, and they also suffered cruel pogroms, although they were fewer than the wild pogroms that frequently hit the Jews in the **Russian** czardom.

Life changed for the better in the 1790s, when the "enlightened" Emperor Josef II introduced a set of progressive reforms (that's why Prague's ghetto is called *Josefov*). Jews were allowed to move outside the ghettos, they were ordered to send their children to public schools and also allowed to take a **surname** and have a family. During the next century, the Czech Ashkenazi diaspora made a huge step towards emancipation. When the Austro-**Hungarian** Empire fell apart in October 1918, most of the 120,000 Jews who were living in Bohemia and Moravia easily reconciled with the fact that they had now become citizens of the Czechoslovak Republic.

The **First Republic** is commonly remembered as a period when the Czech Jewish community flourished. Although reality was probably less rosy, at least for the majority who spoke **German** and not Czech, **Masaryk's** Czechoslovakia indubitably offered its Jewish citizens a more liberal atmosphere than Horthy's Hungary, where Jews faced restricted admission to universities, or Catholic Poland, where anti-Semitism was rife. The Italian novelist Claudio Magris has a telling comparison that illustrates the Czech Jews' strong assimilation. On the day when Nazi troops marched into Austria after the *Anschluss* in 1938, several hundred of Vienna's Jews committed suicide in pure despair. In Czechoslovakia at that time, few Jews believed that their state would fail to protect them.

They were, unfortunately, wrong. Starting in October 1941, Czech citizens of Jewish origin were rounded up and transported to extermination camps in Poland. Many Bohemian Jews, especially children, were first sent to Terezín (Theresienstadt), about 60 kilometres north of Prague. Here, the Nazis turned the former garrison city into a "model" concentration camp, complete with its own orchestra and theatre, which was cynically presented in their propaganda. But ultimately, not even the Terezín prisoners escaped the gas chambers in Poland.

When the war ended in May 1945, 78,000 Czech Jews had been murdered (their names are meticulously written on the walls inside Prague's Pinkas Synagogue). Holocaust's horrors, combined with the Bolsheviks' short-lived love for Israel, made Czechoslovakia in May 1948 one of its staunchest allies in Europe, and it was only thanks to weapons hastily delivered from Brno in Moravia that the young Jewish state managed to fend off the attacks from its Arab neighbours.

Still, the post-war era proved difficult for the Czech Jewish community, who was diminished to 10,000 members. That figure grew even smaller when the communists launched a rabid anti-Semitic campaign that culminated with the monster process against Rudolf Slánský and 10 other Bolsheviks of Jewish origin in 1952 (see: **Horáková, Milada**).

After 1967, when the East Bloc countries broke their diplomatic relations with Israel, the Czechoslovak secret police launched *Operace*

Pavouk (Operation Spider) – a campaign to register and, if needed, harass every citizen of Jewish origin. The goal was obvious – either to silence Jews with fear, or press them into **emigration**. This strategy proved sadly successful. When the Bolsheviks were finally swept from power, the once flourishing Czech Jewish community had dwindled to a group of 1.500 scared and grey-haired people.

In the aftermath of the **Velvet Revolution**, support, both moral and financial, flooded in to help the Czech Jews. After nearly a decade without a formal leader, Karol Ephraim Sidon, a respected writer and **Charter 77** signatory, was named Chief Rabbi of the Czech Republic in 1992. Later, a *Yeshiva* – a Jewish school – and a Jewish home for the elderly were also established in Prague. Another important step has been taken by Czech authorities, who have returned the Jewish communities most of their pre-war property. Thus, hundreds of buildings, acres of land and religious objects, including Prague's world-famous Jewish Museum, are securing their rightful owners a financial base, but also the economic responsibility for countless neglected premises.

Yet there has so far not been any Jewish revival in the Czech Republic – for at least two reasons. First, the strong degree of secularisation (see: **Religion**) also affects the 8,000 – 10,000 Czechs estimated to be of Jewish origin. They simply don't consider this to be an important issue. And if they do, but happen to live outside Prague, Brno, Karlovy Vary or Plzeň, there is no Jewish community that can receive them.

And second, due to the Czech Jews' extensive assimilation, there are many mixed marriages. When their children have taken interest in their origin, they have not always been met with open arms by Prague's Jewish community, which, in religious matters, has been strongly influenced by conservatives hailing from the Mukachevo area of pre-war Czecho-slovakia's most eastern corner (see: **Ukrainians**). This goes, of course, twice if it's a Czech *goy* interested in converting to Judaism.

While American Jews living in Prague in the early 1990s established *Bejt* (The House), open to followers of both liberal and conservative Judaism, there was a growing dissatisfaction in the city's Czech-Jewish community with the hard-line approach of Rabbi Sidon and his backers. In the summer of 2004, the subdued grumbling burst out into an open re-bellion. The liberals forced Rabbi Sidon to step down as religious head of the Prague community (but he is still Czech Chief Rabbi), which in its turn threw the entire community into a bitter quarrel about the future course.

Luckily, open demonstrations of anti-Semitism appear to be a marginal problem in the Czech Republic (although a psychologist, Petr Bakalář, experienced a commercial success when he published in 2003 a book where racist views were masked as a scientific report), propably because the country's repulsive skinheads have so far focused their aggression towards members of the **Roma** minority. The only slightly controversial issue is a lingering debate about the Jews' influence on Czech culture.

While some intellectuals, such as the playwright Pavel Kohout, claim that modern Czech culture is a product of three mixed elements – the

Slavonic Czech, the German-Bohemian and the Jewish (see: **Kafka, Franz**), several Czech **politicians**, most notably President **Václav Klaus**, maintain that multiculturalism is an empty and meaningless term.

Kafka, Franz

Except for **beer** and ex-president **Václav Havel**, there is probably nothing a **foreigner** associates more strongly with Prague and subsequently also the Czech Republic than the writer Franz Kafka. Thousands of **tourists** walk about in the Czech capital dressed in T-shirts with Kafka's portrait on their chests, they sip coffee in the Franz Kafka Café or visit the English-speaking Franz Kafka Theatre. Some of them have even read one of the novels this modern tourist attraction wrote.

The strange thing, though, is that the Czech Republic officially behaved for a long time as if this literary genius didn't have any relation to Prague and the country at all. Just to take one example: almost 10 years passed after the **Velvet Revolution** until Prague's magistrate managed to name a square after the famous artist. But rather symptomatically, "Franz Kafka Square" is in reality a paved passage so nondescript and anonymous that most cabbies don't have the faintest idea where it is located (at the corner of Kaprova and Maiselova streets).

This treatment may seem rather ungenerous. If one also takes Kafka's deep, personal relation to the city into account, it seems almost incomprehensible. Ernst Pawel, one of Kafka's most renowned biographers, puts it like this: "There is one all-important and fundamental fact in Kafka's existence: that he was born in Prague, was buried in Prague, and spent nearly all the 41 years of his life in this citadel of lost causes."

To be precise, he was born in 1883 in a house situated at the very border between the **Jewish** ghetto and Old Town. Bar a short stay in Berlin and a year in the countryside spent with his sister Ottla in Northern

Bohemia, Kafka never left Prague, where he gradually occupied 10 different flats. A small house in the Golden Lane at Hradčany and two rented rooms in the Schönborn Palace (now the US Embassy) at the Malá Strana were the farthest he came from Old Town. When he died prematurely at a tuberculosis sanatorium outside Vienna in 1924, he was living in a flat in the Oppelt House at Old Town Square number 6.

"Prague is like a little mother with claws," Kafka himself summed up his love-hate relations to the city, whose dominant Hradčany Castle most probably served as the physical model for his novel *Das Schloss*, published in 1926. Another famous location, the stone quarry from *Der Prozess* (1925) to which Josef K. was led by his anonymous capturers and subsequently executed, was at Kafka's time situated directly to the west of Hradčany. One might even imagine that the sober bureaucrat Josef K. on his way to work passed Jaroslav Hašek's brilliant idiot Švejk on his way to his favourite *hospoda* The Chalice.

Although born into a Jewish and **German**-speaking family, Kafka came into close contact with his Czech surroundings early on through the family's maid, and the writer's father, Herrmann the ambitious merchant, even regarded Czech as his first language. Franz, on the contrary, was educated in Prague's German schools, so there can be no doubts about his mother tongue, but **Czech language** was an obligatory subject both in grammar school and at the lyceum, and a few Czech-written letters that have been preserved document that he had a very good and lively grasp of colloquial Czech ("… the wind is constantly blowing in our a**es").

Kafka's amicable relations with his Slavonic compatriots were clearly demonstrated in 1918, when Czechoslovakia emerged from the ruins of the Austro-**Hungarian** Empire. While the German management of the Workmen's Accident Insurance Company, where he was employed for most of his life, was fired and replaced by Czechs, Kafka – now a Czechoslovak citizen – was asked to stay and later promoted. Even his **surname**, although written as it is pronounced in German, is as Czech as it gets (*Kavka* is the Slavonic term for jackdaw).

Photo © Jaroslav Fišer

Nevertheless, the Czechs have never come to perceive Franz Kafka as "their man" for two reasons, one national and one political. Combined, they have caused widespread ignorance about the great writer.

The national explanation is rather obvious. Whereas Kafka's Jewish origin is no hindrance to being considered a "Czech writer" (there are lots of them – starting with Karel Poláček and ending with Ota Pavel), his mother tongue definitely was. As a member of the German-speaking minority that lived in Prague in the interwar years, he could, at best, be regarded as a representative of Bohemia's multicultural heritage.

However, after the Jews were murdered in Holocaust, the Germans were kicked out of the country in 1945 and the **Slovaks** – following the separation of Czechoslovakia in 1993 – finally achieved national independence, the Czechs became masters of an ethnically and culturally homogenous state for the first time in centuries. This atmosphere didn't exactly offer a superabundance of interest and tolerance towards the country's multicultural heritage.

Neither is the political reason for disregarding Kafka a mystery. As a prophet of existentialism, describing in details how an inhuman and all-mighty society manipulates the powerless individual, Kafka was seen by the Nazis (unfortunately, correctly) as envisaging the terrible bloodshed soon to be released, and his works were prohibited in Germany in 1933.

Not surprisingly, the Czechoslovak communists, who came to power in 1948 (see: **Communism**), took a similar stance, adding that Kafka was "too pessimistic and decadent" as a writer. Only in 1963, a semi-official literary conference in Liblice north of Prague carefully aired the possibility of making Franz Kafka accessible for Czech readers. Those attempts were mercilessly crushed five years later by Soviet tanks.

Forty years of a publishing ban under the communists and 10 years of ostentatious official ignorance after the Velvet Revolution have taken its toll on Kafka. Today, even fewer Czechs than all those silly tourists with Kafka t-shirts have actually read any of his novels. Ironically enough, the single most palpable trace the shy writer has left is the frequently- used Czech term *kafkárna* – something Kafkaesque.

Yet there are some bright signs of change. In mid-2003, the inexhaustible people behind the Franz Kafka Publishing House managed to complete the translation of all his works into Czech. Some months later, a no less important event took place, when a full-sized statue of Kafka was finally unveiled in Prague. Located on the border between Old Town and the former Jewish Ghetto, the statue is not only a very belated tribute to Kafka, but also a strong, symbolic acknowledgement of Prague's multicultural heritage. Since Prague's mayor personally unveiled the statue, it may even seem that this view at last is being acknowledged officially.

Kajínek, Jiří

In May 1993, a Czech mafioso and his bodyguard were cold-bloodedly executed in a car outside Plzeň in Western **Bohemia**. Nine months later, police arrested the suspected assassin – Jiří Kajínek, a notorious criminal in his late 30s – who was subsequently found guilty in the double murder and sentenced to life imprisonment.

Considering Kajínek's criminal record, neither the verdict nor the life sentence was spectacular, so the prisoner was swiftly transported to the Mírov prison in **Moravia**, a former Habsburg fortress where the Czech Republic's 20-odd lifetime inmates are kept. Because of its high and impenetrable walls and its location on the top of a steep hill, Mírov is commonly known as the Czech version of Alcatraz – an inescapable prison where dangerous convicts like Kajínek are supposed to rot for at least 25 years, until they are eligible for parole.

This scenario dramatically changed in October 2000, when Kajínek managed the unthinkable – to escape from the most heavily guarded prison in the country. Thanks to an amazing display of brains combined with muscles, Kajínek managed to divert his guards' attention, get out of the barred window in his cell, slide on a home-made rope over a wide moat full of specially trained Doberman **dogs**, climb a six-meter tall wall – and then disappear into the forest beneath the fortress.

As one might expect, the incredible escape instantly brought Kajínek national fame. In the following weeks, when literally every single uniform in the country was combing the Czech countryside in search of the escaped prisoner, more and more people came to regard this common criminal as a national **hero**. Even when he was caught after 40 days on the run, he put up a stylish display: a video, which the police released to prove that they really had got him, showed how the athletic and naked Kajínek was overpowered in the bed in a Prague flat belonging to the wife of another Mírov prisoner. "What a pity he didn't hide in my flat," a female television reporter commented half-jokingly (see: **Sex**).

So all's well that ends well? Not really. Kajínek was immediately transferred to another maximum security prison, where a cell was specially adapted to make sure he never again repeated his amazing stunt.

Yet he certainly achieved what he wanted with the escape – to draw attention to his case. Kajínek himself admits that he is not an angel, but neither is he a murderer, and he swears he is not guilty of the crime that brought him to Mírov (after all, what else would you expect from a lifetime prisoner?). Even though police investigators and several judges insist he is guilty, the media regularly question the verdict. As late as

January 2004, Czech journalists presented a so-far unknown witness that can allegedly prove Kajínek's innocence.

The funny thing is that millions of Czechs seem to believe more in Kajínek and the media's version than in the official assurances that he really is guilty.

Romanticism is certainly one part of the explanation – many Kajínek fans are simply confusing him with Harrison Ford or Count Monte Cristo. The other part is less amusing: many ordinary Czechs still nurture a strong and deeply rooted **scepticism** against the independence of the country's judiciary, which for almost half a century allowed itself to be abused as an instrument of the Bolshevik tyrants (see: **Horáková, Milada**).

Klaus, Václav

Some weeks before Czechs were to cast their ballots in the Parliament elections, in the summer of 1998, the conservative Civic Democratic Party (ODS) played one of its campaign trumps: at the Letná Plain, the bluff on Vltava's left bank where the Bolsheviks (see: **Communism**) erected the **world's** largest statue of Stalin in the 1950s, the Czech conservatives, in total earnestness, raised a 5-by-10 meter billboard featuring the face of their chairman Václav Klaus.

Thus, for the next several weeks a gigantic chairman Klaus, complete with his crew cut and close-cropped moustache, overlooked Prague from exactly the same spot as one of the most bloodstained (and definitely more moustached) tyrants in history.

This is, admittedly, a rare example of historic amnesia, but it is pretty illustrative as an expression of the cult that has surrounded Václav Klaus since the early 1990s:

Quite a few people in this country, many of them running small businesses, love and admire Klaus so intensely that they cease to perceive the real world. Others – probably outnumbered by the manic *Klausophiles* – pretend to be his ardent fans out of sheer opportunism (as a political godfather he secured them money, power or both). And then you have a smaller number of intellectuals who simply can't stand the fellow, and do their utmost to forget that he in 2003 was elected the country's president.

In many ways Václav Klaus is everything his predecessor **Václav Havel** isn't. Contrary to Havel, who was born into a bourgeois family of prominent businesspeople, Klaus was born, in 1941, as the son of an ordinary civil servant. While the first Václav started a somewhat **bohemian** career as a self-educated and chain-smoking playwright, who in the 1970s bravely opposed the communist regime (see: **Charter 77**) and subsequently spent four years in jail that ruined his health, the latter excelled as a student of economics and as a sportsman. After several scholarships in the West, he spent the two decades of Bolshevik *normalization* after 1968 as an economist in the Czechoslovak State Bank and later in the Academy of Science.

By the time of the **Velvet Revolution** in 1989, Klaus entered the political scene as one of those clever and adroit Czechs who had never confronted the Bolshevik regime officially (and thus had managed to pursue a professional career) while at the same time avoiding open collaboration in terms of Party membership.

This ultra-pragmatic record was certainly less heroic than Havel's firm opposition, but it was not a tremendous drawback for a **politician** at the start of the post-communist era. On the contrary, while Havel almost seemed larger than life, Klaus embodied the fate of millions of common Czechs who were neither Bolsheviks nor brave dissidents; only ordinary, uncourageous citizens who tried to live a happy life.

Thanks to his image as an ambitious commoner-cum-respected scientist (obviously, he was soon awarded with the **academic title** Professor of economics) and also his brilliant ability to sense exactly what people wanted to hear, Klaus' political career got a flying start. He was the very man for the post of minister of finance in the first democratic government that emerged after the Velvet Revolution. He was, in 1991, the obvious founder and first chairman of "liberal-conservative" ODS, which won the Parliamentary elections a year later by a landslide, making him Czechoslovakia's new Prime Minister.

The Klaus government's battle cry was to effect radical economic reforms that would pull the country out of stagnation. Inspired by Maggie Thatcher and Milton Friedman, Klaus called for a mass privatisation of state industry and the introduction of a laissez-faire economy that in a decade or two would transform Czechoslovakia into **Central Europe's** Switzerland.

Today, seen in retrospect, it's evident that Klaus was far too cautious to introduce reforms that would disturb the social equilibrium of the Bolshevik era. In reality, he promised the reform-minded part of the population the radical changes they longed for, while he calmed those who were scared about the future, because his government avoided any change that would hurt too much. Some observers have called the practical application of this strategy Bank Socialism (Klaus forced state-owned banks to pour bad loans into industrial giants controlled by semi-dubious oligarchs loyal to him), while others prefer Václav Havel's term Mafia capitalism (Klaus' voucher privatisation is estimated to have cost billions in frauds and stripped company assets).

Yet in the first half of the 1990s, Klaus' transformation unquestionably led to economic growth and relatively high employment, which in turn led Klaus, notorious for his arrogance and un-Czech immodesty (see: **Egalitarianism**), to conclude: "While the other post-communist countries are still laying on the operating table, the Czech Republic is already working out in a fitness centre."

Unfortunately for the Czechs, Klaus' reform miracle was a flop. By the spring of 1997, the economy was plummeting, and later that year his days as Prime Minister were terminated as well when businesspeople participating in the privatisation of industry confirmed that they had paid millions of *korunas* directly to the ODS' party coffers (see: **Pepa from Hong Kong**).

A juicy **corruption** scandal mixed with economic crisis would have broken the neck of any ordinary politician. But Klaus is not an ordinary politician – he is the ultimate political survivor.

Basically, his tactics are quite like those of the Bolsheviks: he claims personal responsibility for everything that succeeds, such as the tranquil divorce with the **Slovaks**, while "external forces" (in Klaus' instance his coalition partners or the Central Bank, in the Bolsheviks' case evil capitalists) should be blamed for everything that goes wrong. When it's impossible to blame a debacle on somebody else, such as the embarrassing sponsor scandal in 1997, Klaus is always innocent because "he was not informed by his subordinates".

When questioned publicly on a touchy issue, Klaus' standard reaction is to flood his unlucky opponent with accusations of behaving unfairly, using false arguments or being ill-prepared. Especially troublesome opponents are silenced with selected quotations of "highly respected scientists" (preferably Australian) who nobody ever has heard about. Only once, when asked if he found it ethical that his wife was sitting on the board of a large state company when he himself was running the government (see: **Balkans**), Klaus threatened to smash the impudent journalist's face.

After the Czech miracle was silently buried and Klaus' overt hopes of international recognition as a reform wizard evaporated, he swiftly switched his image as an economics expert to one as an ardent guardian of Czech **national identity** (which he doesn't bother to define), heavily intoxicated by Europhobia.

The Czechs must not, according to Klaus, dissolve in Europe like "sugar in a cup of coffee". The thought that Portuguese officers may one day come to command Czech soldiers in a EU army or that – heaven forbid – **German** police officers will be allowed to operate in the Czech Republic gives him the shivers, and the Euro is, of course, only a conspiracy invented to strip Europe's smaller countries of their last piece of national sovereignty. Logically, when the country on May 1, 2004 celebrated its EU membership, Klaus ostentatiously visited the Blaník Mountain – home of the legendary knights that will save the country in its darkest hour. A few days later he added that the EU's "sneaking federalization" represents a greater threat to the Czechs than the Bolshevik regime.

Incredibly enough it seems that the wily opportunist Klaus once again has found a profitable way to success. The Bolsheviks were strongly attracted by his nationalism, open detest of the supra-national Catholic Church and Europhobia, and only thanks to their support, the Parliament elected him to succeed Václav Havel as president in 2003.

During his first year as head of state, he was manically focusing on two goals: to replace his common image as an unsuccessful politician and honorary chairman of a corruption-tainted party who says peculiar things like "There isn't any practical difference between clean and dirty money" with the image of a mild and caring president (who will certainly be re-elected in 2008); and second, to oppose, with an almost pathological fervour, everything Václav Havel symbolized.

Klaus uses tame newspaper journalists and the trash **TV Nova** to show he has a younger mistress than his predecessor, he ostentatiously throws out most of the art objects that Havel installed at the Prague Castle, and he sincerely claims that the economic seminaries he organized in the 1980s represent a more significant contribution to the fall of communism than that of Havel and the **Charter 77**.

So, what kind of politician is Václav Klaus really? Is he a super-shrewd and opportunistic power technocrat, a Czech version of the xenophobic **Austrian** Jörg Haider, or just another of those populist nationalists that post-communist Europe has been full of since 1990?

He is definitely more educated and cultivated than Slovakia's "terminator" Vladimír Mečiar, and contrary to the ex-Yugoslav Katzenjammer Kids, Franjo Tudjman and Slobodan Milošević, he must be described as a democrat. But when one compares his political rhetoric in the 1990s with the practical results of his governments, he reminds of that type of married man who brags to all his *hospoda* pals that he has found himself a young and beautiful mistress (see: **Sex**), while in reality he is a **homosexual**.

Actually, there is no need to concoct parabolas. Tomáš Ježek, one of Klaus' former colleagues from the Academy of Sciences and later minister of privatisation, once presented in Czech media an alleged real-life story that's even more apt:

During the World Championships in football in Mexico in 1986, Klaus, Ježek and a couple of other academicians were watching the match where Diego Maradona scored with his "magic hand". Everybody agreed that Maradona was a real creep – except Klaus. To him, Maradona had just done everything in his power to win the match, and the only fault was that he got caught. If that story is true, it may seem that the Czech president regards football much in the same way as he regards politics.

Kundera, Milan

If there exists an ultimate and living proof that the biblical words "a prophet has no honour in his own country" correspond to reality, it has to be Milan Kundera. While people all over the globe praise Kundera as a brilliant novelist who more than once has been close to the Nobel prize, in his mother country he seems to arouse more disapproval and downright anger than respect and admiration.

Of course, the fact that he is an **emigrant**, even an extremely successful one (see: **Egalitarianism**), doesn't exactly guarantee him raging popularity among his ex-countrymen. Some would even say that Kundera, in the eyes of the overtly Prague-fixated Czech intellectuals, has a drawback, since he was born in **Moravia**. But this goes deeper.

Both the intensity with which many Czechs revel in hating the star novelist and the contempt with which Kundera treats his Czech readers bear all the signs of a relationship that has turned irreparably sour. It's something like an ex-husband and his former wife soon after an ugly divorce. It's hard to say when it started. The writer Ladislav Verecký, for instance, believes the first tensions appeared after the Soviet invasion in 1968. In a heated debate in one literary magazine, Kundera, at that time 39 years old and famous for several collections of poetry, theatre plays and not least his latest novel, *The Joke*, clashed with another prominent intellectual, **Václav Havel,** in their evaluation of the *Prague Spring's* legacy.

In short: while **Havel** claimed that the attempts to reform the communist regime were meaningless because **communism** was irreformable (history later proved him right), Kundera, who personally engaged himself in the reform movement, felt that such attempts made sense.

According to Verecký, the discord grew stronger after Kundera left Czechoslovakia in 1975 and settled in France. Instead of using his international fame and position as an exiled writer to help promote the **Charter 77** dissidents in their non-violent fight against the Husák regime, Kundera preferred to concentrate on his career as a writer. Later literary successes proved this choice, at least from a pragmatic point of view, to be a wise decision.

However, this petty quarrelling was nothing compared to the hullabaloo that broke out when Kundera published the novel that was to become his biggest success ever – *The Unbearable Lightness of Being*. In his biting travesty of the gloomy daily life in Czechoslovakia under *normalization*, Kundera managed to enrage both the communists as well as the dissidents. The red establishment reacted as expected, and attacked the novel for being artistic trash that didn't hesitate to distort "socialist reality" just to achieve commercial success.

Amazingly enough, the dissidents this time fully agreed with their communist oppressors. In the novel, Kundera's **hero** Tomáš, a brilliant surgeon, was degraded to a window cleaner because of his support for the *Prague Spring* reformists. But Tomáš didn't despair and used the advantages of his new profession (i.e., transparent windows) to conquer a veritable host of willing women. This, the dissidents objected, was definitely not the fate of Czechoslovakia's persecuted! Actually, many of them were forced to work as window cleaners, so maybe the true reason for their rage was an uneasy feeling of being unsuccessful conquerors?

Anyway, the literary values of *The Unbearable Lightness of Being* may be arguable, but one thing remains undisputed: internationally, Kundera's novel – and the screen version which followed some years later – shed more bad light on the Czechoslovak communist regime than any other artistic work in the 1980s.

Unfortunately, the **Velvet Revolution** didn't smoothen the conflict. As a gesture of goodwill, Václav Havel, now as president, nominated Kundera for a state order for his literary merits. But instead of accepting his former opponent's hand, the famous novelist sent his wife to the ceremony in the Prague Castle, while he himself, allegedly, strolled incognito around in the streets, hidden behind dark glasses and a false moustache.

The Ypsilon Theatre in Prague fared even worse when it decided to honour Kundera by staging one of his earliest plays. Only days before the premiere, the theatre's managing director received a telegram from Paris: the author does not give his consent to the re-staging! In their enthusiasm, the Czech actors had failed to notice that Kundera some years earlier had conducted a strict revision of his earliest works and found some of them to be worthless.

Admittedly, an artist of Kundera's calibre can allow himself eccentric behaviour, and the misunderstandings could certainly have been sorted out in a lengthy interview. The problem, however, is that Kundera, since the middle of the 1980s, has stubbornly refused to say a word to the press, let alone grant some journalist – Czech or foreign – an interview.

Do these entanglements sound very petty? After all, why should there be anything else between the author and the readers than his or her books? Well, the core of the problem lies elsewhere. In 1986, Kundera declared that he was a French writer, which obviously doesn't point to what passport he is carrying, but to the language in which he is writing.

Since the author can't stand the thought of letting somebody translate his French novels into his mother tongue, Czech readers who don't speak foreign languages can forget about Kundera's latest novels. And due to the fact that he has started revising all his earlier works, they haven't got access to some of his most famous, Czech-written works – such as *The Unbearable Lightness of Being* – either.

In other words: Milan Kundera has, for different reasons, burnt every thinkable bridge to his former home country. For this, his former compatriots have rewarded him with grumpy and ostentatious oblivion.

Lustration

"What's happened to Franta, why did he leave our office?" a civil servant asks his colleague. "Oh, nothing much, there was only a lustre that fell on his head…"

To a **foreigner**, this joke might appear a bit cryptic, but to the Czechs, it's clear enough: František was one of those who were registered in the archives of the communists' feared secret police, the StB, as an agent, informer or collaborationist. And the chandelier that smashed his head was the *Lustration Law*, which rules that anybody who holds a senior position in the civil service, the army, the judicial system, the police, public broadcasting, the National Bank and companies controlled by the state, must prove the he or she is *"Stb negative"*.

In practice, this means that state employees request the Czech Ministry of Interior to issue a lustration certificate. If that certificate happens to be positive, they are mercilessly kicked out of their jobs. Of course, this also goes for the actual members of the old StB. Bar some allegedly irreplaceable specialists (the precise number has not been published) these *estebáci* have not been accepted by *BIS*, the Czech Republic's new secret service. This might explain why so many of them have started careers as private and – thanks to their contacts from the olden days – often quite successful businessmen.

The Lustration Law was adopted by the then-Czechoslovak parliament in 1991. Its purpose was quite obvious: to cleanse the democratic state's civil apparatus of those persons who had let themselves be used as tools for the totalitarian regime. This is also reflected by the law's name – *lustrum* was a cleansing ceremony, which the old Romans conducted every fifth year.

Even though it was never explicitly stated, the Lustration Law worked as a kind of moral settlement as well. Those who for some reason or other (see: **Communism**) couldn't bear the pressure from the StB and started informing on their colleagues, neighbours, friends etc., have been, at least symbolically, punished. "We don't want you to go to jail, but, on the other hand, because of your collaboration, you've lost the moral credibility required for holding an important post in the civil service," is the Lustration Law's underlying message.

With the somewhat expected exception of the communists, the Lustration Law gained broad support in the Czech population (the **Slovaks**, on the other hand, scrapped it after the separation of Czechoslovakia, while the **Poles** adopted a less rigid law almost a decade after the Czechs). But those who looked forward to a massive cleansing of the public sector have been disappointed. Of the more than 400,000 lustration certificates that the Ministry of Interior so far has issued, less than 5 percent have actually been positive.

Of course, the real number of StB informers was at least four times higher, but many of those who knew they were positive logically haven't bothered to ask for a certificate. In other cases, people who knew they would not pass the screening simply found a suitable excuse to leave their jobs silently.

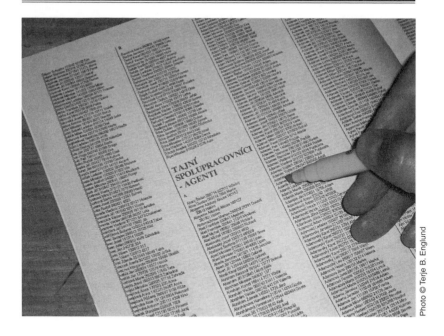

So, does the Lustration Law, almost a decade and a half after it was adopted, serve any purpose? Not if you ask the Council of Europe or the International Labour Organization.

Both of these foreign institutions condemn the law, maintaining that it's unjust and discrimination to a part of the population. Even prominent ex-dissidents, such as **Václav Havel,** oppose the law as a manifestation of the outdated *Berufsverbot*, which was practiced by the communists. As the Polish ex-dissident Adam Michnik puts it: "I was brave under the communists, so I don't have to be brave now when they're gone."

In one respect, the lustration opponents undeniably have a convincing point: the Czech Ministry of Interior has issued more than hundred negative certificates to people who evidently were positive. And, vice-versa, persons who apparently never conscientiously collaborated have been stamped as "StB positive" just because some swindling secret policeman claimed rewards for having acquired "agents" who not had the faintest idea that they had been recruited.

The lustration question is further complicated by the action of a single person. In the summer of 1992, the fervent anti-communist and **Charter 77** signatory Petr Cibulka got hold of computer files containing what seemed to be an accurate copy of the StB's archives. Cibulka was so disgusted by the new democracy's lenient treatment of the Bolshevik regime's loyal servants that he published a list of some 80,000 StB informers, completed with cover names and birth dates. So, since anyone is free to check out Cibulka's lists on the Internet, isn't it time to stop clowning about and close this dreary chapter of Czech history?

Well, a majority of Czech politicians, supported by the highest judicial body in the country, believe it's not. In late 2001, after lengthy negotiations, the venerable judges at the Constitutional Court in Brno (see: **Moravia**) concluded that the Czech Republic still has both the right and the duty to defend its institutions against persons who during the communist tyranny didn't behave loyally to democratic principles.

In March 2003, the Czechs took a further step towards a settlement with the country's totalitarian past when the StB's archives, with all their stories about human bravery and treason, were opened to the public. In other words, *lustres* will be falling on Czech heads also in the twenty-first century.

Mácha, Karel Hynek

The intellectual elite, who in the second half of nineteenth century launched a cultural revival that would subsequently lead to the creation of a Czech political nation, used two literati as their standard bearers.

While one of them, Božena Němcová (see: **Feminism**) wrote a boring, pathetic and from a literary viewpoint completely worthless "novel" about the goody-goody *Babička* (Grandmother), the second, Karel Hynek Mácha was a poet whose brilliance is absolutely unquestionable. His large lyrical poem *Máj* (May) is probably the best piece of literature ever written in the **Czech language**, and his compatriots are too modest when they praise him as Lord Byron's equal.

Incredibly enough, this literary genius is virtually unknown outside **Bohemia** and **Moravia**.

Mácha was born in 1810 in the Czech-speaking family of a poor miller's assistant and grew up at Prague's Malá Strana. As practically bilingual – all schools at that time taught in **German** – the young literate became an ardent fan of Goethe and later also of Mickiewicz, the romantic superstars at that time. When not writing, he enjoyed taking mortally long walks in the idyllic Bohemian nature, visiting castle ruins and, most of all, chasing women. "I'm looking for the ideal in every woman I meet, but I only find women in beautiful creatures," he once complained.

In the early 1830s he finally found her. Eleonora "Lori" Schom was a succulent German-speaking girl who seemed to be as obsessed with life's fleshly delights as Mácha himself was. Although hot-tempered and extremely jealous (to prevent Lori from even seeing other men, he strictly prohibited her to leave her house), Mácha undoubtedly got the inspiration to write Czech literature's ultimate masterpiece from his fiancée.

Máj was published in 1836, in 600 modest copies, and even though his earlier short stories were highly praised by local critics, Mácha had to borrow money to finance the project. Formally, this grand lyrical poem consists of melodious sonnets that are grouped in four chapters and two intermezzos. Its main idea was, according to the author himself, "to cheer the beautiful spring and all the emotions connected to it". Needless to say, a romantic of Mácha's calibre interpreted these emotions as burning love, which he described through the intense and tragic affair between the poem's main **hero**, Vilém, and the beautiful Jarmila.

In complete accordance with his romantic poetry, Mácha never lived to experience *Máj's* unbelievable popularity, but came to a tragic end. Shortly after he was appointed assistant to the municipal judge in Litoměřice (he frequently walked the 70 kilometres to Prague to romp

with Lori), he caught cholera and died a week before his 26th birthday from "suffocation and diarrhoea". He was hastily buried on the same day that he and Lori had planned their wedding. Their son Ludvík, who was born a month before Mácha's death, followed his father to the grave less than a year later.

Measured in tragedy, the poet's real life almost outdid that of his poetry. This fact, in addition to *Máj's* indisputable literary quality, unleashed a virtual Mácha cult among the Czechs. This cult, which still is alive and kicking, is built on two pillars – one nationalistic, and one romantic.

Mácha became a national symbol only days after he was buried in Litoměřice, and a requiem mass was held in the St. Ignatius Church at Prague's Charles Square. More or less the entire cultural elite attended the mass, which consequently turned into a grand manifestation of Czech patriotism. During the following century *Máj* was published in more than 100 editions, and after the **Velvet Revolution** in 1989, his intimate diary, originally written in code, was also made available to the common reader.

Among the entries were laconic pearls such as "Today, only masturbation, damn and blast it!"

Mácha's role as a national symbol was clearly demonstrated after the tragic **Munich Agreement** in September 1938, when Czechoslovakia was pressed to cede Litoměřice and the rest of the Sudeten areas to Nazi Germany. Only days before German tanks rolled in, the poet's remains were hastily exhumed from the graveyard and then transported to Prague. The great poet's second burial in "Czech soil", at Prague's Slavín cemetery (see: **Horáková, Milada**), turned out to be an even bigger manifestation of Czech patriotism than the requiem mass that had taken place more than a century earlier. Since then, Mácha's remains have rested in peace, but three decades later, after the **Russian** invasion in 1968, the Bolsheviks were scared to death that another tragic hero – **Jan Palach** – would cause a similar cult.

The romantic part of Mácha's legacy, however, is both more pleasant and relevant.

Every spring, in the evening of the first day in May, hordes of amorous couples march in the falling dusk up the steep path leading to Mácha's statue on the blossoming Petřín Hill in Prague's Malá Strana. There, they leave some flowers to commemorate the greatest poet in Czech history. And, indirectly, also to demonstrate that Mácha's real message was not that of nationalism, but of love.

Masaryk, Tomáš Garrigue

Any **foreigner** who spends more than 15 minutes in the company of Czechs will discover that they are capable of making jokes about practically anything. The more morbid, cynical and taboo-breaking the jokes are, the louder the bursts of laughter.

There is, however, one inviolable exception: Tomáš G. Masaryk – Czechoslovakia's first president. Only communists could have been suspected of ridiculing "TGM" or "President Liberator", which are the canonized versions of his name, but as everybody knows, the Bolsheviks don't have enough of a sense of humour even to make bad jokes.

Ever since the media after the **Velvet Revolution** started to publish ranking lists of the greatest Czechs of all times, Masaryk (1850 – 1937) has been the unquestioned winner. This is not too surprising, since he is personally regarded as the decisive force in the creation of Czechoslovakia, and he is the unrivalled symbol of Czechoslovakia's **First Republic** (1918–1938). In other words, Masaryk is to the Czechs and also quite a few **Slovaks** what Kemal Atatürk is to the Turks – although he didn't share the latter's love for booze and military parades.

Admittedly, the Masaryk cult has a substantial basis. Compared to the dictators and generals that ruled elsewhere in **Central Europe** in the interwar years, the sociologist and philosophy professor stands out as an uncommonly educated, broadminded and responsible **politician**. Yet the 40 years of Bolshevik rule, when his name was practically erased from the history books and every single Masaryk statue in the country was torn down, make him look almost supernatural today.

The funny thing, though, is that this "greatest Czech of all time" has a somewhat non-Czech origin. His father was a Slovak coachman, working at an estate in Hodonín in southern **Moravia**, which explains his Slovak-sounding **surname** (*Masar* meant "butcher"), while his mother was a Czech with **German** ancestors. According to rumours, though, Tomáš' real father was the owner of the estate where his parents worked, a **Jew** named Nathan Rädlich. Although this would have explained why the bright, but pitifully poor Masaryk was sent first to gymnasium in Brno and then to the University in Vienna for education, these rumours have never been proven.

It's undisputed, though, that his wife Charlotte Garrigue, an emancipated American lady whom he met in Leipzig in 1877, had a very strong influence on him. Charlotte's social democratic viewpoints were not least evident in Masaryk's later stance towards women's liberation (see: **Feminism**), where he admitted that he was "just conveying the opinions of my wife". When he officially took his wife's surname as his middle name Masaryk was branded as the first Czech feminist, and this was cemented when he later formulated a much-acclaimed paragraph in the Czechoslovak constitution of 1920: "No privileges connected to origin, gender or profession will be recognized."

The coming statesman's liberal and progressive image was further fuelled by two "scandalous" incidents. In 1886, he published an article in a Prague magazine claiming that two famous historic manuscripts, which allegedly proved that the Czechs' literary traditions were almost a thousand years old, were actually fakes. Good Czechs had just stomached the fact that Masaryk was right when the hard-hitting professor publicly defended a mentally retarded Jew, Leopold Hilsner, who had been sentenced to death for committing an alleged ritual murder. Thanks to Masaryk's campaign against the hysterical anti-Semites, Emperor **Franz Josef** saved Hilsner from execution, a fact, which Czech chauvinists later never forgot.

"A nation's honour lies in it's ability to find the truth," Masaryk echoed another Czech superstar – **Jan Hus**.

TGM was elected Czechoslovakia's president in November 1918 – at the age of 68, he was older than most Czechs at that time could hope to live – and re-elected for the third and last time in 1934, then almost blind and evidently reduced mentally. Many Czechs still consider the 17 years, during which Masaryk ruled Czechoslovakia as a "republican monarch" (Prague's Hradčany Castle is more majestic than most of Europe's royal palaces) to be one of the highlights in their history. Similarly, when Masaryk died in September 1937 less than two years after he abdicated, his state funeral quite literally symbolized the end of democratic and liberal-minded Czechoslovakia (see: **Munich Agreement**).

The First Republic nostalgia that emerged after the **Velvet Revolution** has had an understandable tendency to glorify both Masaryk and his republic. True enough, Czechoslovakia's policy towards its minorities was, by interwar standards, liberal, but hardly praiseworthy today (Masaryk once described the country's role as that of a bulwark against German expansion). Nobody disputes that Masaryk was a sterling humanist, but he seldom missed a chance to bash the Catholic Church ("theocrats") and publicly praise the Hussites, whom Czechoslovakia's Catholic majority, not least the Slovaks, perceived as chauvinistic Czech nationalists.

"Masaryk was no doubt a democrat, although his interpretation of democracy was sometimes rather peculiar," the historian Antonín Klimek says. "He claimed that democracy, in certain situations, is compatible with dictatorship, and he considered a revival of the **Austrian** monarchy to be a bigger threat than Hitler's ascent to power in 1933."

Yet in the row of Czechoslovak presidents, starting with the alcoholised and syphilis-ridden Gottwald to the senile general Ludvík Svoboda to the tragic Quisling Gustav Husák, Masaryk represents an almost surreal ideal. And contrary to another Czechoslovak president-cum-moral-idol, **Václav Havel**, he has the advantage of not being viewed in a real-life context.

"To many Czechs, the words 'Masaryk's republic' have become a declaration of faith and a mantra they use to declare that they are proud to be a part of this nation," the historian Klimek maintains. "But it's unacceptable when modern politicians glorify the legacy of Masaryk's Czechoslovakia to use it as a whip on the Czech Republic of today."

Mogilevich, Semyon Yudkovich

It's 11 o'clock in the evening, on the 31ˢᵗ of May 1995. At the restaurant *U Holubů* (the Dove) in Prague's Smíchov district, some 80 people, most of them **Russians**, are celebrating a birthday party with loads of caviar, champagne and oysters. Suddenly, the doors burst open. Almost 200

heavily armed policemen from the special squad fighting organized crime storm into the premises. Tables are turned over, furniture smashed, and all the party guests are handcuffed and arrested.

The now-legendary police action, which most Czechs know as the *Raid at the Dove*, was meant to be a daring and devastating blow against the Russian mafia and its operations in post-Communist **Central Europe**. It turned out, however, to be mostly a failure. All the men in Armani suits and their half-naked "hostesses", who were marched to black marias, were released within eight hours, and only three of them were later expelled from the Czech Republic.

And the biggest disappointment: Semyon Mogilevich, the Russian mafia's alleged godfather in Central Europe, was not even present at the party. Because his flight from Israel was delayed, Mogilevich arrived at the spot some minutes after the raid had started (at least, that's what he later told in an interview with the BBC). True to his reputation as a level-headed and resolute fellow, chain-smoking "Seva" immediately caught a cab and didn't stop until he reached Budapest.

Nevertheless, the unsuccessful raid at The Dove confirmed what most Czechs already guessed: the Russian mafia (which in this context should be interpreted *as Russian-speaking*, since its members come from all parts of the former Soviet Union) has a strong foothold in the Czech Republic. They even feel secure enough to gather at a giant party in the middle of Prague. And Semyon Mogilevich, while absent at The Dove, has had the dubious honour of becoming the mafia's "face" in the Czech Republic.

The mafia, however, could certainly have picked a duller boss. Through his rare appearances in the media, Mogilevich – also known as "Don the Brain" – fully confirms the rumours that he is extremely clever, cynical and witty. If he is also guilty of all the crimes which police investigators and secret services in numerous countries accuse him of, he is extremely ruthless and dangerous as well.

The Russian mafia's Central European boss was born in Kiev in the Ukraine in 1946. His parents belonged to the "working intelligentsia", but instead of pursuing an academic career after receiving his diploma at Lviv's Faculty of Economics, young Mogilevich moved to Moscow, where he started working for a state company that ran public toilets at the city's railway stations. The rather unglamorous job offered "Seva" a convenient cover for his real profession as a currency dealer on the black market.

In 1974, Mogilevich was sentenced to three years' imprisonment for his black market activities. This was at the time when criminals in the former Soviet Union started to organize themselves, so when "Seva" was released three years later, he had emerged a boss of a gang now known as the Solomon Mafia. Mogilevich earned his first millions under Gorbachov's *glasnost* in the early 1980s, when Soviet **Jews**, who mass-emigrated to Israel, needed "professional assistance" to get their hard currency and valuables – of course, minus a fat provision for "Seva" – with them across the Iron **Curtain**.

The Soviet Union's implosion in the early 1990s led to an immense boost of organized crime. Mogilevich, who by now carried an Israeli passport, settled in Budapest, where he was protected against deportation through a marriage to a **Hungarian** citizen. Based in the middle of the Carpathian basin, "Seva" and the Solomon Mafia started, according to police sources, to entangle all countries in post-Communist Central Europe in a criminal web. Their alleged main activities were drugs, prostitution, arms, nuclear material, antiques, gold and jewels. The profits that this criminal activity yielded, the police reports, were laundered through a network of legal businesses – including The Dove restaurant in Prague – which all belonged to Mogilevich.

It was his extraordinary capabilities in money laundering that earned Mogilevich his nickname Don the Brain. There are even strong indications that he personally masterminded the Bank of New York scandal, which in 1999 linked the then Yeltsin regime to extensive money laundering. FBI's forensic accountants started investigating the case, but no charges were ever raised against Mogilevich. This is Don the Brain's comment in the interview with the BBC in late 1999:

"If there have been committed crimes and the police suspect that I have committed them, I can only say one thing. Please show your evidence. If I really had been involved in all those criminal acts and the police had disposed evidence of this, they certainly would have put charges against me. But they haven't!"

So, officially, Semyon Yudkovich Mogilevich is only an extremely successful businessman trading in wheat, ceramics and shoes. To most Czechs, however, he remains the very icon of a Russian godfather and a kingpin in organized crime in Central Europe.

According to a Czech police spokesman, **foreign** mafiosi booked, in 2001, a turnover approximating 418 billion *korunas*, which corresponds to 20 percent of the whole country's GDP. Even if this figure seems wildly exaggerated there's no reason to doubt that organized criminals – with or without Semyon Yudkovich Mogilevich's brains – are doing quite well in the Czech Republic.

Moravia

The Czech nation has from time immemorial been divided into three historic regions: **Bohemia**, Moravia and Silesia. As in every other country on this planet, the Czech Republic has also witnessed a certain competition among its regions. A neutral observer may, however, quite often have the impression that the *Vysočina,* the highlands that divide Bohemia in the west from Moravia in the east, is a kind of buffer zone between two implacable rivals.

To be fair, the different character of the two regions is really eye-catching. Bohemia, occupying an area twice as large as Moravia and with almost twice as many inhabitants, is highly industrialized, deeply secularised (see: **Religion**) and completely dominated by Prague, the country's unrivalled economic, political and cultural centre. Moravia is mainly engaged in agriculture or mining (see: **Ostrava**), the Catholic Church with its traditionalistic **values** represents a spiritual cornerstone, and the regional capital Brno is both a nice and pretty city, although its ultra-provincial character is impossible to ignore.

If this makes you think that the average inhabitant of Bohemia can't stand the mug of the average Moravian and vice versa, you are probably too harsh (such a strong repulsion is mostly reserved for **foreigners**). Yet on both sides of the *Vysočina,* people regard it as a matter of honour to pester and insult the clowns on the other side of the highlands.

According to the Moravian stereotype, the classic *cajzl* (originally denoting a person from Prague, but today it applies more or less to anybody from Bohemia) is an arrogant, overpaid, **beer**-drinking fellow who goes to his cottage twice a month (see: **Fridays**) in Moravia to fix his car and bask in the sun. He knows everything better than the local boors, and his treatment of the **Czech language** is despicable. Logically, if you park a Prague-registered car somewhere in Brno, you can bet your boots that local police will give you a fat fine for some completely surrealistic offence.

The average Bohemian's perception of the Moravians isn't much more flattering. True, thanks to their rural roots, many of them are quite jolly and hearty (not least in combination with the locally produced wine), and lots of Moravians still have this funny physical resemblance to the Mongolian Avars that raided the area in the Middle Ages. But their strong religiosity is outdated and rustic, their dialect is ridiculous, and their inferiority complex about Bohemia is as huge as it is justified.

In complete accordance with this view, Czech state Television (based in Prague, of course) has practically only two ways of presenting life in the eastern part of the country: either you see thousands of pious Moravian Catholics attending mass, or a bunch of drunk chaps, who are dressed in folklore costumes and dance around in the village streets during some festival while roaring "I'm not Czech, I'm Moravian!"

Actually, there are also sober Moravians who seriously struggle to put an end to Bohemia's dominance and *Pragocentricism.* The Moravian National Party was established in the early 1990s, and it is working to transfer some of the nation's political decision-making to Brno. So far, only the Constitutional Court and the Anti Monopoly Office have left Bohemia for Moravia, but the MNP's long-term policy goal is to reorganize the Czech Republic into a federation, like Austria and Germany, where the government in Prague will only decide major issues such as **foreign** and defence policy.

The Czechoslovak separation (see: **Slovaks**) was a hard blow to the Moravian nationalist movement. Many ardent supporters discovered that their country had suddenly shrunk almost in the half and could hardly be split into another two parts. Yet their distinctive cultural character is still a touchy matter for most Moravians. In the national census in 2001, more than 1.3 million of the Czech Republic's citizens took great care to declare their nationality to be Moravian, not Czech.

This delicate situation may cause a foreigner some unexpected problems. While the adjective "Czech" in most European languages usually refers to the entire Czech Republic, *český* in Czech refers primarily to Bohemia (*Čechy*) and secondarily to the whole country.

So, if you are speaking about the famous "Czech composer" Leoš Janáček" in Prague, you'll probably be tolerated. Try the same in the composer's native Brno, and you'll be killed on the spot. Or imagine you are sitting with some locals in a wine cellar in charming Valtice in Southern Moravia and then foolishly spoil everything by saying something like "this Czech wine is surprisingly tasteful".

What you actually want to say is that "Moravian wine" is terrific!

Munich Agreement

O nás, bez nás – about us (but) without us. These words of utter despair and powerlessness were spoken for the first time in September 1938, but have later been carved into the brains of more or less every single Czech (see: **National Identity**). They relate to an event most people in this country consider the biggest tragedy in their modern history – the Munich Agreement – and it's no exaggeration to say that it still represents a national trauma for the Czechs.

It all started with the emergence of Czechoslovakia in 1918. The very name of the new state indicated that the country consisted of two peoples, the Czechs and the **Slovaks,** but this cleverly concealed the fact that 3.2 million ethnic **Germans** (compared to only 2 million Slovaks) were also living in the country.

The "Czechoslovak" Germans are a bit inaccurately called *Sudeten Germans* after the Sudeten mountain range, which stretches from the Elbe valley eastwards to **Moravia.** In reality, ethnic Germans, who were invited by the Czech kings to start agriculture in the kingdom's fringe areas, had from the thirteenth century densely populated all border regions in **Bohemia** and Moravia.

Compared to **Central Europe's** minority standards in the interwar years, it's fair to say that Czechoslovakia granted the Sudeten Germans generous rights.

True, they didn't enjoy the status as one of the country's official nationalities, and German was not accepted as one of the state's official languages. But they had cultural autonomy with their own schools, universities, theatres and a multitude of organizations, and ethnic Germans were represented in each and every Czechoslovak government from 1926 to 1938. At one point, the leader of the of the Sudeten German Social Democrats' was a certain Mr. Czech, while the boss of the Czech Social Democrats was *Mr. Němec* (German)!

Yet the economic crisis in 1929 made tensions between the Czech majority and the Sudeten German minority grow rapidly. Export-oriented Czechoslovakia was hit badly, but the Sudeten areas, heavily dependent upon light industry and mining, received an almost fatal blow. Poverty surged, and unemployment in the Sudeten areas was among the highest in Europe – which is one of the factors that explains why Czechoslovakia's Germans became grossly recipient to Hitler's propaganda, not least since *der Führer*, after seizing power in 1933 effected great measures to raise employment.

In the same year, Konrad Henlein, a gymnastics instructor from Karlovy Vary (see: **Carlsbad English Bitters**), established the overtly Nazi-friendly *Sudetendeutsche Partei.*

Officially, the SdP declared its loyalty to Czechoslovakia, but silently it struggled intensely for the annexation of the Sudeten areas into the *Third Reich.* When Nazi Germany swallowed Austria in March 1938, Henlein didn't bother any more to conceal his true goal – to get *Heim ins Reich.* It's undisputed that Henlein was supported by a devastating majority of the Germans living in Czechoslovakia. The SdP itself had 1.3 million members, and in the municipal elections in May 1938 almost 90 percent of the Sudeten Germans gave the party their votes.

In late September 1938, the leaders of Europe's then most powerful nations – Great Britain, France and Italy (but not the Soviet Union) – met up with Adolf Hitler in Munich to discuss the Sudeten question. Prior to the conference, Hitler had made it clear that annexation of the Sudeten areas into Germany was his final demand. Convinced that *appeasement policy* was the appropriate medicine to calm Hitler down, both France's Premier Édouard Daladier and Great Britain's Neville Chamberlain agreed to throw democratic Czechoslovakia to the Nazi wolves.

"They had the choice between dishonour and war," Winston Churchill later commented on his predecessor's behaviour. "They chose dishonour, and got a war."

As a result of the tragic Munich Agreement – or the *Munich betrayal*, as the Czechs call it – Czechoslovakia was forced to cede over 40,000 square kilometres of its territory to Germany (and later smaller areas to the **Poles** and the **Hungarians** as well), with a population of roughly four millions. Some 800,000 inhabitants of these areas were ethnic Czechs, who had suddenly become inhabitants of the Third Reich.

You don't have to be a psychologist to understand how traumatic this blow was for the Czechs (the Slovaks were in another situation, as the later occupation of Bohemia and Moravia enabled them to establish their own state), and it had several important long-term consequences:

After 20 years of independence under the **First Republic**, most Czechs were both eager and determined to defend their country militarily. Actually, Czechoslovakia was not that badly prepared. During the 1930s, the government had poured billions of *korunas* into the construction of a vast network of 260 concrete fortresses along the borders. Moreover, the mobilization that was announced in the autumn of 1938 was greeted with common enthusiasm in the Czech population. With an army totalling 1.1 million men, Czechoslovakia boasted the **world's** largest ground forces after Germany, Japan, France and Italy.

Nevertheless, pressed by the big European powers and haunted by visions of a terrible bloodshed like the one that happened in Spanish

Guernica a year earlier (the Luftwaffe was incomparably better armed than Czechoslovak Air Force), president Edvard Beneš decided to give in without a fight. This led to a widespread contempt for the country's political leadership in general, and to the democratic ones in particular. "I have a plan, or more precisely, an aero-plane," the Czechs spitefully distorted one of the president's remarks after he had fled the country.

The parallel to King Friedrich's flight after another national disaster, the **Battle of White Mountain**, and later also to Dubček's behaviour after the **Russian** invasion in 1968 is striking, and it underpinned the suspicion that Czech leaders tend to collapse when the country needs them as most.

Secondly, both Great Britain, widely admired in pre-war Czechoslovakia, and France, which was even a military ally, failed to help a small and threatened democracy in Central Europe ("Why risk our lives for a country we even can't find on the map?" a British **politician** reportedly asked). Ever since, many Czechs felt that they could not trust the Western democracies that participated in the Munich betrayal.

The Soviet Union, on the contrary, had no Munich blood on its hands. Except for Western Bohemia, Czechoslovakia was even liberated by the Red Army, which was a tremendous propaganda advantage to Stalin's local henchmen, who used the Russians' image as true friends and peaceful liberators to pave the country's way to **communism**.

And finally, the "disloyal behaviour" which the Czechs felt that the Sudeten Germans had demonstrated against their common state before the war led to a rather uncompromising reaction after Nazi Germany was beaten. Already in May 1945, civilian Sudeten Germans were rounded up and harassed by members of the Revolutionary Guards, and then concentrated in large camps.

Later, at the Potsdam Conference in August 1945, Great Britain, France, the Soviet Union and the United States gave Czechoslovakia the formal go-ahead to finish the operation. The Czechs didn't waste their time. By the end of 1946, about 2.9 million Sudeten Germans – including social democrats who opposed Henlein's SdP – had been mercilessly chucked out of the country, without any more belongings than the few things they could carry with them. Historians still disagree, but estimates suggest that at least 23,000 persons died during this "transfer", as it is officially called in Czech.

Within three years of the end of the war, the number of ethnic Germans in Czechoslovakia was reduced to 150,000 persons (less than five percent of the pre-war community), who immediately had to assimilate into their Czech surroundings.

Judged by modern standards, the expulsion of the Sudeten Germans suspiciously resembles collective guilt and ethnic cleansing as lately seen in the former Yugoslavia. To most Czechs, though, it was a fair and deserved repayment for their undeniable participation in crushing democratic Czechoslovakia in 1938. It has also convinced many Czechs, especially older ones, that co-habitation with **foreigners** never brings anything good, and that multiculturalism is Western mumbo-jumbo.

Mushrooms

In one of his lectures, the legendary linguist Vladimír Skalička presented a theory that once and for all pinpointed the quintessential difference between Europe's Germanic and Slavonic peoples.

"There is one decisive criterion," the great linguist maintained. "While the Germanic nations detest mushrooms, the Slavonic peoples cherish mushrooms as a gastronomic delicacy, and use any opportunity to go to the forests and pick them."

The alleged cultural clash between the Germanic peoples and the Slavs definitely belongs in history's graveyard. Yet in one respect professor Skalička was right. The Czechs are downright crazy about mush-

Photo © Terje B. Englund

rooms! In late summer and autumn, a **foreigner** might even get the impression that the number of sponge-hunting Czechs roaming about in the forests with a punnet largely exceeds the possible number of mushrooms.

Why? As the professor said – mushrooms are considered to be a delicacy. If **Czech cuisine** in general appears to be – mildly speaking – a bit dull, this certainly doesn't go for mushrooms. Any decent cook in the country knows at least a dozen ways to transform the fungus into more or less tasty dishes. And lots of other cooks know how to prepare the mushrooms that give you week-long hallucinations...

The advice to the foreigner is therefore evident: you needn't become a mushroom freak, nor even pretend that the fungi dishes taste wonderful. But never speak derogatorily about them! In addition to insulting the Czechs' cultural **values**, you will be perceived as a barbarian!

National Identity

Some years ago a sociologist, Jiří Pacek, confronted the readers of the daily *Lidové Noviny* with an intriguing question: when *Pepa Novák*, the average Czech, is to describe his country's national identity, he normally doesn't pull his punches. The Czechs by and large regard themselves to be a very cultivated, highly educated and broad-minded nation with **golden hands** and a natural flair for **egalitarianism**, improvisation and, not least, humour (see: **Švejk, The Good Soldier**).

However, when the same *Pepa* is to present his views of the individual Czechs who are actually living around him, then he'll probably change his tune completely: "The average Czech is a sly and conformist egoist," *Pepa* would say, "capable of adapting to almost any degree of sup-pression from any rotten regime as long as it gives him some advantages."

How, then, can these selfish anti-**heroes** create such a broad-minded and educated people? Pacek didn't offer any clear answers to the puzzle, except for concluding that the Czechs' view of their national identity doesn't agree much with the view they have of themselves. However, the social anthropologist Ladislav Holý, a Czech who fled to Great Britain after the Soviet invasion, didn't intend to accept this contradiction. As soon as the **Velvet Revolution's** dust settled, he returned to his native country to conduct a broad field survey of how Czechs from various layers of society perceive their national identity.

Later, the results of the survey were presented in a book, which Holý gave the rather striking title "The Little Czech and the Great Czech Nation". As one might expect when Holý was considered a **foreigner**, his conclusions didn't go well down with all his Czech colleagues.

One feature that many Czechs value, according to Holý, is their nation's amazing capability always to survive in difficult times. During history, **Austrians**, Nazi **Germans** and Soviet **Russians** have bullied the

Czechs around. Often, it might seem as if they were loyal to their oppressors, occasionally even as if they were collaborating openly with them (See: **Communism**). But in the end, it always became clear that the Czechs never really gave in to the oppression. Therefore, what some foreigners (particularly the **Poles**) often regard as Czech weakness or even as downright cowardice is considered to be a great strength by the Czechs themselves.

This has led to another peculiarity. As Pacek the sociologist also pointed out in his article, the Czechs can look at their history in two ways, according to what is most convenient for their national pride. When something bad and undesired happens, it's because "somebody else" didn't want the Czechs to succeed and deliberately mucked it up for them. And when they, against all odds, still succeed, it's because of their nation's nature-given genius (see: **Cimrman, Jára**).

As a result, many Czechs tend to view their history not in light of what actually happened (Czechoslovakia was nastily raped by Nazi Germany), but in the light of what could have happened if they hadn't been stopped (thanks to its ingenious system of heavily armed border fortresses, Czechoslovakia would have caused any aggressor serious wounds).

If you still find the contradiction between the very positive picture of the Czech nation and the very bad picture of the individual Czech a bit enigmatic, Holý offers two additional explanations.

First a somewhat obvious reason: each of the two pictures has its origin in different types of experience. While the common Czech's ugly picture of his compatriots is empirically based on his personal meetings with (some of) them, his rosy picture of the Czech nation is entirely mediated by the things he or she has read in glorifying literature. Which, after all, is an attitude familiar in several other European countries (see: **Austrians**; **Danes**; **Hungarians**; **Poles**; **Russians**; **Slovaks**) as well.

Secondly, a more intriguing aspect: Holý maintains that the Czechs' perception of national identity is still based in a nineteenth century, nationalistic tradition, and not in a modern, universal tradition. While liberals in Western Europe regard their nation as a collective of individuals, the Czechs perceive it as a supra-individual entity, or, if you like, the nation is something like a mother.

Thus, Pacek's contradiction makes perfect sense; Czech national identity simply lives its own life, and its quality doesn't need to be identical with that of the average Czech at all. Moreover, when the nation is perceived as a mother, those who leave her are logically perceived as having renounced his or her family, and, logically, don't belong anymore among the nation's true children (see: **Emigrants**).

Nobility

The Czechs often claim about themselves that they are a "nation of plebeians" where the absence of nobility has caused a widespread aversion to any higher ideals. Without the moral guidance of the nobility, the saying goes, the cunning Czechs have developed a strong ability to behave pragmatically under all circumstances, and even adapt to rotten regimes forced upon them (see: **National Identity**).

This characterization is not only unflattering, but also false. There are very few European nations where the nobility, during the last several centuries, was non-existent, and **Bohemia** and **Moravia** (the latter was a margraviate right up until 1918) are definitely not among them. On the contrary, many of the 2,200 or so magnificent castles that are spread around the Czech Republic once belonged to noble families.

Yet when one compares the Czechs with the **Poles** and the **Hungarians**, they do indeed have a different attitude towards their nobility. The not-too-surprising reason for this is to be found in their turbulent history.

After the disastrous **Battle of White Mountain** in 1620 many patriotic members of the Czech nobility were forced to flee the country. They were soon replaced either by noble families from abroad, such as Karl von Liechtenstein, the forefather of Prince Hans Adam, who today runs the tiny Principality of Liechtenstein, or by Czechs, who the Emperor ennobled as a reward for their participation in curbing the rioting Protestants.

In both cases, the nobility – bar some bright exceptions – came to be perceived in the same way as the Catholic Church (see: **Religion**): as a **foreign** element, who often had **German** as their mother tongue and not infrequently behaved disloyally to the "Czech cause". Rather symptomatically, one of independent Czechoslovakia's first actions was to expropriate large chunks of land belonging to the Catholic Church – and to abolish the use of noble titles.

The contrast with Poland, where the church has traditionally been one of the nation's cornerstones, or Hungary, where counts and barons played a significant role in interwar politics, could not be sharper.

The Czechs' ambivalent attitude towards the nobility grew dramatically stronger when Bohemia and Moravia were occupied by Nazi Germany in 1939. It's hard to give precise numbers, but it's undisputed that some of the most high-profile members of the former nobility, such as Count Ulrich von Kinsky, assisted practically in paving the way to the **Munich Agreement** or later collaborated happily with the occupants. But there are also examples of brave resistance. In 1938, on the verge of the Second World War, a group of ten noblemen published a petition to ensure President Beneš of their loyalty to Czechoslovakia, and several families had their estates and personal belongings confiscated by the Nazis because of their pro-Czech behaviour.

To the Bolsheviks, however, nobility was nobility. Without exception, the "people's democracy" expropriated the property of all noble families, irrespective of any Nazi affiliation, and then turned the castles and estates into schools, sanatoria or even military barracks. To make a show of their "classless" justice, the communists also forced the members of the few noble families who didn't leave the country to take utterly

proletarian jobs. Thus, in the 1960s, Jan Stránský, a knight, could be seen busy at work at a filling station in Prague's centre.

This changed after the **Velvet Revolution** in 1989. As all other citizens who had their property stolen by the Communist regime, also members of the former nobility claimed it returned. Their legal position, however, has not been too easy. Firstly, they have had to prove their innocence when it comes to allegations about Nazi collaboration (and not the other way round – that the state has to prove they collaborated). And secondly, they had to fight the common prejudices against **emigrants.**

The result? Fifty-fifty, one might say. Numerous castles and estates have been returned to their original owners. Thanks to this property restitution, ex-Prince Karel Schwarzenberg (during the *normalization,* one of **Charter 77's** most vociferous advocates in the West) has become one of the country's most affluent men and biggest landowners. However, several others, most notably the Walderode family, have either been rejected because their Nazi collaboration is well documented, or they are fighting endless battles in Czech courtrooms to regain the palaces, forests and land they once owned.

This ambiguity also characterizes many Czechs' attitude towards the old nobility. True, the vast majority seem to have far too many problems on their own to care about the fate of Bohemia and Moravia's former feudal families. But many people loathe the idea that popular state castles, visited by thousands of **tourists** every year, may fall into the hands of private owners, who moreover are regarded as foreigners.

Ocean

After years of brutal communist exploitation of nature, many **foreigners** perceive the Czech Republic as the apex of ecological disaster and pollution. In one of his films, the famous Finnish director Aki Kaurismäki even has a scene where a tourist is developing his film in a **Bohemian** river.

This is, by all means, a cruel distortion of reality. The Czech Republic, with its Krkonoše (Giant) mountains, Šumava forest, numerous rivers, green valleys and rolling hills, bound together with charming country roads and alleys lined with fruit trees, can boast amazingly varied nature and countless places of immense beauty.

Still, God forgot to give the Czechs one of Mother Nature's most fundamental elements: the ocean. "So what?" you'll probably object. In his play *The Storm*, William Shakespeare placed the Bohemian kingdom by the sea, and nobody noticed it. And besides that, after the Iron **Curtain** disappeared, you could reach the Adriatic Sea or the Baltic by car from the Czech Republic within six hours, so why make such a fuss about the absence of ocean?

Simply because it belongs to the group of arguments, which Czechs often use to explain some of the most basic features of their alleged

Photo © Jaroslav Fišer

national character. You may, of course, consider this term to be a bit woolly, but in this country, most people take it deadly seriously, so a foreigner should at least know it in theory.

According to common Czech wisdom, the sea is something that literally enhances big visions and great deeds. In a maritime nation, people walk on the seashore and stare out at the endless ocean. Almost physically, they feel there is something bigger and better out there behind the horizon. The Czechs, on the other hand, have at best a small *rybník* (a fishpond) at their disposal. "That's why we are so petty-minded, **sceptical** and timid," the saying goes.

President **Masaryk** put it even more harshly: "Because we don't have any sea, we sit by the pond and croak like small frogs." The poor frogs have even found their way into the **Czech language** in the familiar saying *žábomyší válka* (a war between frogs and mice) which equals the petty and meaningless quarrels which are so often demonstrated by the country's **politicians**.

Of course, the Czechs don't have a monopoly on attaching symbols to entire nations. The Nobel Prize laureate Elias Canetti wrote an essay

206

where he compared the broadminded and fearless Englishmen to the sea, while the **Germans**, according to Canetti, were as dangerous and unpredictable as a deep forest.

To develop this somewhat dubious theory a bit further, let's take a quick look at the map: the Czechs not only lack the ocean's horizons, but mountains or deep forests surround them to the north, west and southwest. Bohemia, it's often said, is even submerged in a basin (which it in reality isn't). To the protagonists of the absence-of-ocean-theory, this has an evident result: even though the Czechs are living in the middle of Europe, geography has made them feel protected from the outside **world.**

Add forty years of isolation behind the Iron **Curtain**, and what do you get? An inwardly-looking atmosphere, unruffled by fresh maritime winds or oceanic perspectives, where the Czechs have been happily chewing their *knedlíks* (see: **Czech Cuisine**), downing **beer** and producing unique characters such as **Jára Cimrman**, **Karel Gott** and **Václav Klaus.**

Ostrava

If Prague and the rest of **Bohemia**, with all their charming *hospodas*, delightful architecture and pretty landscape should become too cosy for you, Ostrava, the Czech Republic's third largest city with about 330,000 inhabitants, will rapidly cure your spleen. Tucked away in the country's northeastern corner on the border between **Moravia**, Silesia and Poland, the former Czechoslovakia's "heart of steel" offers the true flair of the Wild East. As an Australian probably would have put it, this is a city where men are men, and sheep are nervous.

Contrary to most other Czech cities, which were established in the Middle Ages, Ostrava emerged only in the 1920s, when small-town Moravská Ostrava was merged with 30-odd villages in its surroundings. What Ostrava lacked in historic patina, however, it fully compensated for with an incredible ethnic blend. Pre-war Ostrava's population consisted of Czechs, **Germans**, **Jews** and **Poles**, all of whom were in one way or another economically dependent upon the Vítkovice steel mill (established in 1828) and the extensive coal mining industry.

Now, guess what happened to Ostrava when the Bolsheviks came to power in 1948?

Correct: the already heavily industrialized and ecologically disturbed region became even more industrialized and ecologically disturbed. By the end of the 1950s Ostrava had been transformed into Czechoslovakia's unquestioned centre of heavy industry. Thanks to the region's economic importance, local Party bosses had great influence in Prague, and propaganda portrayed Ostrava's miners as the **nobility** of the ruling proletariat.

Surprisingly enough, the city stayed an ethnic hotchpotch also under Bolshevik rule. True, most of Ostrava's Jews were murdered during the Holocaust, and the city's German inhabitants were kicked out of the country right after the war (see: **Munich Agreement**). But these two minority groups were soon replaced by a strong influx from the eastern part of Czechoslovakia – be it **Slovaks**, **Roma** or **Ruthenians**. And since the hordes of industrial labourers needed a place to live, architects relished designing houses according to the Stalinist brutalism style.

As a result, most Czechs tend to see post-communist Ostrava as a living monument to the Bolshevik era's crazy command economy mixed with failed social engineering, while the city's inhabitants, the *Ostraváci*, are often perceived as a mixture of East-European gastarbeiters who didn't make it to the West.

Admittedly, North Moravia certainly belongs among the Czech Republic's most troubled regions. The once so dominant heavy industry is, at best, in deep recession or has already gone bust, so unemployment is souring. With larger **foreign** investments absent, the city has not been able to afford the massive face-lift that most other Czech cities have undergone. Even graver, the consequences of the Bolsheviks' eco-

logical ignorance can still be seen and felt all over the region, and Ostrava's Fifejda district sits directly upon enormous quantities of highly explosive gas.

Yet Northern Moravia's capital is definitely not on its knees. The region, which the rest of the Czech Republic regards almost as the nation's armpit, displays a vitality and devil-may-care attitude that's hard to find elsewhere. It's probably no coincidence that the folk singer Jarek Nohavica, the closest you can come to the desperate **Russian** Vladimir Vysotskij in **Central Europe**, hails from Ostrava. Indeed, there is something desperate about the entire city.

The biggest and certainly wildest pub district in the entire Czech Republic is Ostrava's Stodolní Street. As one might expect, the average *Ostravák* doesn't drink hectolitres of Bohemian **beer** or sip South Moravian wine, but downs one vodka shot after the other (see: **Alcoholism**). In Ostrava, girls take a more no-nonsense attitude towards life than their sisters in Prague, and the boys have bigger cars and definitely harder fists. Local businessmen erect private castles for themselves that dwarf the baroque business-villas that pop up in the rest of the country, and the **corruption** scandals, bank robberies and murders are usually juicier, bigger and far more shocking than the Czech average as well.

In short: in a country where the philosophy of the middle of the road is treated as a holy cow (see: **Egalitarianism**), Ostrava represents a rare oasis of unbridled extremes. *Bon voyage!*

Palach, Jan

It's not hard to understand why Jan Palach's name can be found close to the top on the list of the Czech Republic's most respected national

heroes. His boundless idealism and shocking self-sacrifice in the nation's name is truly amazing in a country that often seems to be dominated by cynical pragmatists.

The 21-year old philosophy student entered Czech history five months after the Soviet Union's Red Army raped Czechoslovakia with the symbolic assistance of four other Warsaw Pact countries. To stage a personal protest against the invasion and his countrymen's growing lethargy, Palach decided to kill himself in public and in the most horrific way possible. Thus, on January 16, 1969, Palach went to Wenceslas Square in the middle of Prague, sprinkled his clothes with petrol, and then set fire to himself (see: **Hus, Jan**). After three days in indescribable pain – when he also had to endure interrogation by the secret police – he died.

In the short term, Palach accomplished exactly what he had intended. His living torch deeply moved occupied Czechoslovakia, and the Western **world** was shocked. The funeral became a nationwide protest against the occupants (see: **Mácha, Karel Hynek**) and their local henchmen. He even inspired others to follow suit. A month later, another living torch blazed up when Jan Zajíc, also a student, committed suicide in the same way and for the same reasons as Palach.

This time, however, the communist regime was better prepared. The news about Zajic' death – and any additional living torch that later may have followed – was painstakingly concealed. Within a year of Palach's suicide, the neo-Stalinists had won a full victory. Palach's remains were secretly removed from the Olšany cemetery in Prague to the graveyard in his home village Všetaty in Central **Bohemia**, and two decades of grey *normalization* fell over Czechoslovakia.

Viewed from a political angle, Palach's tragic sacrifice might seem completely vain and a terrible waste of a young life. This picture, however, is only partly correct. Even if it's hardly measurable, he undisputedly represented a source of comfort for those not-too-numerous Czechs (see: **Communism**; **Charter 77**) who sacrificed their professional careers, material prosperity, mental tranquillity and sometimes even personal freedom for not paying lip service to the totalitarian regime. Symbolically enough, the London-based publishing house that fed Czech dissidents with uncensored literature was called "Palach Press".

In the 1980s, when the communists reached their final stage of agony, the annual manifestations to commemorate Jan Palach turned into wild clashes between the growing opposition and the riot police. What's more, the students who triggered the **Velvet Revolution** would probably have never got so many passive Czechs out of their easy chairs if the alleged police killing of a student had not so chillingly reminded them of Jan Palach's death twenty years earlier.

Naturally enough, the years of post-communist freedom have put a veil of oblivion over Palach's name. True, the park in front of Charles University's Philosophical Faculty has been named Jan Palach Square, which is both an appropriate and highly symbolic change (it was formerly named the Square of the Red Army Soldiers). But as times go by, fewer and fewer people turn up for the annual commemoration at his grave. It's not even commonly known that his remains have been relocated to the original Prague cemetery.

Yet Palach's act still invites reflection. It's nothing new that civilians choose to sacrifice their own lives on the nation's altar, but the goal of such political suicides is almost always to kill as many enemies as possible. Contrary to all those desperate Palestinians, Chechens or Tamil Tigers, both Palach and Zajíc took painstaking precautions to ensure that nobody else – neither **Russians** nor Bolsheviks – was hurt.

As an act of ultimate altruism, their suicides bear a striking resemblance to those committed by Buddhist monks during the Vietnam War. Maybe it's a bit far-fetched, but to many Czechs this underpins the myth (see: **National Identity**) that the Slavs' nature is basically peaceful and non-aggressive. Unfortunately, Palach still serves as a model. In the spring of 2003, a series of self-immolations hit the Czech Republic when six people, most of them young, tragically ended their lives in flames in public places.

Pepa from Hong Kong

Politics in the Czech Republic after the **Velvet Revolution** has had more than its fair share of comical elements, but few of them, if any, can beat the sponsoring scandal that broke out in 1997. Even though Czechs don't have a monopoly on lugubrious relations between businessmen and **politicians** (but they certainly belong in the European Champion League), the way these fishy relations came to light, was quite unique.

The farce started in 1996, when **Václav Klaus'** Civic Democratic Party (ODS), which had played a leading role in all Czech coalition governments since 1992, published a list of its numerous sponsors. Surprisingly enough, among the generous donors were also two **foreigners** – one **Hungarian** and one citizen of Mauritius. When the media checked the names, it appeared that the Hungarian had died ten years earlier, while the chap on Mauritius had heard neither about ODS nor the Czech Republic.

The widespread suspicions that there was something rotten in ODS' finances sharply increased when members of the party's leadership announced that ODS had opened a secret multi-million account abroad. What followed later entered Czech political folklore under the name of the "Sarajevo coup" against party chairman Klaus: while he participated at a conference in the Bosnian capital, several party bigwigs asked him to resign because of the financing scandal. Klaus was hesitant, but his government fell, the ODS split into two parties, and the Czech courts started to sort out the mess.

A sponsoring scandal good as any, one might say. It was indeed – except for the fact that nothing was ever sorted out.

The indications that ODS actually has secret funds in a foreign country are strong, but nothing was proved under the legal clean-up that took place in early 2000. The businessman who hid behind the foreign donors had previously privatised a large steel mill, but investigators didn't manage to find enough evidence to prove that his under-cover sponsorship was more than a matter of sheer altruism. Today, the ODS earnestly profiles itself as a law-and-order party.

But Pepa from Hong Kong took the cake. Asked by a judge about the millions of *korunas* she donated to ODS without telling the tax authorities, a female party supporter answered that the money was not hers, but belonged to a certain Pepa (Czech slang for Josef). Unfortunately, she didn't know where he was living, because she had met him in Hong Kong. And no, she could neither remember what he looked like, nor whether Pepa had given her the millions of *korunas* in coins or bank notes!

To be fair – ODS is probably the biggest, but hardly the only, financial wrongdoer on the Czech political scene. Suffice is to say that for many disillusioned Czechs, Pepa from Hong Kong has become the ultimate icon of the political **corruption** and murky business climate that apparently flourished in the Czech Republic in the 1990s.

Personal connections

Nobody will deny that it can be quite handy to know the right persons in the right places. Most people will probably also agree that, in a European context, the practical importance of personal connections grows stronger and stronger the farther south you go. Therefore, one might expect the Czechs to regard this phenomenon in more or less the same way as their **Austrian** and **German** neighbours.

But that's definitely not the case. Because one of the communist dictatorship's most characteristic features was the ostentatious way in which it bent rules and laws to hand out "advantages" to people who were loyal to them, personal connections became crucial to any slightly ambitious person.

Obviously, Party membership was the ultimate door opener to a high-powered career (it's probably no coincidence that Czechoslovakia's Communist Party had 1.8 million members, which relative to the country's total population of 15 millions made it the largest in the former East Bloc after Romania's Bolsheviks). A less compromising but still effective method was to ally yourself with a *strejda* (literally "uncle", or an important person) who because of your personal relations and sometimes also an envelope stuffed with bank notes would use his influence to obtain certain advantages for you.

Because courts were totally controlled by the regime, it was often pointless for those who were discriminated against to take legal action (that is, unless they didn't happen to be connected to an even more important *strejda*). Logically, the less people trusted state authorities, the more confidence they put into their personal relations – first of all their family, and then their friends and acquaintances. The Czechs themselves call this system "to have protection".

Every reasonable person relied upon at least a handful of "protections": you needed to personally know an auto mechanic (if not, your car might be repaired with used spare parts), a dentist (they were few and all working for the state, so why bother to do a good job?), a gynaecologist (some of them are still ill-reputed for sexual misconduct), a bookseller who put aside William Styron's latest novel for you, and a nice teacher who fed your children with the absolute minimum dose of Bolshevik ideology.

Now, take a wild guess: did this system disappear with the communists? Of course it didn't. Just as **corruption**, which is an extreme version of the protection system, still lives and thrives, so does also the importance of personal connections.

In fact, this tradition has become so ingrained that is doesn't stir the slightest public outcry when **politicians** reward their ex-colleagues with prestigious state jobs or super-lucrative memberships on company boards of directors. When postings for Czech ambassadors are to be filled, formal careers and years of service are not always among the most interesting factors. Similarly, when a young woman was catapulted from total obscurity to a seat in Parliament in the late 1990s, most people found it completely natural, because everybody knew her political qualification was a previous stint as a private secretary for the party boss.

Needless to say, the protection system can be both a curse and a blessing. If you, for instance, find an interesting job announcement in the newspapers and decide to apply, you're probably wasting your time unless you already have "protection" in the company. Logically, the more attractive, interesting and well paid the job is, the greater the need for a *protector*. On the other hand, if you only are a bit unscrupulous, personal connections can secure you huge advantages.

When, for instance, **foreign** journalists call a governmental institution's spokesperson and ask some questions, they'll probably get a useless answer a week later. But if they know somebody in the place personally, he or she might reveal tons of secrets over a few pints of **beer** in a cosy *hospoda*. In short: when it comes to personal connections and their importance as a tool for solving practical problems, the Czechs display a striking resemblance to those **Balkan** countries that they always take such great care to belittle.

Poles

In his bestseller *The Mitrokhin Archives,* KGB defector Vitalij Mitrokhin cites a conversation between the KGB's resident in Warsaw and a Polish general in 1981. When the **Russian** spy indicated that Moscow was seriously considering invading Poland to curb the rebellious Solidarity movement, the general answered calmly: "If you do that, rivers of blood will flow. Remember, we are not Czechs, but Poles!"

Crisply speaking, this is a quite apt expression of how many Poles look at the Czech Republic and its inhabitants. While the Poles are convinced that their own nation has an almost messianic mission, crucified as it is between a "**German** and a Russian criminal", the Czechs are perceived as a small and ungodly state, full of scared *Pepiczeks* who don't care a bit about abstract **values** and moral questions when toadyism can earn them some instant benefits (see: **Švejk, The Good Soldier**).

The common Czech, on the other hand, doesn't have a better opinion of his northern neighbours. True, they reacted bravely when attacked by Nazi Germany in 1939, but what other nation could have thought of launching its poorly equipped cavalry against the advancing tanks? And yes, millions of ordinary Poles eagerly supported the Solidarity trade union in its fight against the communist regime, while only some 1,800 Czechs, plus a few dozen **Slovaks**, signed the **Charter 77** document (logically, many of them became avid Polophiles). But in Czechoslovakia at that time, meat was not rationed and anybody could buy shoes in the shops (see: **Communism**). That could hardly be said about Poland in the early 1980s...

If these stereotypes make you believe that the Czechs and Poles are not exactly on good terms, you're only partly right. In fact, one might find a certain animosity as a natural reaction to communist propaganda, which exhorted both Czechs and Poles to love and admire their fellow socialist countries (all of whom, except Ceasescu's Romania, helped the Russians in 1968 to invade Czechoslovakia). This, however, doesn't mean that today's relations are patently bad. They only seem, at least from the Czech point of view, to be more dominated by differences than the things that bind the two nations together.

So, what do the two nations have in common? Several kings, for instance. Admittedly, some time has passed since the Jagiellon dynasty in the fourteenth century ruled both the Poles and the Czechs, but it certainly represents a relatively bright period in the two nations' bumpy histories.

The linguistic aspect is more significant. Bar Slovak and Lusatian (see: **Czech Language**) no Slavonic language is closer to Czech than Polish. People living along the two countries' 762-kilometre common border usually understand each other without a problem (some 60,000 of the inhabitants of Silesia and northern **Moravia** are of Polish origin, representing one of the largest minorities in the Czech Republic). The Czechs very likely even got their name from their neighbours to the northeast: in old Polish, *Czachy* (dry) described the quality of the land between thetwo major **Bohemian** rivers, the Vltava (Moldau) and the Labe (Elbe).

Yet history's course of events has driven a cultural wedge between the two Slav brother nations. The Reformation movement, which found broad support among the Czechs (see: **Jan Hus**) and led to the country's devastating defeat at the **Battle of White Mountain** in 1620, never held any great appeal for the Poles. Symptomatically, the Catholic League's most feared and violent troops at White Mountain were the Polish Black Battalions.

This split was further deepened in the eighteenth century. While the Czechs in the aftermath of White Mountain were ruled with a firm hand from Vienna and left to a violent Counter-Reformation (which, naturally, didn't make the Catholic Church extremely popular), the once so mighty Polish Kingdom was gradually chopped up by its neighbours, until it ceased to exist in 1795. Exposed to strong suppression from Protestant Prussians in the west and Orthodox Russians to the east, the Poles embraced the Catholic Church – their nation's only saviour – with even stronger fervour.

This religious schism is still very apparent. More than 95 percent of the Polish people regard themselves as practicing Catholics. The Church enjoys significant political influence (remember where Pope John Paul II was born!), which, among other measures, has led the country to adopt one of Europe's strictest bans on abortion.

The Czechs, on the other hand, stand out as one of the continent's most secularised nations (see: **Religion**), and are reputed for their liberal stance in moral matters. As a result, many Czechs view the Poles as a nation of bigoted Catholics and obscurants – not least when it comes to **sex** – while many pious Poles regard the Czech Republic as a European branch of Sodom and Gomorra, which, judged by the amount of brothels close to the Polish borders, seems welcomed by quite a lot of them.

Obviously, the different size of the two nations represents a further problem. Both in area and population, Poland is almost four times as big as the Czech Republic. The same goes, logically, for the country's political ambitions.

In 1919, Poland occupied the Těšín territory, which historically was a part of the Czech Kingdom, but at that time predominately populated by ethnic Poles (55% versus 27%). Prague, as expected, reacted, and some 40 Czechoslovak soldiers died in the military clashes that followed. International pressure forced the Poles to back off (just as the **Hungarians** were pressed to leave Southern Slovakia), but the Czechs have worried ever since about being dominated by their bigger neighbour. This is probably one of the main reasons why the intended plan to federalize Poland and Czechoslovakia after the Second World War failed.

And finally, there has traditionally been a palpable difference between the Poles' and the Czechs' social structure. Thanks to its early and massive industrialization, Bohemia and, to a lesser degree, Moravia already had by the end of the nineteenth century a broad and relatively well-educated working class, while the influence of the liberal middle classes grew rapidly. The vast majority of the Poles, however, were still deeply rooted in the agricultural society, dominated by the Catholic Church and rural traditions.

This changed a bit after the Second World War, when Poland "moved" 250 kilometres to the west (which gave them control over a strong mining industry in the former German Silesia), and the communists launched a massive program of industrialization. Yet about 20 percent of the Polish work force is still employed in agriculture, most of them on small family farms. Thus, many Czechs feel it more natural and in greater accordance to their **national identity** to compare themselves with the urban **Austrians** and Bavarians (see: **Beer**) than with their Slavonic brethren in rural Poland.

Do the Polish-Czech relations prove Robert Frost's words that only "good fences make good neighbours"? Not really. In the post-cold-war era, the fences have gradually become lower, and Poland's economic boom during the last decade has also been felt in the Czech Republic.

The ski resorts in Northern Bohemia's beautiful Krkonoše (Giant) Mountains, for instance, are flooded every winter with **tourists** from the opposite side of the border. In addition to money, this development also brings some funny situations. Such as the elderly Polish skier who some years ago walked into a hotel reception in Špindlerův Mlýn. Unbuttoning his jacked, he declared with a loud voice: *Dzień dobry, szukam pana Tadeasza!*

The receptionist reacted with professional politeness, but the event is, nevertheless, a striking demonstration of the close, yet slightly distorted relations between the Poles and the Czechs.

Politicians

Numerous surveys conducted over the past several years suggest that one of the professional groups that the Czechs least respect and admire, is that of politicians. To be precise, they place them neatly between cleaners and army officers on the social ranking list.

Although depressing to the country's honest and hardworking politicians, this result is not very surprising. The mixture of burgeoning **corruption**, deep-rooted **egalitarianism** and **scepticism** towards anybody who claims to be sincerely fighting for some noble and non-monetary ideals has created a widespread suspicion about any politician's true motives.

Frankly, quite a few of the politicians who emerged after the **Velvet Revolution** have behaved in a way that does not exactly allay the common taxpayer's distrust (see: **Pepa from Hong Kong**).

This common disdain has, obviously, its roots in the era of **communism**, and it can be described in lengthy studies. Here, however, we will put it in a nutshell:

In the communist society that collapsed in 1989, political influence gave you money. In a Western, capitalist society, money gives you political influence. In a post-communist, neo-capitalist country like the Czech Republic, money gives you political influence, while political influence ranks just behind the lottery as the fastest way in which a commoner can get rich without working too hard (see: **Personal connections**).

Religion

The statistics' message is unambiguous: there is probably no other country in Europe with a higher density of atheists and non-religious people than the Czech Republic. In 1991, almost 40 percent of the population stated that they had no religious affiliation at all. Ten years later, the National Census showed that the number of non-believers had reached a record 60 percent of the population! Quite an achievement compared to neighbouring Poland, Bavaria, Slovakia and Austria, where people take great pride in presenting themselves as good Catholics.

Why have the Czechs become so thoroughly secularised? As you might guess, it's not only because the Pope wears funny hats, but because of historic reasons. Let's move some 600 years back in time.

The body of **Jan Hus**, who was burnt at a stake as heretic in July 1415, had barely turned to ashes when wild turmoil broke out among his followers in Prague. The subsequent Hussite Wars raged for two decades. Thanks to the fighting spirit and also appalling brutality demonstrated by the Hussite *Boží bojovníci* (God's Warriors) and their military leader, the one-eyed Jan Žižka, Rome decided to grant the rebellious Czechs certain concessions in 1436.

Most important among them was the revolutionary innovation of letting common believers taste the Communion wine (thus making the chalice the Hussites' main symbol). This period of relative religious tolerance lasted until 1620, when the mainly Protestant Czechs suffered their "heroic defeat" in the **Battle of White Mountain**, and the victorious Habsburgs then launched a forced Counter-Reformation.

This treatment has apparently marked the Czechs' relations to religion forever. The historian Dušan Třeštík puts it like this:

"After the Battle of White Mountain, we found ourselves between two camps – the Catholic and the Protestant. When the Czechs, during the national revival 250 years later, emerged as a self-confident and modern nation, they naturally started to distance themselves from the **Austrian** Habsburgs – and their main ally, the Catholic Church. Since the Czechs supported the liberal ideas of that time, we should logically have become Protestants. But ultimately, we didn't become either Protestants or Catholics, either Liberals or Conservatives, only atheists."

Indeed, when Czechoslovakia emerged as an independent state in 1918, the Catholic Church, because of its close ties with the former rulers in Vienna, didn't exactly enjoy high credit among urban Czechs (but in **Moravia** it did – and still does). As one of its first measures, the Prague government expropriated vast lands belonging to the Church, and symbols of its glory, such as the magnificent Marian column at Prague's Old Town Square, were torn down. On the other hand, the teaching of Jan Hus underwent a certain revival. Feeling that changes were imminent, his followers (see: **Sokol**) had already erected a monument of the Mister on Prague's Old Town Square in 1915.

Five years later, they established the Czechoslovak Church (officially renamed the Czechoslovak Hussite Church in 1971), a liberal Protestant Church, which was to carry on Hus' ideals. Even though the Hussites didn't succeed in their ambitions of becoming Czechoslovakia's state church, they were supported by some of the **First Republic's** most influential persons. President **Tomáš G. Masaryk** himself was an ardent Hussite, and infuriated the country's Catholic clergy every 6th of July by

Photo © Jaroslav Fišer

hoisting a flag featuring the Hussites' chalice outside his residence at the Prague Castle.

The flourishing of religion during the First Republic ended in 1938 with the **Munich Agreement**, which heralded a half-century of tyranny hostile both to the Catholic Church and to their Evangelic and Protestant brethren. True to Lenin's words that "religion is the opiate of the masses", the communists, who seized power 10 years later, did their utmost to complicate life for believers.

In the early 1950s, thousands of Catholic clergymen, monks and nuns were locked up (some of them even killed), and churches of all denominations were held under constant surveillance by the Secret Police. Any Czech, eager to have a career, was better off not turning up to mass. This applied especially if you happened to be a **Jew**. The small community that survived the Holocaust was not only regarded as suspicious because of their religious convictions, but, due to the regime's pro-Arab orientation, they were politically "highly unreliable" as well.

223

Also when it came to religion, the Bolshevik regime played skilfully with sticks and carrots (see: **Communism**). While those members of the clergy who demonstrated personal integrity were mercilessly badgered – Prague's archbishop, Josef Beran, was interned for 14 years, and then, in 1965, deported to Rome, where he soon after died – those willing to pay lip service were richly rewarded. For the Catholic clergy, this meant membership in *Pacem in Terris*, a quisling organization, which was supposed to give the **world** the false impression that Czechs and **Slovaks** enjoyed religious freedom.

It's an unarguable fact that a significant part of the Catholic priests succumbed to the hard pressure (because of softer treatment, the collaboration was not so widespread and apparent among the Evangelic and Protestant clergy). Consequently, while Poland's Catholic church acted as a moral force, which gave ordinary people support and spiritual guidance during communism, many of their Czech brethren (but not all!) confirmed the Church's reputation as more loyal to the rulers – whomever they might be – than to the people. Not surprisingly, when an unofficial list of the Secret Police's agents was published in 1992 (see: **Lustration**), several prominent clergymen were named among the alleged informers.

So, what is the situation today? According to the National Census in 2001, the Catholic Church tops the religious ranking list with 2.7 million members, down from 3.7 million in 1991. The great outflow is commonly explained as a result of the secularisation that is going on in all European countries, and also because of one specifically Czech syndrome – the Church's haggling with the state about the ownership of real estate holdings ("greedy Bible thumpers").

The Catholics are trailed, at a rather significant distance, by the Church of Czech Evangelic Brethren (120,000 members) and the Czechoslovak Hussite Church (100,000) – both of which, interestingly, have a distinct majority of female members. The Christian ranking list is rounded off by the Augsburgian Evangelic Church (29,000), the Jehovah's Witnesses (24,000) and the Orthodox Church (23,000).

According to the Census, there are also some 3,700 Muslims and 1,500 Jews registered in the Czech Republic, but in reality both groups probably number several times as many.

The single largest group, however, is that consisting of the 6.1 million Czechs who don't have any religious affiliations at all.

This, of course, does not necessarily mean they are atheists. There is a palpable interest among Czechs in transcendental questions: the Buddhist Society, for instance, has skyrocketed to 6,000 people; and the virtual army of fortune tellers, healers and clairvoyants who have popped up after 1989 are doing big business. It merely seems that most Czechs, based on their historical experience, are thoroughly **sceptical** of any "official" religion with a clergy that demands their prostrate obedience.

Rhombus

Just like young people all over the globe, Czech youngsters also delight in scribbling dirty words on walls and buildings. **Foreigners** may even understand their meaning, since some of the most frequent obscenities are in English (*"Fuck off komunisty!"*).

But even in this basic and rather uncomplicated area of human activity the Czechs have invented some peculiarities. Most of them are, of course, verbal (see: **Cursing**), but there is also one very popular symbol: a rhombus with a distinct I drawn inside. As any dirty mind will guess, it symbolizes the female genitals, which in a wider context can be translated as "fuck you", "asshole" or "you dirty creep".

Seen from a child's perspective, this is a brilliant invention that allows them to scribble apparently innocent symbols and at the time express things that would have gotten children in other countries three weeks of house arrest had it been written in words. Just bear in mind that when you as a foreigner find a nice rhombus drawn in the dust on your car, it's most probably not an attempt to make you happy with a beautiful decoration...

Roma

On a hot summer evening in 2003, three young **Moravians**, who were downing **beers** in a *hospoda* in the city of Jeseník, suddenly got a bright idea. To have some "good fun", they went to the home of a local Roma couple, a young man and his pregnant wife, kicked the door open, and then silenced the fighting Roma with a knife while they smashed the woman's head with a hammer.

The couple survived the brutal assault, but when the local court tried the scumbags six months later, the victims were dealt another blow: all three bullies got away with a warning, because they had a clean record and, as the judge said, they were basically "nice boys", but excessive consumption of beer had made them a bit naughty.

At first sight, this tragic incident looks like a repetition of a series of similar cases over the last decade: Romas have been physically assaulted – in at least 15 incidents even killed – and the white Czech assailants (often skinheads) have received a hair-raisingly lenient punishment from the courts. The Jeseník incident, several activists maintained, proved that the Czech Republic still tolerated violent racism towards its Roma minority.

Fortunately, the shameful court ruling caused a wave of angry protests in the national press, a spokesman of the Czech government publicly questioned the judge's competence, and even good Jeseník burghers expressed their solidarity with the Roma couple, rejecting the city's image as a racist haven. Ultimately, the young hooligans were re-tried by another court, and one of them was sentenced to prison.

Still, the co-habitation between the Czech "gadja" majority and the Roma (meaning "human being" in Romani, a term which has replaced the old "gypsy") is strained and their **communication** is full of misunderstandings.

Take for instance the fact that nobody knows for certain how many Roma there are in the Czech Republic. According to the national census in 2001, only 12,000 Czech citizens declared themselves as Roma (the law prohibits officials from deciding a person's nationality) while Roma organizations, obviously eager to look as big as possible, boost the number to more than 300,000 individuals. Sociologists and field workers, however, estimate that there are about 200,000 Roma, which in a relative ranking (two percent of the population) places the Czech minority among the larger ones in Europe.

To make the picture even more complicated, the overwhelming majority of today's Czech Roma minority have roots in Slovakia. Prior to the Second World War, only some 6,000 Roma were living in **Bohemia** and Moravia, and more than 5,400 of them were murdered in Nazi concentration camps. It says a lot about the communist regime that this Roma Holocaust was officially fully acknowledged only after the **Velvet Revolution**.

After the war, poor Roma from Slovakia (where no mass extinction had taken place) started to migrate westwards, often to the Sudeten region, which offered an abundance of empty houses, left over from the three million ethnic **Germans** that were kicked out in 1945–46 (see: **Munich Agreement**). The increasing Roma migration was speeded up after 1948 by the communists, who needed lots of unqualified labourers for their newly-established heavy industry.

The result of this policy can be seen all over North Bohemia today: large numbers of Roma, who until the 1950s had earned themselves a living as tinkers and travelling craftsmen, were moved together in towns and cities that were completely **foreign** to them. Still, after half a century in the area, many Roma feel that their roots are in the hilly landscape of Eastern Slovakia, and not in polluted North Bohemia's industrial ghettos.

Pavel Říčan, a researcher at the Czech Academy of Sciences, depicts the communist era as both a curse and a blessing for the Roma. Among the nice aspects was a regular wage for unqualified work, a place to live, free health care, schooling for children and a wide range of social benefits. But they paid a high price: indigenous Roma culture was almost totally eradicated, their language was banned (most young Roma don't speak Romani, yet their command of Czech is often far from flawless), their traditions were ridiculed and their old crafts forgotten.

"Throughout their forty years in power the communists taught the Roma that it paid to lie and steal," Říčan concludes. That verdict may be a bit too harsh, but it's undisputed that the Roma, who always had relied on themselves, became totally addicted to help from the state.

Not too surprising, then, that the transition to a market economy has been especially difficult for the Roma. Official figures are hard to come by, but according to the researcher Říčan, some 60 percent of children in Czech orphanages are Roma, and more or less the same ratio applies for

inmates in Czech prisons. The average Roma is in substantially worse health than the average "gadja", the great majority of Czech Roma are jobless (here, widespread discrimination also plays a certain role) and only one in five adult Roma has completed elementary education.

These facts are certainly not too encouraging, but Milena Hübsch-mannová, the Czech Republic's most renowned expert on Roma culture, is still quite optimistic. In her opinion, it's obvious to everyone that the Bolsheviks' forceful integration – an attempt to turn the Roma into dark-skinned Czech proletarians – was a complete fiasco. Now, voluntary assimilation has become the new gospel, and if this is to succeed, the Roma need to establish their own intellectual elite – which is currently emerging.

"In the last years, our Roma have been undergoing a cultural revival, and I'm curious what social impact this will have," Hübschmannová recently told *Reflex* magazine.

The troubled process of creating a Roma elite has been accompanied by a no less important change in political attitude. While the **Klaus** governments in the early 1990s proclaimed that the Roma, like everybody else, now had to help themselves (many Roma interpreted this as a disguised attempt to force them back to Slovakia), later governments have realized that the Roma never will succeed in dragging themselves out of the backwater if they don't get practical assistance.

Yet this process will certainly take several decades, and setbacks are bound to occur. Some critics, many of them foreigners, even claim that Czech authorities could have been far more persistent in helping their Roma. They are probably right, but, on the other hand, is there any country at all that can serve as an integration model for Europe's seven million Roma?

Russians

If there is one nation that can surprise most Czechs only in a positive way, then it's the Russians. And honestly, their shabby image is very understandable.

For more than 40 years, Czechoslovakia was practically ruled (or rather misruled) from Moscow. When the Prague Spring, in 1968, was crushed by Soviet tanks, thousands of Czechs fled the country (see: **Emigration**), while those who stayed had to put up with Soviet soldiers all around the country and official propaganda praising everything Russian. Only masochists – or communists – could find anything positive about the giant to the east (see: **Ice Hockey**).

Yet the Czechs have not always despised and feared the Russians. On the contrary, when the national revival (see: **Czech Language**) blazed up during the second half of the nineteenth century and the question of Czech emancipation from the **Austrians** became a political issue, many leading intellectuals turned to their big Slavonic relative for support and comfort.

One of the most notorious pilgrimages to Russia took place in 1867. Only months before Emperor **Franz Josef** was to be crowned **Hungarian** king in Budapest's St. Stephen's Cathedral, two leading Czech nationalists, František Palacký and František Rieger, went to St. Petersburg to meet Czar Alexandr II, who greeted the Czechs as "brothers from a nation of brothers", thereby demonstrating that mighty Russia did not approve either that the Hungarians were given a more privileged position in the Danube Empire than its Slavonic citizens.

Karel Kramář, a prominent politician who alongside **Tomáš G. Masaryk** played a key role in the struggle for Czechoslovak independence, went even further. Convinced that the Slavonic **world** should unite, he dreamt of turning **Bohemia** and **Moravia** into a monarchy ruled by a member of the Russian Romanov dynasty. Luckily, Kramář's visions were not fulfilled (instead, he and his Russian wife built the beautiful villa on Prague's Letná Plain that is now the Czech Premiers' residence). The Czechoslovak republic that emerged in 1918 led an overtly Western oriented policy, and was among the last European states to recognize the Soviet Union.

Masaryk's **First Republic**, however, didn't hide its strong sympathy for the Russians who opposed Lenin's Bolshevik dictatorship. In 1920, Czechoslovakia invited some 10,000 Russians loyal to the dethroned Czar to settle in the country, but in short time almost 40,000 "white Russians" arrived. Many of them belonged to Russia's former elite, be it as members of the banished **nobility**, high-ranking officers or scientists and intellectuals.

Thus, interwar Czechoslovakia soon became a centre for the White Russian diaspora. This was especially visible in Prague, where most of the Russians settled. Renowned academics, such as Roman Jakobson and Nikolay Trubetzkoi, made the Prague Linguistic Circle famous internationally, while Nikodim Kondakov established one of the world's leading scientific institutes of Byzantine arts. Russian lyceums, schools, housing complexes, churches, cemeteries and even a military academy popped up in many places around Bohemia and Moravia.

And most Czechs didn't seem to mind. On the contrary, thanks to their relatively high educational standards, linguistic adaptability and outspoken loyalty to the Czechoslovak state, the Russian minority was commonly treated with respect.

This smooth co-habitation lasted for only 20 years. The **Munich Agreement** in 1938 and Nazi Germany's subsequent occupation of Bohemia and Moravia represented a direct threat to the Russian emigrants (although thoroughly anti communist, they were, after all, Russian patriots). Some of them managed to flee to the West or hide themselves in the countryside, but many others were sent to **German** concentration camps.

Unfortunately, the Russians' bad luck didn't end here. Immediately after the liberation of Czechoslovakia, Stalin's Red Army started to silently round up White Russian emigrants who had survived the war. In 1946, 12,000 Russians (many of whom by now had become Czechoslovak citizens) were transported to the Soviet Union without a single word of protest from the Prague government. Back "home", the emigrants were without exception imprisoned in gulags. Less then 4,000 of them ever saw Czechoslovakia again.

As relatives of the abducted emigrants' recently told *Týden* magazine, this horrible injustice didn't arouse any popular upheaval. After France and Great Britain's treason in Munich in 1938, which paved the way for six years of brutal Nazi occupation, the mood in post-war Czechoslovakia was, not surprisingly, strongly pro-Soviet. Stalin had not stabbed Czechoslovakia in the back. On the contrary, his victorious Red Army's soldiers had liberated the country from its occupants (later it appeared that they also had raped quite of lot of women). As a result, even non-communist Czechs were convinced that Soviet Russia was the only nation they could really trust.

It's fair to say that a majority of post-war Czechs tolerated the strong fixation on Soviet Russia as long as it didn't affect the economy (as it

Photo © Terje B. Englund

started to do in the 1960s). Symptomatically, most people didn't react to the Russians' violent invasion in Hungary in 1956 (see: **Communism**), but this changed dramatically when the Czechs themselves, in 1968, were treated with the bitter medicine that the Hungarians had tasted twelve years earlier.

Contrary to the Hungarians, the Czechs didn't put up an armed fight against the invading Russians, but the resistance was still heroic. Almost 30 protesting civilians were shot dead by the invaders (many of whom apparently believed they were curbing an American-supported revolution), over 70 others were killed in accidents caused by the invaders, and thousands of civilians were wounded, some severely. The Czechs' peaceful attempt to create "socialism with a human face" was crushed by blunt and brutal force. **Jan Palach's** self-sacrifice was an extreme reaction, but his immense despair was shared by millions of Czechs.

The invasion in 1968 and the following deployment of a 75,000-strong occupation force in Czechoslovakia ruined the Russians' image for generations. As so often before, the majority of the Czechs didn't express their deeply felt revulsion for the rulers openly (see: **Communication**; **National Identity**). Neither did they stop reading Chekhov or listening to Tchaikovsky. Instead, they poked fun of and ridiculed the Russians in private, just as **Švejk** in the past had ridiculed the Austrians.

Most of the jokes were based on one comical fact: while the official propaganda portrayed the Soviet Union as a frontrunner in almost every thinkable area of human activity, the Czechs knew perfectly well that the Eastern Empire, stripped for its nuclear arms, was in reality hopelessly backwards. As one common joke went: We'll follow the Soviet Union to eternity, but not a second more!

So, have the Czechs' relations to the Russians changed after the fall of the Iron **Curtain**? The answer seems to be both yes and no.

On a political and economic level, the relations have indubitably improved (that is, from a Czech point of view). A milestone was passed in June 1991, when the last Red Army soldier left Czechoslovakia, and few Czechs shed tears when the Soviet Union was dissolved a couple of months later. Then add Germany as the Czech Republic's main trade partner, membership in NATO and the EU, and the picture gets clear: Moscow has to treat the Czechs as any other smaller, Western country.

Yet the common suspicion of everything Russian still persists. Now, many Czechs believe, they are not threatening us with their tanks or political pressure, but with their criminals!

It's hard to judge whether these allegations are exaggerated or not. Yes, the enormous privatisation, the lack of official control, and the legal chaos that characterized the Czech Republic in the first half of the 1990s attracted criminals from every corner of the world, including the former Soviet Union. The question, however, is whether "Russian-speaking persons", which is the official Czech euphemism for inhabitants of the former Soviet Union, are over-represented among **foreign** criminals.

When it comes to ordinary street crime, police statistics suggest that they are not. However, after Prague police (in 1995) made an unsuccessful attempt to arrest **Semyon Y. Mogilevich,** an alleged Mafia godfather, otherwise sober observers concluded that that Russian Mafia has picked the Czech Republic as the centre of its illegal operations in **Central Europe**. Money laundering, often through property acquisition, is said to be one of their favourite activities, but it is not a kind of crime that represents an acute threat to ordinary citizens.

What's undisputed, though, is that life in the Czech Republic again has become attractive to affluent Russians. While their mother country is mired in economic turbulences and political unpredictability, the Czech Republic offers stable conditions in a relatively safe environment, only a few hours' ride from Germany. In addition, the language barrier is minimal, and cities like Prague and Karlovy Vary have a cosmopolitan atmosphere, so it's quite easy for the Russians to adapt to local conditions.

Combined, these factors have led to a repetition of the Russian migration to Bohemia and Moravia during the **First Republic**. Currently, about 12.000 "New Russians" have settled in the Czech Republic, and like the interwar wave, most of the newcomers have university degrees or thriving businesses – a majority of the hotels in the spa city Karlovy Vary, for instance, are owned by Russians (see: **TV Nova**).

Still, history has left a deep scar. Contrary to the immigrants from post-Czarist Russia, the immigrants from post-communist Russia are not treated with respect, but with suspicion and often even silent contempt. Most Russians, on the other hand, don't bother to integrate in the Czech society, and tend to create their own islands within it.

But there are evident signs of some timid changes. In 2002, many Czechs were flabbergasted by media reports that the most generous private contributors to the planned reconstruction of the Charles Bridge – Czech statehood's most revered symbol – were actually members of the local Russian community. **Sceptical** Czechs certainly concluded that local Russians were only buying themselves a better image. But even so, the mere fact that the Russians have started to care what the Czechs think about them is an undisputed improvement.

Sandals and Socks

If you see a photo from the most recent EU summit and wonder which of the politicians is the Czech representative, here's a clue: go for the guy who has paired his business suit with sandals and white socks.

This is, of course, a slight exaggeration (and maybe also a bad joke), but the fact is that the Czechs, partly because of the 41 years of communist isolation (see: **Ocean, Absence of**), and partly because they have made such a fetish out of *pohodlí* (comfort) have developed a dress code with a few rather extravagant components.

Probably the most widespread and frequent of these extravagances is Czech men's long-lasting love affair with the aforementioned sandals. As soon as you can sniff the vapour of spring in the air and the thermometer climbs to a few degrees above zero, practically any Czech male is capable of putting on sandals. And even more intriguing – the sandals are almost always combined with socks, preferably white.

A **foreigner** might argue that the weather is either so hot that you wear sandals on bare feet, or it's so cold that you wear socks and normal shoes. But that's not the Czech way of reasoning. The most die-hard sandal freaks will keep both sandals and socks on their feet nearly until Christmas, and for hordes of puzzled foreigners, the sandals have been elevated to a place alongside **beer** as the very icon of Czech culture.

It's hard to give a satisfactory explanation of Czech sandal frenzy. Perhaps it has political reasons – just as the Iranian Ayatollahs urge men not to wear Western neckties, the Bolsheviks discreetly filled stores with sandals because they represented the proletarian antipode of capitalist patent-leather shoes. Or maybe it's just an uncompromising war against foot sweat, although Czech men usually don't seem to mind sweat from other parts of the body. In any case, a foreigner should be prepared for the fact that the average Czech man regards sandals as completely ordinary shoes and may wear them on practically any occasion.

A special division within the Czech sandal army is formed by the *otužilci* (literally "hardy fellows"). These are often young and always very tough men who have hardened themselves (or at least pretend they have) against cold weather, and therefore wear nothing more than sandals, shorts and a t-shirt all year round.

The roots of the *otužilec* tradition go back to the nineteenth century **Sokol** movement, which promoted the ancient ideals of a sound (and patriotic Czech) soul in a sound body, and it was wholeheartedly endorsed by the Bolsheviks, who regarded the *otužilci* as Czech followers of the crazy **Russian** tradition of ice bathing. In the 1970s and 1980s the movement found a very visible "face" in František Venclovský, the first Czech swimmer to cross the English Channel. Notwithstanding all his toughening up, Venclovský unfortunately didn't get to be very old, but his fellow *otužilci* are still walking around in the middle of winter dressed in bermudas without attracting the slightest attention.

As one might expect, Czech women are far more clothes-conscious than men, and many of them miraculously managed to be fashionable even during the super-dull communist era (see: **Golden Hands**). Yet local streets and squares still offer a view now rare in Western Europe: hordes of women mincing along dressed in miniskirts so short and ultra-tight that they might be confused with bikinis. And just as white socks are the obligatory accessories to men's sandals, the mini-skirts are usually complemented with a half-transparent blouse, bleached hair, and black pumps.

"Aha! The Czech edition of Hustler has just held an audition nearby," a confused foreigner might think. But that reaction is strongly determined by the Western perception of **feminism**. In a Czech context, it's not only fully accepted that women show off their physical qualities, they are almost expected to do so! To be considered an object of men's (or women's, for that sake) sexual interest is not, as Western political correctness dictates, humiliating or discriminating, but downright desirable.

Thus, the super-sexy, mini-skirted ladies are ordinary women (well, at least most of them) on their way to ordinary jobs. True, not all of them are exceedingly tasteful, but there are certainly far worse elements of the communist era's pop culture (see: **Gott, Karel**) that still are alive and kicking.

Some Czech peculiarities apply to both genders. One of them is the importance of wearing nightclothes. If you are to spend a night at somebody's house or cottage (see: **Fridays**) and don't want to give the impression that you are either an uncivilized primitive or a sexual deviant, be sure to bring pyjamas or a nightgown. During the weekend, when people are relaxing at home, both men and women often wear tracksuits. This is not because they are working out, but because the tracksuits make it more comfortable to drink beer and eat chips in front of the telly. They are also obligatory for inmates in Czech prisons.

Footwear represents the ultimate super-dangerous pitfall for a foreigner. If you visit a block of flats, you will often see several pairs of shoes lined up outside each flat. Contrary to Moslems, who are driven by religious considerations, the Czechs only take practical precautions not to smear their **Balkan**-inspired wall-to-wall carpets with all the niceties that flood local streets (see: **Dogs**). According to the **sex** researcher Radim Uzel, some men also take advantage of the fact that there is an alleged correspondence between shoe size and the length of the penis, and therefore place shoes twice their actual size outside, just to impress their female neighbours.

No matter what you think about the shoe/sexual organ link, if you are invited to a Czech home and your hosts urge you not to take off your sneakers, they are almost certainly expressing courtesy to their guest (see: **Communication**) and expecting you to say something like "Oh, that's alright", and then leave your shoes by the doorstep. If you don't, and march into their flat with your shoes on, you'll risk eternal damnation. Most Czech households have extra pairs of slippers, which guests are supposed to put on their feet during the visit.

And finally, when you travel by public transportation, go shopping, or just visit a restaurant, you may get a very palpable sniff of human bodies. Or, to put it plainly: many people, regardless of their gender, are proud to smell of sweat. Lots of those who don't smell are happy to put up with the odour, and deodorants are still widely perceived as the privilege of **homosexuals** or social climbers. However, if you complain about the smell, you'll only make a fool of yourself. This leaves you with two options: either pretend not to notice the stench, or start smelling yourself!

Scepticism

One of the main features of the alleged "Czech national character", which many people in this country are firmly convinced exists (see: **Golden Hands**; **National Identity**) is a strong inclination towards scepticism. For instance, when polls only months before the EU enlargement in May 2004 suggested that the Czechs were the least enthusiastic of all new member states, nobody was too surprised. "Jesus Christ, what else could you expect from Europe's biggest sceptics?" common wisdom calmly commented.

To assign certain personal character traits to an entire nation of 10.3 million individuals is certainly rubbish. And if the Czechs are so thoroughly sceptical, how is it that they are among the **world's** most fervent buyers of overpriced junk from tele-shops? If the word scepticism, however, is interpreted as somewhat cautious behaviour combined with doubt about the truth of noble ideals (see: **Religion**), then the number of Czech sceptics may really be higher than the Western European average.

Those who revel in the myth of Czech scepticism usually explain its existence by pointing to the country's turbulent history. From the disastrous **Battle of White Mountain** in 1620 to the **Munich Agreement** in 1938 to the Soviet invasion two decades later, radical changes have tended to be for the worse. Add forty years of **communism**, when people had very limited possibilities to influence their own lives, and you understand why the philosophy "a bird in the hand is worth two in the bush" has got so many followers in this country.

While this generalization is too strong when it comes to the entire Czech population, it fits quite well as a characterization of political development during the first decade after the **Velvet Revolution.** On the rhetorical level, **Václav Klaus** and his "right-wing" ODS promised more radical reforms than in any other post-communist country. In the real world, however, many changes were milder, slower and more considerate than in other transition economies. In other words, it was crucial to avoid dramatic changes and maintain the social equilibrium. If it was disturbed, even pro-reform voters might be turned off.

Today, however, the subject "Czech scepticism" has started to live its own life. In important international questions, such as the Czech Republic's NATO membership in 1999, the EU enlargement in 2004, and the war in Iraq, people are almost expected to take a wait-and-see attitude, because "a sceptical approach is the Czech way of doing things". However, making a fetish out of scepticism at a time that belongs to the brightest in Czech history resembles more closely an excuse for remaining passive.

Sex

One of the first things that meet you when you cross the borders into the Czech Republic is an enormous number of "erotic clubs", which is the local euphemism for an institution most other countries know as brothels. Actually, they are not limited only to the border region. Every Czech city with some self-respect boasts at least one erotic club, a massage parlour, or hotel with "extended services", where men (there are erotic clubs for women too, but rather few) are helped to rid their flesh of lust.

This may lead you to conclude that the Czechs are completely obsessed with sex. Unfortunately, that's not entirely correct. Instead, the incredible congregation of brothels primarily reflects the fact that the Czech Republic after the **Velvet Revolution** has become one of Europe's major destinations for sex-tourism (see: **Germans**). And the reason for this is not only the geographical proximity to Western Europe and a pleasant price tag, but also the country's traditionally liberal attitude towards moral issues (see: **Religion**), which has led to an equally relaxed relationship towards sex – including the kind available for money.

Where sexual habits are concerned, the Czechs seem to be perfectly in the middle of the road. Recent surveys show that the average Czech has sexual intercourse 144 times a year, which is less frequently than the average American (who is exaggerating, as always), but more often than the Japanese (who's probably ashamed to tell the truth). The Czechs have their first sexual experience somewhat later than the average Scandinavian (at 18 for both men and women), but earlier than what is common in Italy and Spain, while the percentage of **homosexuals**, logically, corresponds to the average in Western Europe.

The condom producer Durex places the Czech Republic in a European context with these words: "The Czechs have sex as often as the French, they start their sexual life as early as the Dutch, and they fear venereal disease as little as the Italians."

Still, the Czechs can book one sexual **world** record: few other countries can boast a more liberal attitude towards marital infidelity. A survey conducted by the company TNS Factum in 2003 showed that Czechs, on one hand, consider "life in a happy family" to be of the utmost importance. On the other hand, they tolerate – and conduct – marital infidelity to an extent that is matched globally only by the Bulgarians and **Russians**. What's the reason for this anomaly?

It's certainly not too wild to guess that it has its root in the era of **communism**. Many ugly things can be said about the Czechoslovak Bolsheviks, but they shall be credited for one thing: they lavishly financed the establishment of families; i.e. of marriages. As the sociologist Jiří Černý explained in an article in *Lidové Noviny* daily, the goal of this policy was to turn the family into a social instrument that produced new labourers, took care of the elderly, and stuffed each citizen into collectives that discouraged him or her from "dangerous individualism". The state even encouraged young people to marry by offering them "marital loans", which secured young Czechs an economic head start that Westerners of similar age could only dream of.

In this area, the communists were extremely successful. While young people in Western countries happily enjoyed the fruits of the sexual revolution, young Czechs often married the first sexual partner in their life. As late as 1988, the average bride was 21 years old, and her husband-to-be three years older. Since men regarded the use of condoms as a nuisance and women – quite justifiably – feared the locally produced hormonal contraception, they also had children at a significantly earlier age than in the West.

Marriage was, in other words, the only officially tolerated means in which two young Czechs could live together. What's more, it also became an economic necessity. With next to no flats rented to singles and a wage level that granted the individual only the most modest existence, marriage represented financial security. Besides that, it gave children a good start in life (surveys show that the otherwise liberal Czechs still are pretty intolerant of children born out of wedlock). During the ultra-pragmatic *normalization* in the 1970s and 1980s, the economic aspect of marriage became so important that it wholly overshadowed its other ingre-dients. This attitude still lingers on.

In addition to the utilitarian attitude towards marriage, the grey and dull life in communist Czechoslovakia did little to enhance marital fidelity. It was hard to travel abroad, it took extreme efforts to get hold of consumer goods that were common to every Westerner, and it made no sense to pursue a career (it often required great humiliations, and your pay didn't rise much anyway). So what did you do? Enjoy all the fleshy temptations that life could give. The writer **Milan Kundera** does not have many fans in the Czech Republic, but he's at least credited for one thing: in his novels, he gave a vivid picture of how the Czechs used sex and promiscuity as a remedy against their *Weltschmerz*!

The fall of communism has brought about some interesting changes. Marriage rate has plummeted from 90.000 weddings in 1990 to some 49.000 in 2003 (which means that marital infidelity, and not necessarily promiscuity, is becoming less widespread), and the average Czech is getting married at a later age than ten years ago. Simultaneously, Czech women now have unlimited access to Western hormonal contraception, as well as the possibility of pursuing a career that secures them economic independence. As a result, the number of women preferring to remain single and have casual sexual relations instead of getting married has sky-rocketed. Currently, every third child is born to an unmarried mother.

The most palpable change, however, is that the communist regime's silly prudery has been replaced by a strongly liberal attitude towards anything that smacks of sex. What a decade and a half ago was shrouded in deepest privacy is now demonstrated openly on every street and corner.

In that respect, it was hardly a coincidence that in 1995 the Czech broadcaster **TV Nova** became the first in Europe to feature naked weather forecasters. The reactions that this revolutionary innovation evoked are equally telling. Hordes of female viewers bombarded the TV station with letters to express their anger. Not about the nude forecasters, but about the fact that they were all women! Some weeks later, Nova admitted its guilt, and introduced nude males as well...

Slovaks

Anyone who has a younger brother or sister knows how most Czechs regarded their Slovak neighbours and ex-compatriots until just recently: somebody we are fond of and can lean for support in bad times, but generally, an impulsive individual who behaves immaturely and sometimes downright stupidly. So that's why we, the elder, wiser and more experienced, consider it our constant duty to correct the young fool and give him our well-intended advice and directions.

Fortunately, public expressions of this paternalistic attitude have weakened since Czechoslovakia split in January 1993. Yet many Czechs still have an ambiguous feeling towards their eastern neighbours: "There is no other nation on this planet that is so close to us than the Slovaks. Their language is basically a Czech dialect, and we share 74 years of common history in Czechoslovakia. But compared to us, they are more emotional and, well, less sophisticated," the *hospoda* wisdom goes.

Such generalizations can hardly be taken seriously, but some striking differences between the two nations are evident. Slovakia has traditionally been an agricultural society, while **Bohemia** – and to a lesser extent **Moravia** – have been industrial. The Slovaks drink less **beer** and more wine than the Czechs, their traditional folk songs and dances reveal more temperament than those sung and danced to in Bohemia, and most Slovaks cling to the Catholic Church, while the average Czech treats **religion** as a waste of time. And, yes, while God gave the Czechs an amazing number of pretty women (see: **Beauty Contests**), he gave the Slovaks even more.

Czechs often refer to Slovakia as a nation without history. This is, of course, a ridiculous offence, unless it's interpreted as follows: barring a half-mythical kingdom in the tenth century and six years as a Nazi puppet state during the Second World War, the Slovaks have never experienced national sovereignty (which doesn't mean that they don't have any history). From the tenth century right up until 1918, the **Hungarians** ruled Slovakia as the province of *Felvidék* (Upper Hungary) and at times, they behaved as if all its inhabitants were Magyars.

Partly because of harsh pressure from Budapest and partly because of its deep roots in agrarian society, both economic and cultural developments were slower in Slovakia than in the rest of **Central Europe**. "To the urban Czechs of the nineteenth century," the writer Pavel Kosatík comments, "a trip to Slovakia was almost like a safari to an exotic and picturesque country, where the natives happened to speak a Slavonic language they understood very well."

It's fair to say that the emergence of Czechoslovakia in 1918 meant a giant leap forward for the Slovaks. The government in Prague made great efforts to develop the eastern and more backwards part of the young state (see: **Ruthenians**), not least by building a functioning educational system. After 1948, the communist regime followed suit with the large-scale industrialization of agricultural Slovakia, so by 1969 Slovakia's standard of living had risen more than any other East Bloc country. Many Czechs, however, credited this amazing achievement more to generous financial contributions from better-developed Bohemia than to the Slovaks' industriousness.

But didn't the creation of Czechoslovakia also lead to the creation of Czechoslovaks? This was certainly the goal of the country's "founder" and first president, **Tomáš G. Masaryk**, who had a Slovak father and Czech mother. The great national enthusiasm that flared after independence and lived on during the **First Republic's** early years strongly suggested that a Czechoslovak **national identity** was under formation. But this process would take time – Masaryk himself suggested 50 years.

Unfortunately, history had other plans. The infamous **Munich Agreement**, which the governments of Great Britain and France signed with Hitler in September 1938, was practically a go-ahead for the Nazi **German** occupation of Bohemia and Moravia six months later. Millions of embittered Czechs could never forget that the Slovaks - or more precisely, their political leaders – exploited this tragic event to establish an "independent" Slovakia lead by Jozef Tiso, a Catholic priest.

Seen in retrospective, it appears that the Slovak and Czech political elites chose different paths at almost every important crossroads in the twentieth century. The divergence manifested itself not only in 1939, when the Slovaks ostentatiously preferred national sovereignty to solidarity with the Czechs. The same schism appeared in Czech and Slovak attitude towards **communism**.

In 1946, in the first elections after the war, a staggering 36 percent of Czech voters supported the Communist Party, and thus enabled them to establish a government. In Slovakia, however, the agrarian Democratic Party won in a landslide with 62 percent support. In other words, while the Czechs largely paved the way to the communist dictatorship themselves, the Slovaks got it stuffed down their throats.

Peculiarly enough, by the time of the political thaw of the late 1960s, the roles had changed completely. Now, a vast majority of the Czechs enthusiastically supported the Prague Spring's reforms, while most Slovaks expressed reservation and sometimes even condemnation. The fact that the only Prague Spring reform that survived the invasion was the federalization of Czechoslovakia – the country was formally transformed into two republics – didn't make the Slovaks particularly popular with the disillusioned Czechs. "While we have to put up with the Soviet occupation troops, they got their federative republic, which we subsidize with billions of *korunas* every year!" the Czechs groaned.

Given this background, it's not too mysterious that Czechoslovakia finally fell apart once the **Velvet Revolution** put an end to the communists' grip on power.

Sure, the Czechs had no intentions of breaking up the federation. They only took it for granted that Czechoslovakia consisted of two equal nations, and they were a bit more equal than the Slovaks. And yes, a majority of Slovaks wanted to keep the benefits (not least the economic ones) that the federation offered, but at the same time dreamt of international recognition of Slovakia's sovereignty. Basically, the Slovak stance in the early 1990s was strongly reminiscent of Winnie the Pooh's famous slogan: Yes please, I'll have both milk and honey!

Another obstacle was the two nations' diverging perceptions of how the communists' command economy should be transformed into a market economy.

The Czechs declared that they wanted to move quickly and implement immediate reforms to regain what was lost during the communist stagnation. The Slovaks, on their side, knew perfectly well that a substantial part of their economy was based on heavy industry and military production, both of which were hard to reform overnight. A slow pace for reforms, they argued, was necessary to avoid social distress. What's more, Slovakia's Catholic Church, traditionally an important opinion maker, skilfully used people's distrust of the market economy by warning against the godless Czechs' addiction to consumerism.

If the Slovaks and Czechs had lived in a marriage, a therapist would have probably concluded: "The marital partners have never managed to establish a common identity. They have been living side by side for twenty years, and now their personal interests have become stronger than their will to keep the marriage together. Divorce is the most sensible solution." And that's how it ended. The Czechs and Slovaks conducted a divorce that was almost as smooth and quick as the Velvet Revolution four years earlier. Quite an achievement compared to the terrible slaughter that was going on in Yugoslavia.

So how has the separation affected the relations between the Czechs and Slovaks? As one might expect, lots of Czechs were maliciously pleased when the lugubrious Mečiar government in the middle of the 1990s led "separatist Slovakia" into international isolation and thousands of liberal-minded Slovaks into Czech exile. But the incredible work later governments in Bratislava have done to change the course has evoked great respect among most Czechs, and there is no more paternalistic talk about spoiled little brothers.

The same attitude also seems to apply for the Slovaks. Gone are the days when they could blame the "damned bureaucrats in Prague" for everything that went wrong. Now, the Slovaks can only rely on themselves, so in one sense, it seems that the separation has made relations between the Slovaks and Czechs better than they were before.

And, of course, not all ties from the Czechoslovak days have been broken. Some 300,000 of the Czech Republic's citizens still regard themselves as Slovaks. What's more, Slovaks make up the largest group of **foreigners** in the country (officially 61,000), and the Czechs are the largest minority in Slovakia – excepting the indigenous Hungarians living alongside the Danube.

Sokol

You can find the building in practically every town and city in the Czech Republic. Centrally located and often with rich architecture, the *Sokol* (Falcon) gymnasiums have been a cornerstone of Czech cultural life for almost 150 years. True, their importance has somewhat faded with the years, but in the collective consciousness of what it means to be Czech (see: **Beer**; **Cimrman, Jára**; **Golden Hands**; **Ice Hockey**; **National Identity**), *Sokol* is still an institution to be reckoned with.

The Falcon was born in Prague in 1862, when Miroslav Tyrš and Jindřich Fügner founded the Prague Gymnastics Union. Tyrš was a renowned aesthete and university professor who, inspired by contemporary trends in neighbouring Germany, worked out a program of gymnastic exercises, while Fügner was a wealthy banker willing to finance the start-up of the organization. In addition to promoting the ancient ideal of a sound soul in a sound body, *Sokol*, as the Union was soon renamed, also had a nationalistic mission: to foster "energetic, self-conscious and hardy Czech men".

Tyrš and Fügner definitely struck a chord among the Czechs. *Sokol* clones popped up all over **Bohemia** and **Moravia**, among Czech **emigrants** in America and even in other Slavonic cities in the Austro-**Hungarian** Empire. The growth was so impressive that in the 1880s *Sokol's* leaders decided to restructure the organization according to a military-like system. Individual clubs were renamed battalions and grouped in regional entities, which were headed by a *náčelník* (chief commander) on the national level. To make *Sokol's* paramilitary (and overtly anti-Imperial) character completely visible, the members were also equipped with uniforms resembling those carried by the Italian revolutionary Garibaldi's soldiers in the war against the **Austrians.**

As the Czech national revival (see: **Czech Language**) grew ever stronger in the second half of the nineteenth century, so did *Sokol*. By the turn of the century, the organization consisted of 630 battalions with more than 50,000 members, and its regular displays of mass gymnastics, called *sleti*, at Prague's Letná Plain turned into giant demonstrations of Czech national self-consciousness. Of course, *Sokol's* importance didn't diminish after Czechoslovakia's foundation in 1918. During the **First Republic,** the movement was given official blessing as a nation-building instrument and expanded to Slovakia.

Being a *Sokol* member equalled being a Czechoslovak patriot and a supporter of president **Tomáš G. Masaryk**. Since this axiom also applied to the Hussite Church (see: **Religion**; **Jan Hus**), one may deduct that a typical Czech patriot in the interwar years equalled a Protestant *Sokol* member, although numerous **Jews** were also fervent supporters. The country's Catholics, on their part, reacted with establishing a competing organization, *Orel* (Eagle), which enjoyed some support in Moravia.

Given *Sokol's* patriotic-Czech image, it was no surprise that the Nazi occupants in 1941 banned the organization. Since totalitarian regimes of different ideologies have much in common, it was also not surprising that the Bolsheviks followed suit by dissolving *Sokol* and incorporating its members into an all-national sports organization. However, to give some impression of continuity, they "kidnapped" the *Sokol's* national *sleti* and gave them a communist wrapping. Thus, every five years from 1955 until 1985, a *Spartakiada* was arranged at Prague's giant Strahov stadium, where thousands of half-naked men and women from all corners of Czechoslovakia met to perform gymnastics according to the original *Sokol* recipe.

Yet, in the forty years of dictatorship, *Sokol* never ceased to exist as a fixed concept. Parents sent their children to do gymnastics in the *Sports club*, but called it *Sokol* when speaking about it at home. The exercises still took place in the original *Sokolovna* – the *Sokol* buildings, which also housed events ranging from Christmas bazaars to pet exhibitions and discos. In rural areas, the local *Sokolovna* often doubled as town hall (as they still do), so, when *Sokol* officially re-emerged in 1989, the changes had mostly formal character.

The once-so-proud Falcon does, however, show unmistakable signs of wear and tear. Many children still attend gymnastics after school, but it's no longer a mass organization. Its paramilitary base looks pretty outdated (some wits joke that Adolf Hitler once applied for *Sokol* membership, but was rejected because he wasn't Czech!). That also goes for its overt collectiveness and cadaver-discipline, which is none too palatable in a nation struggling to forget its communist past.

Nevertheless, *Sokol* must be credited for one everlasting success: this relatively small nation of 10 million beer drinkers (see: **Alcoholics**; **Hospoda**) would probably never have reached such impressing results in the international sports arenas if Tyrš and Fügner not had contributed to the national emancipation by turning physical education into a mass movement. And neither would the Czechs still be greeting each other with *Sokol's* traditional cheer: *Nazdaaaar!*

Surnames

Imagine you are at the airport. Suddenly an announcement sounds from the loudspeakers: *Mr. Frog, Mr. Hippopotamus and Mrs. Pouched Marmot, please come to the information counter. Mr. Scratch-His-Head, Ms. Jump-On-The-Field and Mr. Don't-Eat-Bread are waiting for you.*

Very likely, you'll assume somebody is practising a weird sense of humour. However, if this happens in the Czech Republic, it may not be a joke at all. It simply reflects the fact that probably no other nation on the planet can boast such an incredible number of peculiar surnames.

Most of the approximately 40,000 surnames currently used by Czechs originated in the period between the fourteenth and the eighteenth centuries. The habit of using a second name to express that you belong to a family was introduced by the **nobility** and then spread to the middle classes and free farmers, whose number rapidly increased when the **Austrian**

Empire abolished serfdom in 1781. Five years later, Emperor Joseph II issued a decree ordering every single citizen in the empire to take a surname, which was to be hereditary.

For most Czechs, this didn't represent any great problem, because they had already been given a surname when they were christened for several centuries (even at this point, women had the suffix *–ová*, equalling the genitive *'s* in English, attached to their father's and later husband's names). For the **German**-speaking **Jews**, however, it was not all that easy. For obvious reasons, they did not acquire informal surnames by baptism, and even though they were known to be among the Habsburg Empire's most fervent supporters, only the eldest son in the family was allowed to marry and have a family of his own.

As a result of Emperor Joseph's decree, the **Jews** were given surnames by the authorities, so it was small wonder that **corruption** flourished. The witty writer Pavel Eisner documented many cases where affluent people received impressive names such as *Saphir, Diamant* and *Edelstein,* while the poorest ones ended up as *Regenschirmbestandteil, Nasenstern* and even *Notdurft.*

The largest group of surnames used by Czechs today have their origin in different occupations and crafts. As nearly every other European nation, Czechs are also named *Krejčí* (Tailor), *Truhlář* (Carpenter), *Kovář* (Smith), *Soustružník* (Turner*)*, *Řezník* (Butcher), *Mlynář* (Miller*)*, *Kramář (Shopkeeper), Malíř* (Painter), *Muzikant* (Musician) and *Bubeník* (Drummer).

In the nineteenth century, however, the influx to **Bohemia's** cities was so enormous that these names soon became ubiquitous. Therefore, to distinguish among individuals, people were named after the product they made or the tools they used in their crafts. Thus, tailors became *Jehla* (Needle) and *Náprstek* (Thimble), carpenters *Kladivo* (Hammer) and *Sekyra* (Axe*)*, blacksmiths *Palice* (Sledgehammer), bakers *Chlebíček* (Sandwich) and *Rohlík* (Croissant), and innkeepers *Vomáčka* (Sauce), *Kaše* (Gruel), *Voda* (Water) and *Pivko* (**Beer**).

As the leading onomatologist Dobrava Moldanová points out, almost all of the objects we use in everyday life have produced Czech surnames. That goes for mints, buildings, shoes, vehicles, weapons, musical instruments, and even pieces of clothing, such as *Kaftan* (Caftan), *Rubáš* (Shroud) *Kabát* (coat) and *Kalhoty* (Trousers). Abstracts like *Válka* (War) *Láska* (Love) *Svatba* (Wedding) and *Masopust* (Carnival) are also highly represented, not to mention animal names.

These surnames are so frequent that it's possible to compose an entire zoological classification table based on an average Czech telephone book. It's simply unbelievable how many human hedgehogs (*Ježek*), bullocks (*Volek*), hares (*Zajíc*), frogs (*Žába*) and entire flocks of birds (*Drozd, Holub, Vorel, Skřivan, Čermák*) you can find in Bohemia and **Moravia**.

Even tropical animal names abound. Many Czech families carry surnames like hippopotamus (*Hroch*), ostrich (*Pštros*) and elephant (*Slonek*). This does not mean that hippos, for instance, once used to swim in the Vltava. Instead, many buildings in Prague's older parts were named after these exotic creatures. When the Czechs started to leave the countryside and settled for work in the capital, they simply assumed surnames from the buildings where they lived.

However, the most unique and fantastic Czech surnames are those created from verbs. In other words, they describe an action. Take, for instance the common surname *Vyskočil*, which literally means *jumped out*. It's hard to say who jumped out of what, but Moldanová the onomatologist believes it originated when the first *Vyskočil* jumped out of a window during a brawl in the local *hospoda*. The stories behind surnames such as *Dupal* (Stamped his feet), *Navrátil* (He who returned), *Stejskal* (He who grumbled), *Pospíšil* (He who was in a hurry), or *Stojespal* (He who slept standing on his feet) are less clear.

Logically, when people received surnames because of something they did, they could also perfectly well receive surnames because of something they didn't do, as, for instance, *Nesnídal* (He who didn't eat breakfast) and *Netušil* (He who didn't suspect anything).

The imaginativeness and keen humour of Czech surnames is simply unique. Nobody has expressed the magic of Czech surnames better and more precisely than Pavel Eisner, who knew Czech culture as thoroughly as its German and Jewish counterparts:

"The Czech nation's history manifests its tragedy by forcing tragic situations and experiences on a people whom nature has equipped with a large, mental supply of tragedy. Therefore, they are far more than other nations susceptible to life's bright sides, to smile and laughter, and to mockery and ridicule."

Švejk, The Good Soldier

The **Hungarian** writer Péter Esterházy once said that a place in **world** literature only is available to those countries that can boast at least one work with such reputation that it bulldozes the way for others. Where Czech literature is concerned, there can be no discussion that Jaroslav Hašek's four books about the Soldier Švejk represent such a bulldozer. Since their publication in the early 1920s, the Švejk books have been translated into more than 50 languages, and the slack-jawed and boozing anti-**hero** is still considered to be one of the Czechs' largest contributions to world literature.

This, however, does not mean that the Czechs themselves regard Jaroslav Hašek as a brilliant writer and Švejk as a national treasure. Just like two other writers with roots in **Bohemia** and **Moravia** – **Franz Kafka** and **Milan Kundera** – Hašek and his Good Soldier also generate more controversy than praise. But unlike German-writing Kafka or now French-writing Kundera, the controversy is not because Hašek doesn't fill the requirements to be called a proper Czech. The problem is, as the historian Jan P. Kučera points out, that he is linked more closely to the Czechs and Czech culture than most people find pleasant.

The objections against Hašek and his literary hero can be sorted roughly into two groups – those related to the author, and those linked to Švejk's morality (or rather his astonishing lack of it).

Admittedly, Hašek's personal biography would be a nightmare to any good burgher anxious about his country's good image. During his 40-year life – coincidentally, he was born in 1883, the same year as Franz Kafka, and died only a year earlier – Hašek held a fixed job for only six months, when he worked as a clerk at Slavia Bank. For the rest of his turbulent life, he existed on the very fringe of society, earning a living as a freelance writer based in Prague's *hospodas*.

Besides being a well-known drunkard, hooligan, jailbird, anarchist and provocateur (typically, *The Party for Moderate Progress within the Framework of the Law*, which he established, struggled to promote nationwide alcoholism), Hašek was a bigamist – during the First World War he married a **Russian** woman without having been divorced from his Czech wife – while his real sexual orientation was very likely **homosexual**.

Just to complicate his personality, he suffered from manic depression, which explains his desperate alcoholism (Kučera quotes him saying that his brain didn't work without booze) and his premature death in 1923. In Hašek's lifetime, Švejk was published in flimsy booklets, which were sold at local *hospodas*. His international breakthrough, largely facilitated by Kafka's friend Max Brod (see: **Germans**) took place only several years after Hašek had left this world.

Now, one might rightfully object that an author's biography, however shocking, shouldn't have any relevance to his literary work. The problem, however, is that most Czechs find too many similarities between Hašek and his hero Švejk to distinguish between them.

Just like his inventor, Švejk also is an extremely vulgar, anal-fixated, cheating, and boozing liar who is constantly churning out anecdotes and unbelievable stories. Švejk leaves the impression that he either is a complete idiot or at least very good at pretending to be one, while Hašek often maintained "in this world, only an idiot can enjoy real freedom". As a soldier in the Austro-Hungarian Army during the First World War, Hašek defected to the Russians, where he even served as a Bolshevik commissary in the Siberian town of Bugulma. His alter-ego Švejk uses his brilliant idiocy to ridicule the Army, and ends up presenting cowardice as a great virtue.

Even worse, readers all over the world regard the "brilliant idiot" Švejk as something of a proto-type Czech. The writer Karel Hvížďala puts it like this:

„... Jaroslav Hašek has succeeded in something most literates dream about all their life: to create a figure who is both a unique individual and a representative of a certain kind of people."

Other pundits were less enthusiastic. Leading Czech critics during the **First Republic**, most notably the feared and respected F.X. Šalda, found Švejk so vulgar and folksy, that they refused even to consider it as proper literature, and another famous critic, Václav Černý, took Hašek's hero as living proof of his thesis that the Czechs were "either flunkeys or louts". Despite Švejk's overtly anti-**Austrian** stance, President **Masaryk**, in a very rare confluence of opinion with the Catholic Church (see: **Religion**) found him totally unsuitable as an ideal for newly-established Czechoslovakia.

Given Hašek/Švejk's utterly proletarian background, the communists naturally embraced him with open arms. In the 1950s, the regime financed several grandiose screen versions of the books, plus the final "authorized" publication of Švejk, complete with Josef Lada's wonderful illustrations. Inevitably, the Bolsheviks' intense love affair with Švejk only strengthened the Czechs' ambivalent relation to Hašek and his hero.

These mixed feelings have lasted more or less to this day. A large chunk of the population – including, not surprisingly, almost every single woman in the country – detests Švejk and finds it both disgusting and offensive that someone can think of this "repulsive figure" as an icon of everything Czech. A smaller, but very vocal group of male intellectuals with a deep sense for **beer** and the Czech *hospoda* culture openly revere everything connected with Hašek and Švejk. And then there are the businesspeople who don't care a bit about literature but are making good money on selling Švejk articles ranging from beer tankards and caps to dolls and toilet paper to stupid **tourists**.

What's undisputed, though, is that Švejk has become a living part of modern Czech culture. In newspapers and discussions, people constantly quote golden phrases from Švejk, such as *To chce klid* (Take it easy), *Přísnost musí bejt!* (Discipline is needed!) or *Kristus Pán byl také nevinnej* (Jesus Christ was also innocent). "Švejkologists" and "Haškologists" meet regularly to drink beer and compete in reciting as many phrases as possible, and the verb *švejkovat* (to behave like a sly shirk) has become an oft-used part of the **Czech language**.

So, if Czechs really have a dual perception of their **national identity** – one that idealizes this industrious, democratic, open-minded and highly educated nation, and another that depicts a bunch of egotistic, mean, and cheating individuals with a keen sense of cynical humour – then Švejk represents the ultimate personification of the latter.

Tourists

This probably sounds cruel, but you just have to face it: as a tourist in the Czech Republic, you'll never be loved. If you happen to be in a famous tourist centre, such as Prague, Karlovy Vary or Český Krumlov, you can almost bet your boots that some waiter, hotel receptionist, or shopkeeper will take great care to signal that he or she considers your presence in the city as no more than a barely-tolerated nuisance. And local taxi-drivers, notorious for their ruthlessness, regard tourists in pretty much the same way that the wolf regarded Little Red Riding Hood.

This situation certainly isn't too encouraging, but you don't exactly need to be a psychoanalyst to understand the reason for it.

Even without tourists, the Czech Republic is one of the most densely populated countries in Europe. Add several million screaming, reeling, and gaping tourists, and the result, at least in Prague, is that all of the narrow streets in Old Town (where many people actually still live) are virtually clogged from the beginning of March to late October.

In the middle of the summer, it gets even worse. To move reasonably fast from one point in Prague's centre to another, you'd better wear shoulder protectors and a helmet. Sometimes only a machete can help. And when you finally have made your way to your favourite *hospoda*, dripping with sweat and only seconds from a nervous breakdown, all tables are occupied by noisy and drunken tourists who splash Czech *korunas* about as if they were Monopoly money.

To common Czechs, the flood of tourists feels so strong and all-embracing that when the national news agency *ČTK* reported some years ago that 55 million **foreigners** visit the country annually, not a soul reacted with mistrust. A **German** journalist, however, took the effort to verify the *ČTK* report. If the estimate were correct, he concluded, there would be 3.4 persons sleeping in each and every hotel bed in the country every night. Considering the Czechs' relatively relaxed attitude to **sex**, you can't exclude the possibility that this actually occurs from time to time, but the Freudian message in the somewhat exaggerated ČTK report should instead be interpreted as follows:

"Our small and beautiful country is drowning in tourists. On the one hand, they are a holy terror; on the other hand they bring so much money to the country that we should clench our teeth and put up with them for a while longer."

By the way, any psychoanalyst will probably conclude that it's perfectly natural to hate something or somebody, on whom you feel more or less dependent upon.

There are, however, a few practical precautions a tourist can take to better his or her odds, such as trying to react quickly when in a crowded shop. To the local population, there's nothing so irritating as a seemingly lobotomised foreigner who halts the queue with silly questions ("How much will that be in dollars?") and eternal fumbling with money. If you manage not only to keep your money ready and pick up your stuff without halting the queue for an eternity, but also to utter *Dobrý den!* when you enter the shop and *Na shledanou!* when you leave, then you have contributed significantly to the improvement of tourists' reputation in this country.

The same applies to foreign tourists who desperately press themselves into a tram, metro, bus, shop, or whatever without first letting the people inside get out (in the metro during rush hour, this can be downright dangerous). And similarly, when you are riding in a tram, metro, or bus, or visiting a shop, don't detain the people who are waiting to enter, but get out as soon as possible.

Those are the easy rules. Others can be more challenging. For instance, when using any kind of public transport, younger passengers are expected to let older ones have their seats. But what age is required to have this privilege? In luckier instances, the elderly person (who can be practically of any age) waves some kind of ID to make you get up. In other cases, you just have to leave it to your judgement – or compassion.

Here, you should be aware of an especially tricky problem: pregnant women. Ignoring an expectant mother in need of a seat is (rightly) considered the zenith of bad taste and a really rude offence. On the other hand, you may commit an almost equally rude offence if you signalise that you believe a woman is pregnant by jumping up from your seat when she actually isn't (see: **Czech Cuisine**). So, if the tram or metro you are riding is full of young, swollen ladies, you'd better not sit down at all.

What's more, all public transport companies use controllers to catch passengers without tickets. To increase the effectiveness of the system, the *revizoři* (they identify themselves by flashing small badges which they hide in their palms) are paid according to the number of passengers caught, so quite logically, they systematically prey on confused and easily scared tourists. In fact, the chances you'll meet a *revizor* are even greater than the chances you'll be lifted by a pickpocket (which is rather high, and on tram No. 22 from Charles Square to the Prague Castle, close to 100 percent).

On principle, the *revizoři* don't speak foreign languages, and they can be quite brutal, so unless you are fluent in Czech or carry a black belt in karate, don't forget to buy a large number of tickets – and get them stamped! – before entering the metro, bus or tram.

When riding in a taxi, however, you risk trouble even if you behave like Mother Theresa. As already mentioned, Prague's cab drivers are an amazingly ruthless bunch of predators, and innocent tourists with their pockets full of money and an inability to find their way in the city, are their favourite food.

The classic situation occurs when a foreign tourist stops a cab in the street, asks to be taken to some place four kilometres away, and then is charged 1,000 *korunas* for a trip that would normally cost a maximum of 200 *korunas*. Quite often, tourists who have dared to protest have gotten their faces smashed. Some years ago, it was even revealed that the most shrewd cabbies had installed electric wires in the passengers' seats, so that rebellious passengers could be easily "convinced" to pay up with the help of a few volts shot to the scrotum.

Lately, the situation is said to have improved a bit, but tourists are still cheated on a massive scale. According to media reports, almost every other taxi operating in Prague is equipped with *turbos*. This is a device that makes the taximeter count kilometres with incredible speed, so when you ride from Wenceslas Square to the National Theatre, you risk paying for a trip from Prague to Plzeň.

There is only one protection against Prague's cab mafia: never stop a taxi in the street. Order one by phone from a dispatcher, and always insist on getting a signed receipt. In such cases, any complaints may be addressed to the taxi dispatcher, who can check whether the bill is doctored, or not.

Finally, just one urgent recommendation: if you really want to confirm Czechs' prejudices about stupid and clueless tourists, buy yourself a Soviet military cap or over-sized plush hat, and be sure to wear it in every museum, gallery and theatre you happen to visit. You'll be loved!

TV Nova

Launched in 1994 with American money and much media fuss, TV Nova, the Czech Republic's first nationwide private television channel, was an instant success. After only three months, Nova had beaten the pants off of dull Czech state television – ČTV – in the number of viewers, and advertising revenues were skyrocketing. From a commercial point of view, TV Nova can rightfully claim the title as one of the most lucrative media projects in all of post-communist Europe.

This tremendous success, however, was not a miracle. In a country where the media had been under strict state control for 50 years, a private and commercial television channel was regarded as a revolution, not least because Nova churned out a lethal mix of American sitcoms, Argentine soap operas, aggressive news releases, and home-grown innovations such as naked weather forecasters and talk shows about **sex**.

The only people taken by surprise by this low-browed mega-success were Czech intellectuals, who still lived under the delusion that the Czechs were an uncommonly cultivated lot (see: **National Identity**). However, if Nova was an unpleasant reminder of Czechs' genuine cultural preferences, it also revealed some nasty truths about the country's political realities.

First, when a sponsor scandal forced **Václav Klaus** to resign as Prime Minister (see: **Corruption**; **Pepa from Hong Kong**) in 1997, Nova's news program reported that the ex-Premier had secretly bought himself a luxury villa in Switzerland. The allegations eventually appeared to be undocumented, and Klaus demanded a staggering 100 million *korunas* from Nova in damages. However, after a private meeting with Nova's charismatic boss Vladimír Železný, he suddenly dropped all charges. Is it a mere coincidence that Nova's news releases from that day on have been strongly biased towards Klaus and his ODS party?

Secondly, when CME, Nova's American investor kicked Železný out of his job as Nova's managing director two years later, the shrewd professional launched a daring counterattack: after acquiring fresh capital from unknown sources (Aleksandr Rebyonok, a **Russian** businessman based in Karlovy Vary, has been mentioned), he took a majority of the reporters with him and started up a "new" Nova. Despite vociferous protests from the Americans, who claimed Železný had behaved like a pirate and violated international rules, the Czech government at the time let him get away with his trick. The International Commerce Court in Stockholm, though, was not as tolerant. In 2003, it ruled that the Czech Republic must pay CME a staggering 10 billion *korunas* in compensation.

And third, when Czech authorities awarded a broadcasting license to Nova, they understood that the channel (based on a proposal by a group of respected sociologists) would deliver a mix of high-quality films, operas, and educational programmes that would "arouse envy" all over Europe. The reality, as became soon apparent, had not the slightest resemblance to culture. This is not so surprising, given that Nova was a commercial station from the very beginning, but it's evident that the Nova people beat their competitors with a fraudulent bid.

Well, one might object, some corner-cutting could hardly be avoided when a market economy was created almost overnight, so there's no reason to moralize too much. That's certainly true, but the case of Nova is still exceptional.

Not only have Czech authorities let Nova get away with a blatant license fraud. Today, hardly anybody criticises Vladimír Železný for having caused the Czech state budget to lose 10 billion *korunas*. On the contrary, in June 2004 Železný was elected member of the European Parliament! The station's hair-raisingly biased and professionally flawed news programs (unfortunately, the naked weather-ladies are gone) are still the most popular in the Czech Republic, and just to give the country's most watched television an official blessing, Václav Klaus held his first New Year speech as president both on the state ČTV and Nova.

All in all, this makes TV Nova something more than an ultra-commercial, lowbrow TV station. It perpetuates the self-deception (see: **Gott, Karel**) that a majority of Czechs so nimbly practiced during the Bolsheviks' *normalization* in the 1970s and 1980s: you know that something is stinking, but pretend that you don't notice it.

Ukrainians

Officially, only 260,000 **foreigners** with a permanent residence permit were registered in the Czech Republic as of the beginning of 2004. Even though foreigners, because of illegal immigration, indubitably make up more than the official 2.6 percent of the population, the Czech Republic still has a markedly smaller share of immigrants than the average Western country.

This is not too puzzling, since economic immigrants still find **Bohemia** and **Moravia** more attractive as a transit area than a final destination. There is, however, one spectacular exception: Ukrainians. Because of the hopeless situation in their home country, where a tragic mixture of political mismanagement, **corruption** and souring criminality have wrecked the economy and caused immense social problems, Ukrainians have been flowing to the Czech Republic since the beginning of the 1990s. Officially, they number about 60,000, closely trailing the **Slovaks** as the largest foreign community in the country, but the unofficial number is very likely much higher.

Basically, Ukrainians have found what they were looking for: jobs. But the price they pay is high. Just like Turks in Germany in the early 1960s, the Ukrainians are doing work that Czechs don't want, because of low pay or hardship or both. So, in all parts of Bohemia and Moravia you can find Ukrainians, some of them with **academic titles**, digging ditches, laying bricks or cleaning septic tanks for wages that often don't exceed what the average Czech is paid in unemployment benefits. This drudgery is also dangerous. When a tragic accident happens at some construction site (which practically means every other day) you can bet your boots that the poor guy killed or crippled for life is a Ukrainian.

Needless to say, Czechs don't regard these low-paid, hardworking and often also hard-drinking (who can blame them?) drudges with too much respect. According to the common and utterly cynical perception, a Ukrainian is a poor fellow who is overjoyed by the chance to do unqualified labour in a civilized country. A hundred years ago, thousands of Czechs flocked to Vienna (see: **Austrians**) to do the same kind of work, but that's mostly forgotten today. "Ukrainian", to most Czechs, has become synonymous with "miserable Gastarbeiter".

The Ukrainians have, however, one effective image-saver at their disposal.

In 1918, when Czechoslovakia emerged from the ruins of Austria-Hungary, Trans-Carpathia (or Ruthenia), which is the westernmost region of today's Ukraine, was declared a part of Czechoslovakia. The Czechs, who had suddenly become masters not only over the Slovaks, but also over some 450,000 Ruthenians, started to develop their new and (compared to Bohemia) backward province with great fervour. In the capital Uzhgorod, a Czech governor was installed, and Czech teachers, gendarmes, and engineers were stationed all over the small province (the writer Ivan Olbracht has written several wonderful short stories from Czechoslovak Ruthenia).

In 1939, **Hungarian** troops regained control over the region, which until 1918 had been ruled from Budapest for more than eight centuries, and thus scotched the Czechs' promising career as colonizers. After the Second World War, Ruthenia became a part of Soviet Ukraine, but the Czechs have not forgotten their former eastward expansion. In school, children learn that the 20 years of Czech rule in Trans-Carpathia were the happiest and certainly most democratic in the Ruthenians' long and thorny history.

So, to get to the point: any Ukrainian living in the Czech Republic who claims that he (almost all of them are men) hails from Ruthenia and that he deeply regrets that the Czechs had to leave, will no longer be regarded as a miserable *Gastarbeiter*, but as an unlucky Slav brother longing for democracy and prosperity!

Urination

Nobody would be particularly surprised to learn that the Czechs urinate in the same way as people in all other European countries. What's surprising, though, is the incredible benevolence with which the Czechs tolerate urination in public places.

Take, for instance, this real-life situation: you are travelling by bus to a village in Western **Bohemia**, when the bus-driver stops suddenly because the car **driving** in front of you pulls over and blocks the narrow road. The chap behind the wheel jumps out of his Škoda, takes a few steps towards the ditch - and starts urinating blissfully in front of the fifty bus-passengers. Not a single word of condemnation is uttered, be it against the car driver's tasteless behaviour or the delay he causes.

Basically, public urination is confined to two segments of the Czech population: children and adult men (most **feminists** would probably say that this is practically the one and the same group).

When it comes to children, the tolerance towards public urination is both understandable and praiseworthy. Contrary to Western countries, where children use diapers almost until they become teenagers, Czech parents regard it as a matter of personal honour to teach their children to use the toilet before they reach the age of two. From time to time, this inevitably implies the use of a bush in a public park or even the gutter as an improvised toilet, but thanks to the educational character of the act, nobody complains.

The tolerance towards men's public urination, though, is not that simple to understand. Obviously, it's fair to assume that the extremely high frequency of this phenomenon is somehow connected to Czech men's equally extremely high consumption of **beer**. Consequently, the bladder of the average Czech male tends to be under far greater pressure than male bladders elsewhere.

Nevertheless, this pressure should not give them carte blanche to terrorize their surroundings through urination. Even the most run-down *hospoda* in the country has a lavatory of some kind, and the network of public toilets is often better than those in Western Europe (see: **Central Europe**). Why, then, do so many Czech men so often feel free to dispose of their bodily fluids in public places?

It's hard to give a scientific answer. Some pundits would claim that it's because the Czechs, not influenced or morally guided by any strong and visible **nobility**, are an utterly plebeian nation with plebeian behaviour. In this connection, there is a well-known story about the time that Jan Masaryk (see: **Defenestration**), Czechoslovakia's ambassador to Great Britain in the interwar years, was invited to dinner at an English nobleman's mansion. "Maybe you would like to wash your hands," the host suggested before dinner started, discreetly hinting that the ambassador might need to visit the toilet. "Oh no, that's not necessary," replied the quick-witted Masaryk. "I just washed them behind the tree in your garden!"

According to a less widespread theory, the public urination-syndrome merely reflects the domination of Czech society by male chauvinists, who don't care about their surroundings. And then, of course, there are those who see it as a nation-wide problem with **alcoholism**. In any event, a **foreigner** in the Czech Republic should better be prepared: a man, who is waving his genitals in public, is not necessarily an exhibitionist, but more likely an ordinary chap on his way home from the local *hospoda*.

Values

After the fall of the Iron **Curtain**, Europe has become a marvellously messy place. True, the Oder and Neisse Rivers still divide the richer half of the continent from the poorer, but apart from economic power, the east/west antagonism used during the forty years of the Cold War has evidently become outdated. But if Europe has changed politically, have its inhabitants changed mentally?

In an attempt to sort Europe into groups of regions where people share the same beliefs and values, sociologists have conducted annual surveys since the beginning of the 1980s that are presented regularly in *European Values Study*.

Here, inhabitants of countries stretching from Iceland in the north to Greece in the south and from Portugal in the west to Russia in the east, are asked to present their opinions on matters such as **religion**, **sex** and openness about sexual matters; their acceptance of **foreigners**; the importance they attach to family relations, law and order, social security, and material goods; and whether they prefer liberal or authoritarian relations between children and parents, respectively between pupils and school teachers.

When the answers to these value-related questions are sorted out, the Cold War distinction becomes meaningless. Europe is not divided east/west, but north/south. Or to put it more precisely: when it comes to attitudes towards life, Europe has two anti-poles – the **Balkan** and the Scandinavian attitude.

According to the extreme Balkan model, it's crucial to maintain "traditional values" (fathers as the unrivalled head of family, children blindly obeying their parents), religion is very important, and neither foreigners nor "new ideas" such as **feminism** are very welcome. In school, teachers are supposed to maintain strict discipline, and sexual matters, let alone **homosexual** ones, are not to be discussed in public.

267

The extreme Scandinavian model, on the other hand, is characterized by a very strong openness and a liberal attitude towards everything from children and education to sex and religion. Contrary to the southerners, the northerners don't cry for more law and order, they don't attach too much importance to material goods (maybe because they are too spoiled), and their negligence of family ties often results in social isolation and even loneliness.

So, where do the Czechs and **Central Europe** fit in?

As one might expect, the answer is not entirely ambiguous. In some matters, Czechs display downright extreme tendencies. Few nations in Europe have less confidence in official institutions (see: **Kajínek, Jiří**; **Scepticism**), and the Czechs are generally distrustful towards other people – be it foreigners or compatriots. When it comes to religion, only the former East Germany can boast more lax relations with God, and where sex is concerned, the Czechs confirm their reputation as extremely broadminded. In family matters, on the other hand, they tend towards the traditional model, which is especially apparent when it comes to education (see: **Dancing Schools**).

The survey targets numerous other areas as well, but when all of the answers are tallied the conclusion is quite apparent: the Czechs end up much farther to the north than their geographical position indicates. So while the **Poles**, because of their strong religiousness and respect for traditions, end up in the near vicinity of the Romanians and Bulgarians, the Czechs (and also the Slovenes!) land not far away from Sweden.

This, of course, should only serve as an indication that the old Cold War divisions are practically irrelevant in real life. And the Czechs themselves, **sceptical** as ever, would certainly remind you not to put too much confidence in what people declare in different surveys. As Winston Churchill, the inventor of the term Cold War, once confessed: I only trust statistics that I have forged myself!

Velvet Revolution

Almost 50 years of totalitarian rule, when disgusting crimes were hailed as heroic actions while heroic actions where condemned as disgusting crimes (see: **Horáková, Milada**), have left the Czechs utterly suspicious of any officially "verified" explanation of the many dramatic events that have taken place in their country.

This widespread distrust has given rise to a wild array of historic myths. All of them have one common denominator: events that seem to have a simple and perfectly logical background are, in reality, the result of a conspiracy conducted by "dark forces". This is not entirely inappropriate when it comes to the 1950s and early 1960s, when conspiracies evidently flourished. However, it's more surprising that an event as relatively recent and significant as the Velvet Revolution in 1989 is also entangled in a mesh of myths.

According to the official version, the Velvet Revolution started on November the 17th, when the Socialist Youth Organization (SSM) arranged a demonstration in Prague's Albertov district to commemorate Jan Opletal, a medic who was shot dead by the Nazi occupants in 1939. After some brief speeches, the students marched to **Karel Hynek Mácha's** grave at Vyšehrad – and then towards the centre of Prague.

By the time they reached the end of the Národní Avenue, where special riot police forces blocked access to Wenceslas Square, the students were accompanied by tens of thousands of ordinary citizens, who peacefully chanted freedom slogans. Yet the Special Forces reacted with a brutality uncommon even to the Bolshevik regime. When the savage beatings ceased an hour later, nearly forty demonstrators had been rushed off to hospitals, and one student was even reported murdered by the police.

The violent action on the evening of November the 17th later became known as the "Massacre on the Národní Avenue" (a rather pathetic monument to commemorate the event has been installed in the arcade outside Národní 16). The word "massacre" may seem a bit exaggerated, since the only dead demonstrator, as it was established some days later, was actually a fake (although the alleged police murder served as an effective reminder of **Jan Palach**). Nevertheless, the regime's brutal behaviour against defenceless students triggered a strike among Czech actors and subsequent demonstrations and civic protests in nearly every city and town in the country.

In the following days, the Bolsheviks were forced to renounce one privilege after another. After two weeks of mass demonstrations – some of them attended by almost one million Czechs – the regime collapsed entirely. "Love and truth" had finally defeated "lies and hate", and the Czechs had added a bright – and much-needed – chapter to their modern history.

Or was everything different? Visit any *hospoda* in this country, and you'll probably hear another version. To quite a few Czechs, the Velvet Revolution was, in reality, a reform-communist putsch that failed.

One of the best "proofs" of this conspiracy theory is that the students, participating in the demonstrations on November the 17th were led to the centre of Prague by an agent from the secret police, or StB (see: **Lustration**) who acted as a radical SSM agitator (the agent's presence was later documented). At Národní Avenue, the same secret agent supposedly played the role of the student who was beaten to death by the police. The purpose? To publicly discredit the orthodox leadership of the Czechoslovak Communist Party and thus help the Party's reform wing gain power.

In other words, Czech secret police staged the Velvet Revolution with political backing from Soviet leader Mikhail Gorbachov and his reform-minded comrades in Czechoslovakia. Both the students and dissident movement (see: **Charter 77**) were exploited as unknowing instruments, but for some reason or other, the plot didn't succeed.

An intense, but not particularly credible, spokesman for this theory is Miroslav Štěpán, Prague's last Party boss (see: **Communism**). The much-hated Štěpán allegedly deposes witnesses who claim that

Gorbachov's private secretary Gennadij Gerasimov mentioned "the coming events in Czechoslovakia" one month in advance. The conspiracy theory is further based on the report that several KGB generals were supposed to have visited the Prague police's operations centre on the 17th of November. Why would they, goes the argument, if the KGB and the Soviet reform communists didn't orchestrate the demonstrations that went on in Prague's streets?

No matter how intriguing these theories might sound, the evidence is next to nothing. True, KGB top brass did reportedly visit Prague in mid November, and, yes, the Czech secret police did infiltrate the student movement. But this, of course, doesn't prove that the outbreak of the Velvet Revolution was directed from the Kremlin.

Another theory, which has spread to even more *hospodas* than the previous one, is that **Václav Havel**, during the negotiations that started a week after November the 17th, struck a secret deal with the communist leaders.

Exactly what this deal was supposed to contain often depends on the intoxication level of the person propounding the theory, but one allegation seems to enjoy particularly strong support: the **Havel**-led opposition promised the communist bigwigs immunity if they were nice guys and left power without making any trouble. And then there are a host of conspiracy theories that can't be described as anything other than downright insane, such as the notion that the Velvet Revolution was orchestrated by Zionists and freemasons (see: **Karel Gott**).

It's puzzling, but the most obvious interpretation of the Velvet Revolution's origin is the one most seldom heard: that it wasn't a revolution at all, at least not in the traditional sense of the word. It was, rather, the collapse of a rotten regime.

Just look at the background: the communist regime didn't receive their final blow on the 17th of November. Earlier that autumn, Hungary started to dismantle the Iron **Curtain** along its borders with Austria, and Prague was flooded with refugees from Eastern Germany on their way to

Photo © Jaroslav Fišer

the West. The air was virtually heavy with the scent of freedom. And then, one week before November the 17th, the Berlin wall – the most tangible symbol of Europe's division – fell, and Big Brother in Moscow didn't lift a finger (see: **Russians**).

Many bad and ugly things can rightfully be said about the Czechoslovak "normalizors", but when it came to power politics, they were realistic. Even the moronic Party boss Miloš Jakeš understood that this time, no Soviet tanks would come and save them. They also knew they were too weak, morally corrupt and despised to stay in power on their own. If the student demonstration hadn't triggered the communist collapse, it's fairly safe to assume that some other event would have done the job.

Therefore, it might seem most appropriate to describe the Velvet Revolution as the climax of a long-lasting process that started with the uprising in Poland in the beginning of the 1980s, and then hit its stride when the new Soviet leadership abandoned the Brezhnev doctrine of propping up ideologically and economically bankrupt dictatorships in **Central** and Eastern Europe.

But, of course, this doesn't change the fact that for millions of pestered Czechs, the Velvet Revolution represents one of the brightest moments of their lives.

World

After decades of isolation behind the Iron **Curtain**, it's perhaps only natural that the common Czech perception of the world abroad is still influenced by certain outdated stereotypes. Africa is often referred to as "the black continent", and television reporters don't hesitate to speak about "typical Asian cruelty" or "Nordic emotional frigidity".

What's more interesting, though, is the way in which Czechs speak about their own country in relation to the rest of the world: while most other languages use the opposites *at home – abroad*, Czech use *doma* (at home) versus *venku* (outside).

One shouldn't read too much into this peculiarity, but to some observers it substantiates the view that the Czechs historically have perceived their home country as something closed and insulating that protected them from all of the dangers threatening on the other side. Logically, everybody inside the shelter is one of us, while everybody outside is a potential intruder (see: **Foreigners**).

The Czech Republic in Figures:

National day:
October 28th

Head of State:
President, elected by the Parliament for a period of five years

Government:
Parliamentary republic, Constitution adopted December 1992.

Legislature:
Parliament with two chambers – Chamber of Deputies (200 members)
and Senate (81 members)

Population (2002):
10.28 million (81.2 percent Czechs, 13.2 Moravians, 3.1 Slovaks,
2.5 percent Roma/Poles/Germans/Hungarians)

Area:
78,864 square kilometres

Historical regions:
Bohemia 52,062 km^2/6.27 million inhabitants
Moravia and Silesia 26,808 km^2/4.07 million inhabitants

Administrative divisions:
13 regions plus Prague Capital Region,
76 districts, 6,196 municipalities

Density:
131 persons per km^2, ca. 75 percent in urban areas

Biggest cities:
Prague (1.2 million), Brno (390,000),
Ostrava (327,000), Plzeň (172,000)

Borders:
Germany (810 km), Poland (762 km),
Austria (466 km), Slovakia (252 km)

Highest mountain:
Sněžka 1,602 m

Lowest point:
The Elbe River at Hřensko (German border):
117 m above sea level

Longest river:
Vltava (Moldau) 433.2 km

Biggest lake:
Černé jezero: 18.4 ha

Hottest mineral spring:
Karlovy Vary (Carlsbad) 72 °C

Average temperature (Prague):
January -3 °C, July 18 °C

Closest distance to the sea:
Šluknov – Baltic Sea (326 km)

Biggest national park:
Šumava (685,2 km^2)

Longest railway tunnel:
Špičácký in Šumava (1,747 m)

Shortest crew cut:
3.7 mm (Václav Klaus)

Life expectancy:
Women 78.1 years,
Men 71.4 years

Live births per 1,000 population (2003):
9.2

Infant mortality per 1,000 births (2003):
3.9

Abortions per 1,000 population (2003):
4.1

Deaths per 1,000 population (2003):
10.9

Fertility (children:women):
1.14

Natural population growth (2003):
-1.7

Children born to unmarried mothers (2003):
28.4 per 100 births

Divorce rate (2003):
48 per 100 marriages

Most fatal decease:
Cardio-vascular deceases (55.7 percent), cancer (23.3 percent)

Religion:
No affiliation 6.1 million, Roman Catholics 4.1 million,
Protestants 410,000, Orthodox 20,000

GDP per capita (Average Exchange Rate, 2003):
USD 6,815

GDP per capita (Purchasing-power Parity, 2003):
USD 15,797

GDP per capita (PPP) compared to OECD average (100 percent):
Portugal 64 percent; Czech Republic 58;
Hungary 53; Slovakia 50; Poland 42

Sources: Czech Statistics Office, OECD, Eurostat, Všeobecná Encyklopedie

Czechoslovak/Czech Presidents and Prime Ministers:

Presidents:

Tomáš Garrigue Masaryk: 1918 – 1935

Edvard Beneš: 1935 – 1938

Emil Hácha: 1938 – 1945 *(Protectorate of Bohemia and Moravia)*

Edvard Beneš: 1945 – 1948

Klement Gottwald: 1948 – 1953

Antonín Zapotocký: 1953 – 1957

Antonín Novotný: 1957 – 1968

Ludvík Svoboda: 1968 – 1975

Gustav Husák: 1975 – 1989

Václav Havel: 1989 – 2003

Václav Klaus: 2003 –

Prime Ministers:

Marian Čalfa (Civic Forum): 1990 – 1992

Jan Stráský (Civic Democratic Party): 1992

Václav Klaus (Civic Democratic Party): 1992 – 1997

Josef Tošovský (Transition government): 1997 – 1998

Miloš Zeman (Social Democratic Party): 1998 – 2002

Vladimír Špidla (Social Democratic Party): 2002 – 2004

Stanislav Gross (Social Democratic Party): 2004 –

List of Literature

Albright, Madeleine: *Madam Secretary: A Memoir,* New York 2003

Andrews, Christopher and **V. Mitrokhin**: *The Mitrokhin Archive,* London 1999

Blažek, Petr: *Rozpačitý epilog Charty 77,* LN 14.2.2002

Bojko, Olexandr and **Vladimir Gonec**: *Nejnovější dějiny Ukrajiny,* Praha 1997

Czech Beer and Malt Association: *Czech Brewing and Malting,* Praha 1997

Čechtický, Tomáš: *Blafáky praotce Čecha,* Týden 15. 5. 2001

Černý, Václav: *Paměti,* Brno 1994

de Bray, R.G.A.: *Guide to the West Slavonic languages,* Columbus 1980

Durex: *Sexual Activity – a global survey.* In NEI Raport, Praha 2003

Eisner, Pavel: *Chrám i tvrz,* Praha 1946

Englund, Terje B.: *M. Štěpán: Et spill bak fløyelsteppet?*
Morgenbladet, 18. 3. 1994

Englund, Terje B.: *C. Munck Birch: Adapting to Western Standards,*
Nordic News 3/2001

Gellner, Arnošt: *Národy a nacionalismus,* Praha 1993

Gut, Karel a Jaroslav Prchal: *Český hokej 1909/2003,* Praha 2004

Holý, Ladislav: *The Little Czech and the Great Czech Nation,* Cambridge 1996

Hašek, Jaroslav: *Osudy dobrého vojáka Švejka za světové války,* Praha 1987

Havel, Václav: *Letní přemítání,* Praha 1991

Husák, Petr: *Budování kapitalismu v Čechách,* Praha 1997

Hvížďala, Karel: *D. Třeštík: Projevujeme se jako moralizující snílci,*
MfD 29. 5. 2002

Hvížďala, Karel: *Švejk, knižní postava i národní povaha,* MfD 28. 1. 2004

Institute for East-West Studies: *The Roma and Europe,* Štiřín 1998

Institute of Jewish Affairs: *Anti-Semitism – World Report 1995,* London 1995

Kaplan, Karel: *Pravda o Československu 1945–1948,* Praha 1990

Karlsson, Ingmar: *Minoriteter utan moderland*, I&M no. 5, Stockholm 1994

Keane, John: *Václav Havel. A Political Tragedy in Six Acts*, London 1999

Kejř, Jindřich et al.: *Prague, a Journey through its History*, Prague 2003

Klimek, Antonín: *Co zbylo z Masaryka*, Respekt 44/2003

Komárek, Martin: *P.Pithart: Vždy jsme byli tak trochu doleva*, MfD 8. 11. 2001

Kovář, Pavel: *Blinkačky zmizely, antabus zůstává*, Reflex 45, 2003

Knoflíček et al.: *Pivovarské muzeum v Plzni*, Plzeň 1990

Kohout, Pavel: *Vážení spoluobčané – čeští i rakouští*, Salon Právo 3/2002

Kratochvíle, Antonín: *Brauereien in dem Königreich Böhmen*, Brno 1996

Kučera, Jan P.: *Švejk. Jiné čtení*, Reflex 29.11. 2001

MacDonald, Callum and K. Kaplan: *Praha ve stínu hákového kříže*, Praha 1995

Magris, Claudio: *Dunaj*, Praha 1992

Mangold, Tom: *Interview with S. Y. Mogilevich*, ČTV 4. 1. 2000

Moldanová, Dobrava: *Naše příjmení*, Praha 1983

Opát, Jaroslav: *Filozof a Politik T.G. Masaryk*, Praha 1990

Ottův slovník naučný, I–XXIV, Praha 1888

Pawel, Ernst: *The Nightmare of Reason, A Life of Franz Kafka*, London 1988

Polišenský, Josef: *Tisíciletá Praha očima cizinců*, Praha 1999

Ripellino, Angelo: *Magická Praha*, Praha 1996

Rybár, Ctibor: *Jewish Prague*, Prague 1991

Rytter, Olav: *Slavisk malreising*, Oslo 1971

Seibt, Ferdinand: *Německo a Češi*, Praha 1996

Skála, Jaroslav: *Jsem půl století bez alkoholu*, LN 26. 11. 2002

Šatava, Leoš: *Národnostní menšiny v Evropě*, Praha 1994

Skilling, H. Gordon: *Czechoslovakia's Interrupted Revolution*, Princeton 1976

Székely, András: *A Brief History of Hungary*, Budapest 1973

Steigerwald, Karel: *P. Tigrid: Ve svízelných situacích se neosvědčujeme*, MfD 23. 11. 2001

Thiele, Vladimír: *Úsměvy Jana Masaryka*, Praha 1969

Vachalovský, Přemysl: *Kato. Příběh opravdového člověka*, Olomouc 2000

Verecký, Ladislav: *Spisovatel, který se skrývá*, Magazin Dnes 48/2001